CREATING
Gem, Beaded & Bonsai
WIRE TREES

Sal Villano

FIRST EDITION

TREES
by: Joyce Kilmer (1886-1918)

I think that I shall never see
A poem lovely as a tree.

A tree whose hungry mouth is prest
Against the earth's sweet flowing
breast;

A tree that looks at God all day,
And lifts her leafy arms to pray;

A tree that may in Summer wear
A nest of robins in her hair;

Upon whose bosom snow has lain;
Who intimately lives with rain.

Poems are made by fools like me,
But only God can make a tree.

CREATING
Gem, Beaded & Bonsai
WIRE TREES

Sal Villano

Copyright 2013
Sal Villano

Printed in The United States of America
PO Box 827
Milford, Ohio 45150
www.salvillano.com
salvillano@gmail.com

No part of this publication may be reproduced, copied,
transmitted or stored in any form, without the
written permission of the author.

With Love
To Mary

for everything I am,
or ever will be.

Introduction

This book is the result of more than 3 years of work. My inspiration for writing my third book on the subject of creating wire trees and other pieces using wire, came to me while showing my work at many art and craft shows and in art galleries. Interested people would ask me how I got started, *(you can read the answer to this question on page 132)*, and how do I make my wire creations. And, some people, who were really interested in my work, said I should write a book showing how I create my pieces. In 1999, at one of my art shows on Long Island NY, the owner of a nursery that grows and sells living Bonsai trees and supplies asked me if I would be interested in selling my wire tree sculpture in his shop and on his website. He also asked if I had a book on the subject. I did create several wire Bonsai trees and placed them in his shop and on his website and also started writing my first book. To date, my tree sculpture and my book are still offered for sale on his website at: http://www.bonsaiboy.com

My first book titled "How To Create Tree Sculpture" showed how to create 3 different types of small wire trees. My second book titled "How To Create Beaded and Wire Tree Sculpture" showed how to create 5 different types of tree sculpture. After the publication of my first 2 books, I was amazed at the response and good reviews they received. My second book is now also available as a PDF down load version and as a KINDLE version. Hundreds of people have written to me saying how easy it is to follow the steps in my books and how much they enjoy creating with wire.

I have taken great care in creating this third book, not only adding many more different types of sculpture, but also adding many extras I think you will find very helpful. I not only explain and show you how to create each piece, I also show or explain how to use a basic item to create many more variations of that item. This book contains over 400 photos and illustrations. You will also be able to create tabs to add onto the pages so that you can easily find the information you are looking for. Plus, based on my over 30 years of creating and showing my work, I have added pages in the book that I call "Extras". These extras will help you with many different topics, such as: *Photography, Pricing your work, Shipping your work, Accepting commissions, Attending art and craft shows, Consigning your work, Promoting your work, Planning for a show, Creating a website, Working with an agent, Finding suppliers* and a few more. The book also contains forms that you can photocopy and use to help you get and stay organized, such as: *Consignment Agreement, Certificate of Title, Certificate of Authenticity, Follow Up Letters, Art Application Request, Price Conformation & Delivery, Press Release, Link Exchange Request, and a few more.*

If you have any comments, suggestions or questions, please do not hesitate to contact me. The best way to get in touch is to go to my website at: www.salvillano.com and go to my contact page. *No phone calls please.*

I hope you find this book helpful and you will always enjoy creating!

Trees,
with their roots intertwined,
imbedded in, and embracing the earth;
in winter they show their structure,
in spring a burst of gentle buds,
in summer an incredible canopy of green,
and in fall, a magical kaleidoscope
of ever changing color.

Beauty, pure beauty.

Table of Contents

The story of Bonsai 2
How to use this book 3
Before you start any project 4
Create a "Lies Flat Book" 5
Index page tabs 6
Create these pieces 7
Tools needed 9
Materials needed 10
Different types of wire 11
Different base styles and objects 12
Preparing a base for a tree sculpture 15
Creating a mini tree sculpture 21
Making the jig to create a tree sculpture 22
Wrapping the wire to create a mini tree sculpture 24
Creating a root system for a mini tree sculpture 27
Wiring the trunk and branches for a mini tree sculpture 29
Forming a mini tree sculpture 30
Thickening a mini tree sculpture 31
The final branching of a mini tree sculpture 32
Creating the root anchors for a mini tree sculpture 33
Mounting a mini tree sculpture onto a base 34
Adding color to the root mound 38
Creating the style of mini tree sculpture you want 39
Weeping willow mini tree sculpture 39
Upright willow mini tree sculpture 40
Beaded mini tree sculpture 41
Adding beads to a tree sculpture 43
Oak mini tree sculpture 44
Wind swept mini tree sculpture 46
Bonsai with leaves mini tree sculpture 47
Bird nest with pearl eggs 48
Jade leaves for a tree sculpture 53
Jade leaves mixed with glass beads 57
Attaching jade leaves to a tree sculpture 58
Cascade on rock wire tree sculpture 60
Mini jade leaf cascade wire tree sculpture 76
Wall art sculpture 81
Tree on a sea shell wire tree sculpture 86
Glass bonsai wire tree sculpture 91
Bird nest in a branch 101
Adding manufactured leaves 104
Creating larger trees 106
Extras (charts, tables and forms) 107
Shipping tree sculpture 108
About Sal Villano 132

The Story of Bonsai
*From Wikipedia,
the free encyclopedia*

Bonsai is a Japanese art form using miniature trees grown in containers. Similar practices exist in other cultures, including the Chinese tradition of penjing from which the art originated, and the miniature living landscapes of Vietnamese hòn non bộ. The Japanese tradition dates back over a thousand years, and has its own aesthetics and terminology.

"Bonsai" is a Japanese pronunciation of the earlier Chinese term penzai. A "bon" is a tray-like pot typically used in bonsai culture. The word bonsai is often used in English as an umbrella term for all miniature trees in containers or pots. This article focuses on bonsai as defined in the Japanese tradition.

The purposes of bonsai are primarily contemplation (for the viewer) and the pleasant exercise of effort and ingenuity (for the grower). By contrast with other plant cultivation practices, bonsai is not intended for production of food, for medicine, or for creating yard-size or park-size gardens or landscapes. Instead, bonsai practice focuses on long-term cultivation and shaping of one or more small trees growing in a container.

A bonsai is created beginning with a specimen of source material. This may be a cutting, seedling, or small tree of a species suitable for bonsai development. Bonsai can be created from nearly any perennial woody-stemmed tree or shrub species that produces true branches and can be cultivated to remain small through pot confinement with crown and root pruning. Some species are popular as bonsai material because they have characteristics, such as small leaves or needles, that make them appropriate for the compact visual scope of bonsai.

The source specimen is shaped to be relatively small and to meet the aesthetic standards of bonsai. When the candidate bonsai nears its planned final size it is planted in a display pot, usually one designed for bonsai display in one of a few accepted shapes and proportions. From that point forward, its growth is restricted by the pot environment. Throughout the year, the bonsai is shaped to limit growth, redistribute foliar vigor to areas requiring further development, and meet the artist's detailed design.

The practice of bonsai is sometimes confused with dwarfing, but dwarfing generally refers to research, discovery, or creation of plant cultivators that are permanent, genetic miniatures of existing species. Bonsai does not require genetically dwarfed trees, but rather depends on growing small trees from regular stock and seeds. Bonsai uses cultivation techniques like pruning, root reduction, potting, defoliation, and grafting to produce small trees that mimic the shape and style of mature, full-size trees.

How to Use This Book

1. Select the piece you want to create. Each piece in the book has a "Difficulty Scale". Number 1 is the easiest to create and number 10 is the most difficult. If this is your first attempt at creating a tree sculpture, I would suggest you start with a difficulty level of either 1 or 2. You will find that it takes some time to get accustomed to working with the different types of wire and the tools. If you have created tree sculpture using any of my other books, you are most likely able to try a higher difficulty level.

2. Read all the instructions and steps completely before you start. Look at all the photos and illustrations to be sure you understand how the piece will look as you create it. As they say, "a picture is worth a thousand words"

3. Gather all the tools and materials needed and have them close at hand. The first instruction page of each piece lists all the tools and material needed to create and decorate the final piece. *Page 9* shows photos of most of the tools needed and *Page 10* shows photos of the materials needed.

4. After you have read and understood all the instructions, I suggest you bookmark the pages you will need to refer to as you create the piece. You can use the tabs I provided on *page 6*. Or, you can use "Post It" type bookmarks or, create you own.

5. This is how the "*Fig. 2/23*" numbers are used. The number to the left of the "/" is the actual figure number, the number to the right of the "/" is the page number on which the figure appears. Therefore, the example above is "figure 2" on page "23".

A Word of Encouragement
The photo below, is the first tree sculpture I made in 1977. As you can see, I have come a long way to get to the point where I can write several books on the subject. I have kept my first tree sculpture creation to remind me, and to show to others, that art is an ongoing, never ending process! Do not get discouraged if your final sculpture does not look like mine. Remember, I have created thousands of tree sculptures since I started many years ago, and I only show my successes!

The wire used for the twigs is too thin

The spacing between the branches and twigs is too irregular

The branches and twigs are not shaped properly

The twigs go in too many different directions

The overall shape of the tree is too flat

The trunk is too small in proportion to the rest of the tree

Wrapping of the trunk is too sloppy

The roots should be thicker

The rock is unsteady

The tree is not securely bound onto the rock base

The photograph is not lit properly

Before You Start Any Project

Before you start this or any other art or craft project be sure you keep safety as a major part of your procedure. Always protect your eyes, lungs, and skin with quality made protection devices. When you are using any chemicals, always be sure to read all the directions and warnings listed on the package label or on the "Safety Sheet" included with the product. Always work in a well ventilated room, with plenty of light. When you are finished with your project for the day, make certain you have replaced any caps or closed any carton you were working with. You should also be very careful to keep all chemicals and tools out of the reach of children. Keep the phone number of the poison control center in you area handy. The number for the National Poison Control Center is:

1-800-222-1222

All the material and tools necessary to create any of the pieces in this book are available from general supply sources, such as: Arts and Crafts stores, Hardware stores, Florist supply companies and Nature. If you take this book with you when you are shopping for your supplies you can refer to it and see exactly what is needed. Although I do not recommend or promote any store or company, If you are having difficulty obtaining any material or tool described in this book, please contact me and I will be happy to give you the names and addresses of the suppliers I use. I can be contacted at:

Sal Villano
PO Box 827   Milford, Ohio   45150
Website: www.salvillano.com
email: salvillano@gmail.com

I would strongly recommend that you read this entire book before you start to create any of the pieces shown. This will help you to understand the steps before you start.

When you are selecting the type of wire you wish to use to create your piece, you should know how the thickness or "gauge" of the wire is indicated. The gauge of the wire is represented by numbers, such as: 26 gauge, 30 gauge, 36 gauge. It's very important to understand that the SMALLER THE GAUGE NUMBER - THE THICKER THE WIRE! For example:

26 gauge wire is THICKER THAN 30 gauge wire!
See page 125 for a wire gauge chart.

You should also know about the type of wire you may be using. **See page 11** Wire, in general, may change color through the years, but this color change will not affect the strength of the sculpture. The sculptures that are bonded onto bases or into pots using sea sand, pebbles or rocks are for indoor display only. Since the bond is created onto a porous material, a water soluble glue is used. Therefore the sculptures should never be submerged in water, left outdoors, or cleaned in a dishwasher. You can clean and dust your finished work using a damp, soft, lint free, cloth. Or you can use a feather duster for the branches and base. You can also use a hand held steam cleaner. If you are using the steam cleaner, set it on the lowest setting and do not over-wet the base.

Create a "Lies Flat" Version for this Book

If you think you will be creating several different pieces I think it would be very helpful to create what I call a "Lies Flat Book". I have created many of these types of books for each of the many projects I have worked on. In fact, the book you are now using was edited using this system. The "Lies Flat Book" is simply a standard 3 ring binder with clear plastic page protectors in it. I insert each page of the book into the page protectors then I add standard plastic self stick tabs to help me find the exact page I am looking for. The page protectors not only reduce wear and tear on the pages, they also make the individual pages in the binder turn very easy to turn. You can also add notes to any page you want by using *"Post-It Notes"* or other types of self stick papers. To create the pages I use a single edge razor blade to cut each page out of the book. You can also carefully rip each page in the book apart, then insert each page into the plastic page protectors. Creating this book may seem like a lot of work, but once you use it and see how helpful it is, you will realize that the effort used to make the book is well worth it!

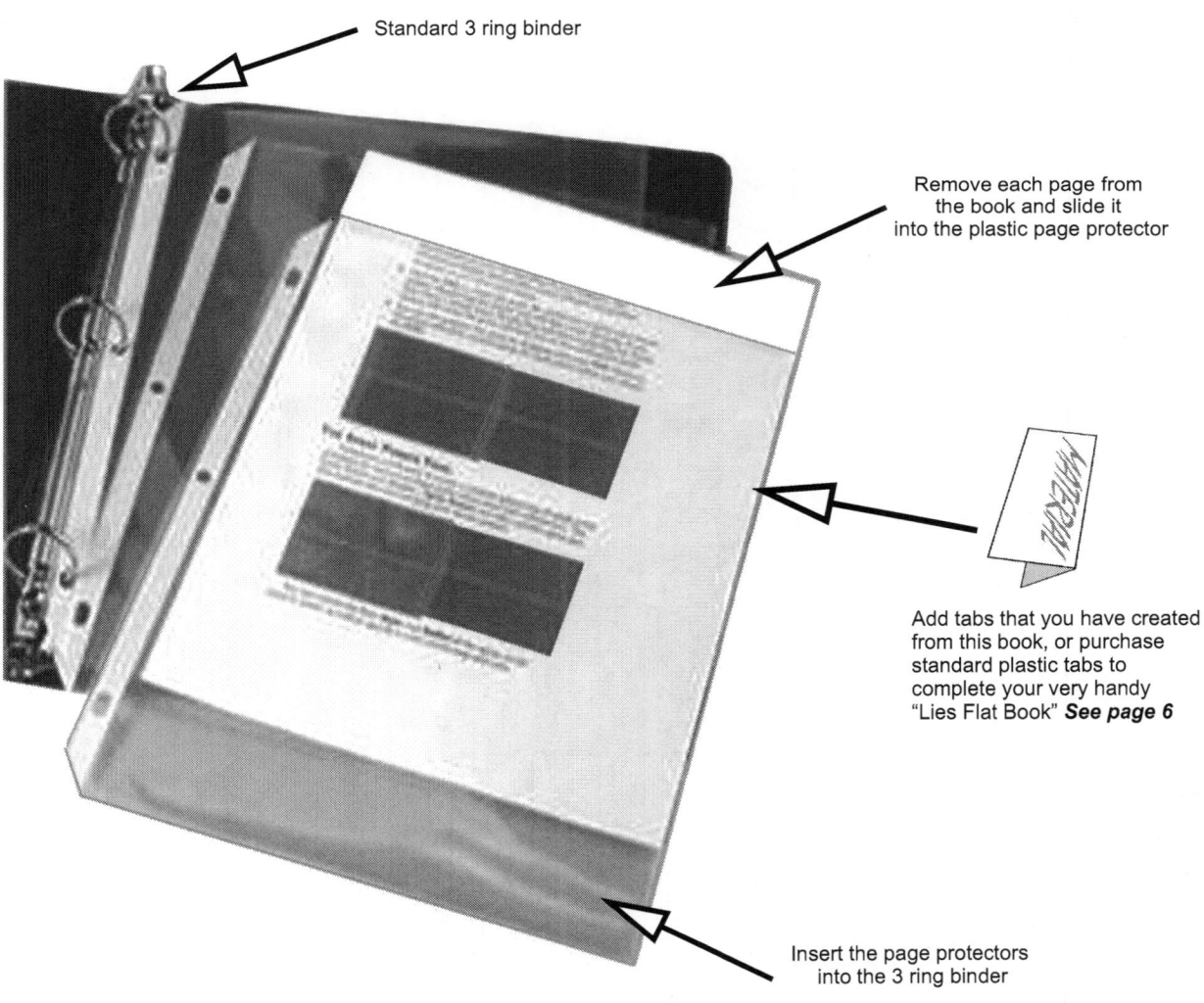

Standard 3 ring binder

Remove each page from the book and slide it into the plastic page protector

Add tabs that you have created from this book, or purchase standard plastic tabs to complete your very handy "Lies Flat Book" *See page 6*

Insert the page protectors into the 3 ring binder

Index Page Tabs for this Book

To make it easier to find the different sections in this book I have created bank tabs so you can write the name of the section on it and tape it on the appropriate page. This will be a great help when you need to refer to different pages as you are creating your piece. The best way to do this is to photocopy this page, then cut out the amount of tabs you need. Write or type the heading on front and back of tab. Fold on dotted line. Tape onto the outside edge of the page.

Write on both sides.
Fold on dotted line.
Tape onto the outside edge of the page

Create these Pieces Using this Book

Using the instructions, and the over 400 drawings and photographs in this book you will be able to create the pieces shown on the following two pages. Plus, by altering and adding to the detailed instructions, you can also create many variations of these basic pieces. I would suggest you read the entire book before you start.

Weeping Willow
Page 39

Beaded
Page 41

Wind Swept
Page 46

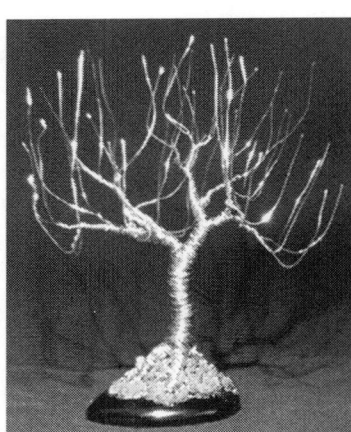
Upright Willow
Page 40

Oak Tree
Page 44

Bonsai with Leaves
Page 47

Bird Nest in a Branch
Page 101

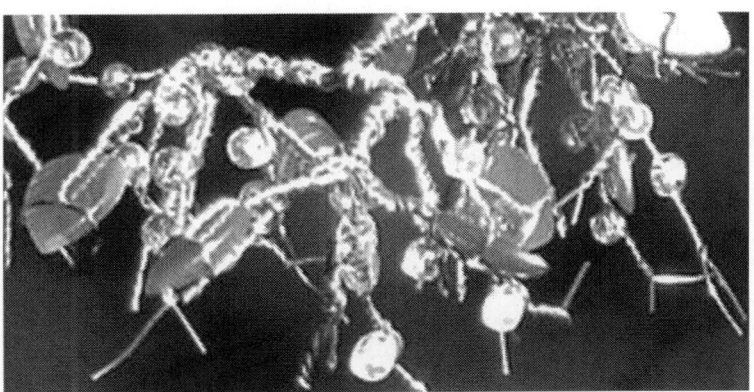
Jade Leaves Mixed with Glass Beads
Page 56

Cascade on Rock *Page 60*

Mini Jade Leaf Cascade *Page 76*

Glass Bonsai *Page 91*

Tree on Sea Shell *Page 86*

Wall Art Sculpture *Page 81*

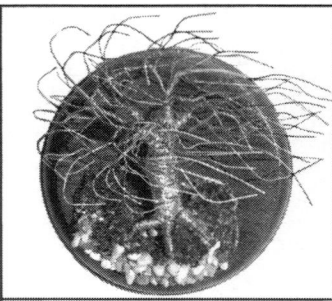

Wind Swept on Round Base

Beaded on Round Base

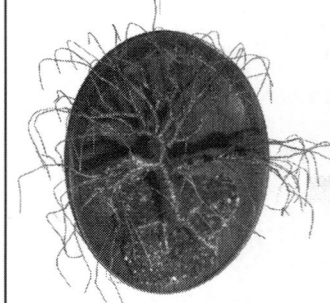

Oak on Oval Base

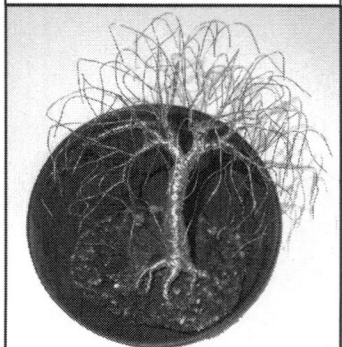

Willow on Round Base

Tools Needed

The following is a list of most of the tools I have used to create all my work. You may not need all of these tools for every piece you create, but I have listed them just to show you what they look like. At the beginning of the instructions for each item, you will find a complete list of all the tools and materials necessary to complete that item. You may also be able to use some tools you may already own that serve the need just as well, for example, a pair of pliers that are also able to cut wire will work. Or a small regular hammer will work as well as a ball peen hammer. And the broad side of a large hammer will work as well as an anvil. If you find a tool that does the job for you, use it. As you may have noticed, I have not suggested or recommended any company or manufacturer as a source to get any supplies. That is because since the advent of the internet and the effectiveness of the search engines it has become very easy to find anything in the world you may need. Simply log onto any search engine, type in what you need, and in a matter of seconds you will have an incredible amount of choices. However if you do not have access to the internet I will be happy to send you a list of the suppliers I use. You can contact me at: *salvillano@gmail.com (No phone calls, please).*

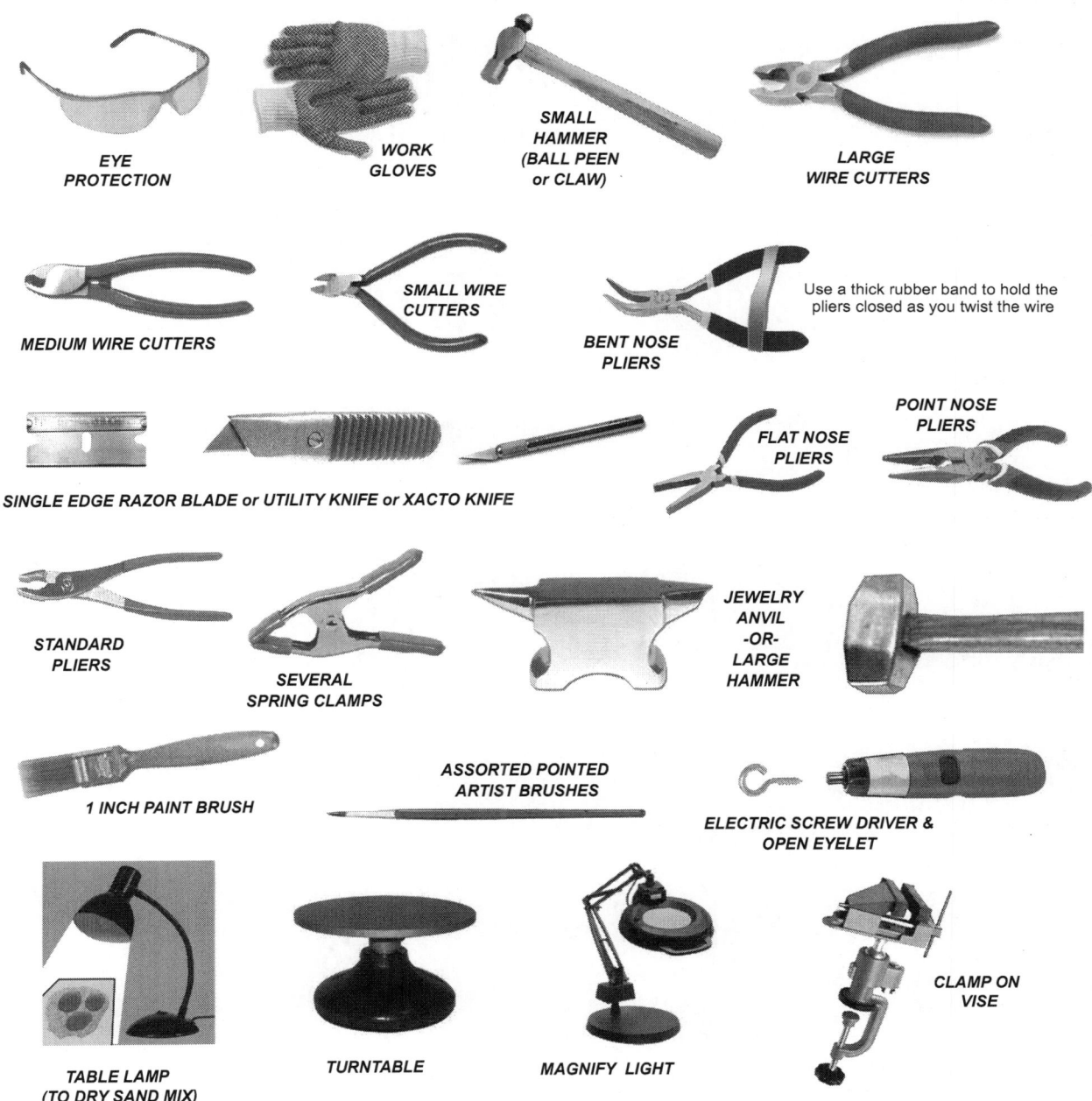

Materials Needed

The following is a list of some of the materials I have used to create my work. You may not need all of these materials for every piece you create, but I have listed them just to show you what they look like. At the beginning of the instructions for each item, you will find a complete list of all the tools and materials necessary to complete that item. As you may have noticed, I have not recommended any company or manufacturer as a source to get any supplies. That is because since the advent of the internet and the effectiveness of the search engines, it has become very easy to find anything you may need. If you don't have access to the internet, I will be happy to send you a list of my suppliers.
Contact me at: *salvillano@gmail.com* (No phone calls, please).

Different Types of Wire

Most of the wire I use ranges in gauge (size) from 30, the thinnest, to 18 the thickest. I have found that any wire thinner than 30 gauge is too weak and will break very easily and any wire thicker than 18 gauge is too thick and difficult to work with. In general I use the thicker wire in the core of the piece and the thinner wire over it to create more detail and a finer look. Wire can be purchased in many forms, from small spools to large reels. Generally, the larger amount of wire you purchase at one time, the less it will cost. **See pages 124 & 125.**

ALUMINIUM - Aluminium wire is very easy to shape and work with. This is an excellent choice of wire if you are going to create trees or loose branches that will have hammered leaves on the ends. The wire is available not only in its natural color but also is produced in many glossy and matte colors.

BRASS - Brass will turn a dark brown color, tarnish and patina creating a very nice finish.

COPPER - 100% copper wire will oxidize slowly and change color or patina into a darker copper color or a dark green color. This is a very nice effect, and will add to the character of the piece. Copper is my favorite wire to work with, and most of my work and commissions are created using copper wire.

CRAFT WIRE - Non-tarnishing craft wire is available in many colors and gauges, such as Gold, Silver, Copper. This wire has a clear lacquer coating that will prevent tarnishing for many years. For the most part, this wire is soft and easy to work with. However if you are going to create any piece that requires hammering the wire flat, the hammering will destroy the protection and the wire will tarnish where you hammered it.

GOLD - Creating a sculpture of gold I'm sure would be beautiful. However considering the price of gold, even gold plating, I have yet to create any tree sculpture out of gold. Perhaps if the price comes down I will create one. I have created a bird nest of gold wire and placed a pearl egg in it. This effect is really beautiful.

PLASTIC COVERED WIRE - This type of wire is available in many different gauge sizes, type of metals and colors of plastic coverings. It is sold in most large hardware stores. After I create the tree, I strip off about 1/8 inch of the plastic on the tip of the wire, then flatten the end to create a leaf. **See page 47** to create a leaf.

SILVER - Silver is very easy to work with. It's relatively soft and will hold a shape. However, as I'm sure you know it will tarnish. If you do choose to work with silver and need to get rid of the tarnish, you will have to submerge the entire piece in a liquid de-tarnishing solution. This may be a bit tricky if you have placed the piece on a base that cannot be subjected to the de-tarnishing liquid. I have never created a piece of silver wire.

STAINLESS STEEL - Stainless Steel wire is very hard and rigid and is more difficult to work with and to cut. The finish of the wire is much like platinum. The wire will not rust.

STEEL - Galvanized steel wire will not rust but will slowly turn in color from a dull silver to a dull gray. This change in color can create some very interesting colors. Ungalvanived steel wire will simply rust to produce a brown color rust.

NOTE - I have also created some tree sculpture using different types of wire in the same piece. For example, using copper wire for the larger inside core, then wrapping the outer surface of the tree with thinner gauge black aluminium wire and letting some of the inner copper wire show through. This technique creates a very interesting effect and will work with almost any two types of wire that are in contrast.

Different Base Styles and Objects

There is literally an endless amount of items that can be used as a base to showcase your creation. I feel that the selection of a base is a very important part in the creation of your overall piece. Some of the items I have used are: solid glass candle holders, actual pots used to grow bonsai, rocks and even driftwood or sea shells. I have listed some of the items I have used, and where I got them. I am always looking for new bases to use.

DRIFT WOOD BASE
Source: Beach on Long Island.

FREE FORMED GLASS
Source: Floral Supply Store.

ROUND BRASS TRAY
Source: Craft Shop.

SMALL FLOWER POT
Source: Garden Store.

SOLID ROUND GLASS
Source: Garage Sale

ROOFING SLATE
Source: Found

ROUND STEEL POT
Source: Gift Shop.

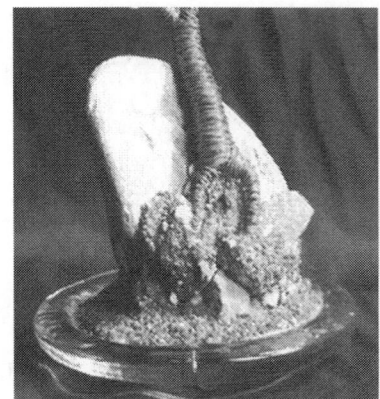
ROUND GLASS TRAY
Source: Gift Shop.

To see completed pieces in Full Color, visit my website: www.salvillano.com

CHINESE CERAMIC
Source: Garden Shop.

ROUND WOOD STAND
Source: Gift Shop.

SQUARE PLATE GLASS
Source: Home Store.

CLIPPED EDGE GLASS
Source: Garage Sale.

ROUND WOOD STAND
Source: Asian Gift Shop.

GLAZED POT on BAMBOO
Source: Asian Gift Shop.

PLASTIC PLANTING TRAY
Source: Garden Shop.

FLAT TERRA COTTA TRAY
Source: Garden Shop.

To see completed pieces in Full Color, visit my website: www.salvillano.com

These are some of the other items I have used as bases for my tree sculpture. I am always looking for interesting objects and bases to which I can add a tree sculpture.

Preparing a Base for a Tree Sculpture

There are many different types of bases that will add to the beauty of your tree sculpture. Before you start to work on the creation of the tree, it is a good idea to prepare the base. There is a considerable amount of time required for drying between each step. You can work on the base, then as each step is drying, you can work on the rest of the tree. For this piece I have chosen a tan colored ceramic "Bonsai" type of base with an interesting shape. What I also do is to have several different types of bases ready to accept the sculpture, then after a tree is completed, I just decide which base looks the best. Plus, having several bases always on hand gives me different ideas for tree shapes and sizes.

See page 14. I also consider the color of the wire I am using as it relates to the color of the base. For example. I would use gold color wire in a white base. It is important to be sure the base you choose has enough mass and weight so the tree does not fall over due to being top heavy. I always use a rock as the main support inside the base.

The following photos show the steps necessary to prepare a Bonsai pot as a base. These instructions can be applied to any type of container you wish to use. Be sure the material the container is made of will accept the white craft glue you are using. You can use plain sand or sand mixed with small pebbles to mix with the glue. I always use the mix, I think it adds more interest to the piece.

See page 19 to learn how to prepare a flat or irregular surface to accept the tree sculpture.

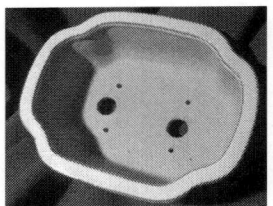
1. If the base has holes in it, you will need to plug them up.

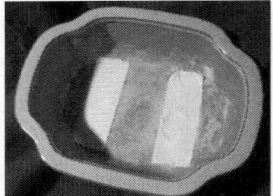
2. Cover all the holes with Masking Tape.

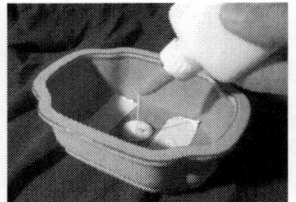
3. Place about 10 to 12 drops of white glue in the pot.

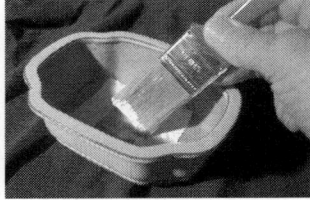
4. Spread the glue all over the bottom of the pot.

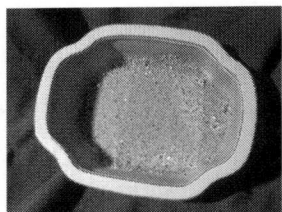
5. Cover the glue with sand. When dry, dump excess sand.

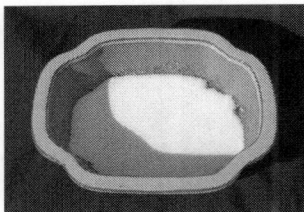
6. Fill the bottom of the pot with about 1/4 inch of glue.

7. Cover the glue with sand. When dry, dump excess sand.

8. Repeat steps 5,6,7 until sand is about 1/2 inch from rim of pot.

9. Create a glue puddle in the middle of the pot as shown.

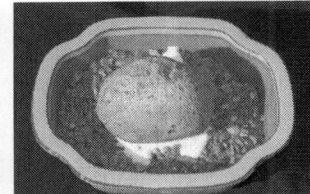
10. Put a support rock into the glue, fill with sand. Let dry then dump out excess sand.

11. Repeat until the rock is about 1/2 covered with sand.

12. The base is now ready for the tree sculpture.

As illustrated on **pages 12, 13 & 14** you can use many different types of materials as a base for your tree sculpture. You can actually use any porous material to mount your tree sculpture on. Some of the irregular shapes and items I have used are: *Driftwood, Marble, Ceramics, Wooden Trays, Found Rocks, Slate, Sea Shells* and many more. Just be sure the base you select is compatible with the white craft glue you are using. Before starting, read the label on the package and it will list the type of surfaces the glue will bond with.

When selecting the size and shape of the base, be sure the base does not visually overpower the size and shape of the tree. And also be sure the base is not too large for the tree. After you have created the tree and mounted it on the base, should you find you are not pleased with the results, you can separate the tree and the base by placing them in a container of clean warm water. Since the glue you used is water soluble, it will dissolve and release the roots from the mound. After the tree is completely dry, you can try again.

SMALL FREE FORMED GLASS BASE - For small tree sculpture, about 3 to 4 inches tall, I use pieces of free formed glass. This type of glass is also called "flat marbles" or "flat floral glass". You can use just one piece for a base, **Fig. 1/16**, or you can assemble several pieces together to form a larger base. **See page 17, Fig. 2/17.** I like to use this type of glass base because it is available in many colors and I can create a base using a color that will work with the wire I am using for the tree sculpture. The glass is made with a flat bottom and a round top. It is very stable, and has a nice irregular contour. Another interesting characteristic of the glass is that it reflects and amplifies light. This quality of the glass is most effective if you are creating a tree sculpture that has beads or gems on it. You can also use the basic instructions that follow, if you want to use rocks or other items as a base. Just be sure the items you are using will bond with the glue.

Fig. 1/16

CREATING THE ONE PIECE BASE -
The single piece of glass I use for this base is about 2" x 1.5" x .25" thick. The thickness of the base is what makes it so strong.

1. Place a dab of glue, about the size of a quarter, onto the top center of the glass. **Fig. 1/16**

Fig. 2/16

2. Add sand, with or without pebbles mixed in it, around the edges of the glue. This will stop the glue from running down the sides. **Fig. 2/16**

3. After you are sure that no glue is running down the sides, cover the entire glass base with more sand.

4. Let the entire assembly dry in place overnight. When all is dry. Remove excess sand. You will have created a solid mound on the center of the glass base. This is the foundation for the tree sculpture. **Fig. 3/16**

Fig. 3/16

CREATING A MULTI PIECE GLASS BASE - For medium size tree sculpture, about 5 to 8 inches, I use several pieces of free formed glass bonded together. These pieces can all be flat, next to each other, *Fig. 1/17* or you can lie one or more pieces on top of each other. *Fig. 2/17*. To create this type of base you will need to assemble all the parts on a non-stick cookie sheet. This is necessary to prevent the glue from sticking to the surface you are working on. I will explain the steps and show the photos for creating the flat multi-piece base. To create a layered base, you need only to bond more pieces to the completed flat base. You can also use the basic instructions that follow, if you want to use rocks or other items to create a base. Just be sure the items you are using for the base will bond with the glue and the sand mixture.

Fig. 1/17

Fig. 2/17

1. Place the pieces of the base about 1/4 inch apart, with the rounded side up. I show three pieces, you can use more if you like. Be sure you are assembling this base on a non-stick cookie sheet. *Fig. 1/17*

2. Gently apply a 1/16 inch layer of sand, with or without pebbles mixed in, between and around the entire assembly. Try not to move the separate pieces as you do this. This is an important step, if you move the pieces too far apart or too close together, you may have a problem with later steps. *Fig. 4/17*

3. Apply the white glue into the center of the pieces and about 1/4 of the way onto the top of each piece of glass. *Fig. 5/17*

4. Cover the entire assembly with more sand. Let this dry overnight. It is very important that you allow the glue to dry thoroughly before you proceed to the next step.

5. Gently brush the sand off the top of the glass pieces. Do not remove the sand from the sides. To test if the glue is dry, gently slide the base on the cookie sheet about 1/4 inch. If any of the pieces start to pull apart, the assembly is not yet dry. Let the base dry for several more hours.

6. After you are sure the base is dry, leave all the sand that is around the perimeter of the base. Now create the actual mound onto the base the same way you created the mound on the single piece base. *See page 16, Fig. 3/16*

Fig. 3/17

Fig. 4/17

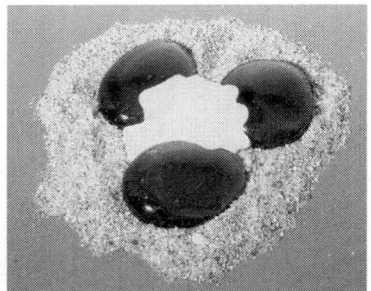
Fig. 5/17

The following pages will show the beginning steps necessary to prepare other objects you may want to use as a base for your tree sculpture. I will show you how to set up the item and begin the process. Since the ending steps are the same for all the items, you can then refer to *page 16,* to see how to finish the final steps for creating the root mound that will accept the finished tree sculpture.

DRIFT WOOD - The instructions to create the base using drift wood, can also be used to create any irregular shaped base, such as coral, found rocks, sea shells, chipped edge glass. Be sure the white craft glue will bond to the object you have selected.

I have used pieces of drift wood many times for my bases. I collected the pieces from beaches I visited, until I discovered the best place to get the drift wood is from a pet supply shop. You can purchase beautiful pieces that have been cleaned and disinfected. Usually it is in the tropical fish or bird department of the shop.

1. Place the piece or pieces of drift wood into a container that has four sides on it. This is so the sand you use will be contained *Fig. 1/18*

2. Build a sand dam upon the area where you want the tree sculpture to sit. *Fig. 2/18*

3. Fill the inside of the dam with the white glue. *Fig. 3/18*

4. Cover the entire glue area with sand and let the entire piece dry overnight. *Fig. 4/18*

5. After you are sure the entire piece is dry, remove the excess sand. You will now have a rock in a mound on which you will attach the tree sculpture. *Fig. 5/18*

6. If you feel the root mound is too small, repeat steps, 3,4, and 5. It is actually better to add to a root mound that is too small, then try to chip away at a mound that is too large. For instructions to mount your finished tree sculpture to this type of base, **See page 71**

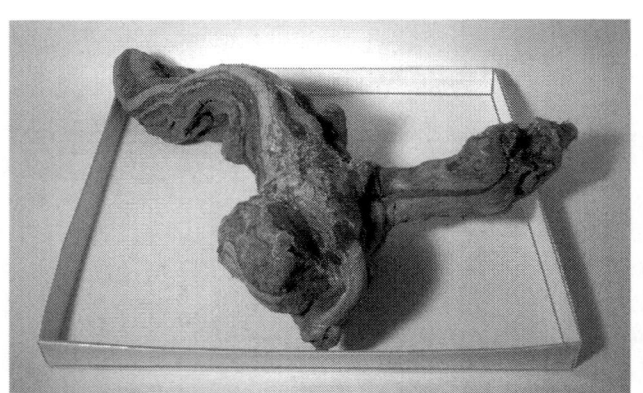

Fig. 1/18

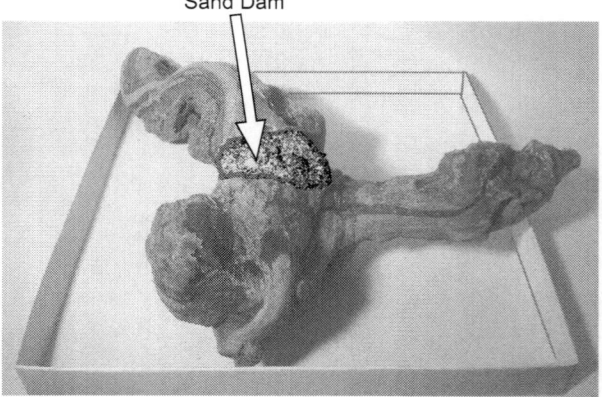

Sand Dam

Fig. 2/18

Fig. 3/18

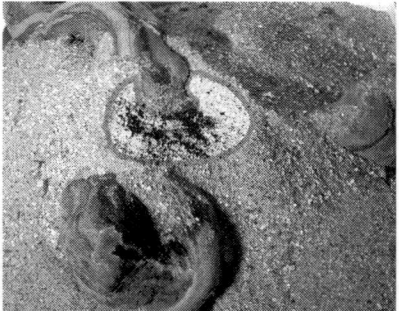

Fig. 4/18

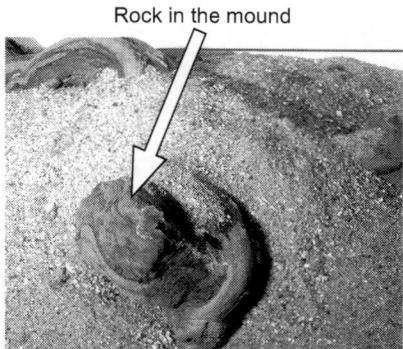

Rock in the mound

Fig. 5/18

The following pages will show the beginning steps necessary to prepare other objects you may want to use as a base for your tree sculpture. I will show you how to set up the item and begin the process. Since the ending steps are the same for all the items, you can then refer to *page 16* to finish the final steps to create the root mound that will accept the tree sculpture.

GLASS CANDLE BASE - The instructions to create the glass candle base, can also be used to create a base on any flat surface area. Be sure the white craft glue will bond to the object you have selected. I often use clear glass candle bases as a support for many of my tree sculptures. This type of base looks very nice especially when the tree that sits upon it is made using glass beads in the branches, *See page 43,* adding beads.

There are many different types, and sizes of candle bases that will work very well with tree sculpture. Sometimes I leave the root area flat and other times I add a rock or shells or even pieces of broken glass to add more interest to the piece. The following instructions will show how to create this base using a rock in the center. *Fig. 4/19*

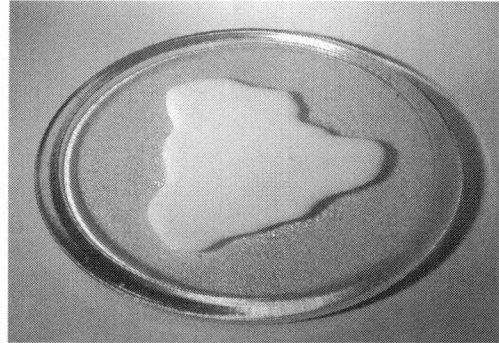

Fig. 1/19

1. Apply white craft glue in an irregular pattern to the area of the base in which you wish to place the tree sculpture. If you want a more defined area as your root mound area, you can brush on the glue to the exact place you want it. *Fig. 1/19* Be sure you wash your brush as soon as you finish applying the glue. If not, you will have a rock hard brush.

2. Using sand, create a dam around the edges of the glue area. *Fig. 2/19*

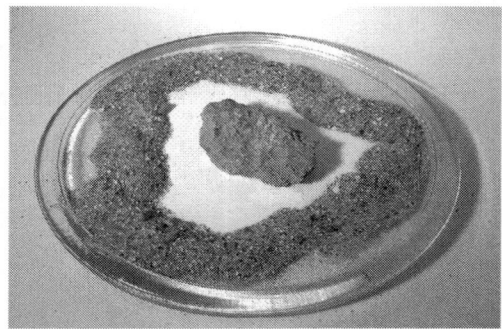

Fig. 2/19

3. Add about 1/8th inch of the white glue within the perminter of the edges of the sand dam. Place the rock or other object you wish to use, in the center of the glue within dam area. Then cover the entire glue area and the base of the rock with more sand. If you notice any of the glue seeping through any part of the mound, add more sand to stop the seepage. *Fig. 3/19*

Fig. 3/19

4. Let the base dry overnight, When you are sure the entire area is dry, remove all the excess sand. *Fig. 4/19* You have created a sand mound with a rock in the center. You can mount the tree directly on the rock or cover the rock with more sand. To mount your finished tree on the base, *See page 71*

Fig. 4/19

FREE FORMED SAND BASE - A free formed base is one that has an irregular shape and is not bonded to any other object. This type of base can be created using only a sand & pebble mix and white craft glue. Or, you can start with a free formed piece of 1/8 inch thick piece of cork and build the base on top of it. The cork is used to prevent the dried sand and pebbles from marring any surface the base is on. If you choose to create an entirely free formed base, you will need to put several felt pads on the bottom to prevent

1. On a non-stick cookie sheet create the outline of the shape of your free formed base, using the white glue. *Fig. 1/20*

2. Using the sand (with or without the small pebbles mixed in), create a dam around the outline of the white craft glue. *Fig. 2/20*

3. Add a 1/8 inch deep puddle of the white craft glue inside the sand perimiter. *Fig. 3/20*

4. Cover the entire area with the sand mix. Let all dry overnight. *Fig. 4/20.*
Note: This base may require more drying time. To help speed up the drying time, you can place the entire piece under a lamp to create more heat for faster drying.

5. When you are sure all is dry, remove the excess sand. If you wish to add an object in the middle, like a rock or a shell, you may add it now. Create another sand dam around the object you added, and repeat steps **3** and **4**.

FREE FORMED CORK BASE - This base is created on a piece of 1/8th inch thick piece of cork. The cork on the bottom of the base prevents the sand from marring any surface.

1. Cut out a piece of 1/8th inch thick cork to the shape of the base you want. *Fig. 5/20*

2. Place the cut out cork onto a non-stick cookie sheet.

3. Apply the white craft glue all around the perimiter of the cork base. *Fig. 6/20*

4. Repeat steps **3, 4,** and **5** from the free formed sand base section above.

For instructions to mount a finished tree sculpture to these types of bases, **See page 71**

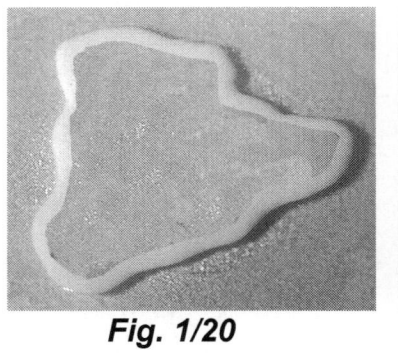
Fig. 1/20

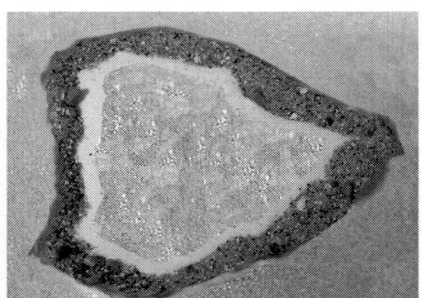
Fig. 2/20

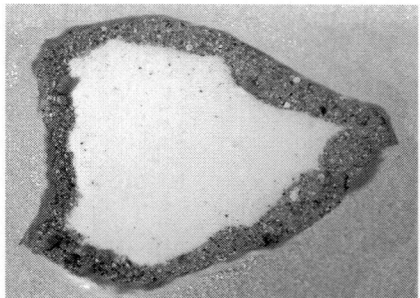
Fig. 3/20

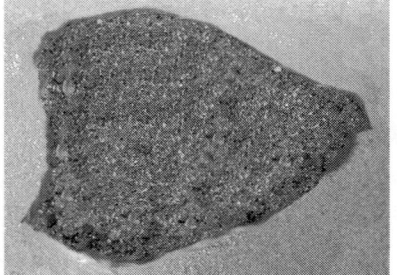
Fig. 4/20

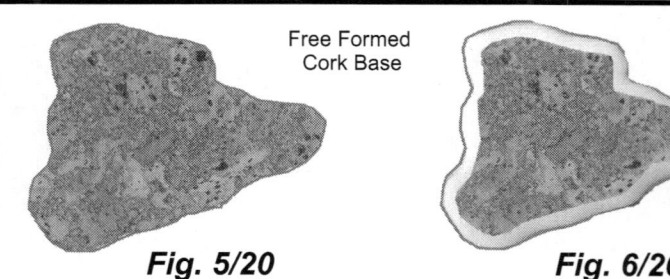
Free Formed Cork Base
Fig. 5/20 *Fig. 6/20*

Creating a Mini Tree Sculpture

This next section, will show you the steps necessary to create the Mini Tree Sculptures. I would suggest you read the entire section before you start. I would also suggest that you create several of the mini trees before you move on to the larger pieces. By doing this you will get a feel for working with the wire and the tools, how to bond the tree to the base, and how to add color to the root mound. I think you will be very pleasantly surprised to see how each of the trees you create will be better than the one before. These mini trees can be put into a large variety of bases. ***See pages 12, 13 & 14*** for more base selections.

You will start by making a jig ***See page 22*** and finish by shaping the basic structure into the style of tree you want. These are the 6 mini tree sculptures which you can create:

Weeping Willow
Page 39
The easiest of all the trees to form it requires very little additional cutting and shaping.

Beaded
Page 41
This decorative tree is created by adding glass fringe beads to the Weeping Willow tree.

Wind Swept
Page 46
To create the Wind Swept you will need to re-shape the trunk, branches and trim some of the branches and twigs.

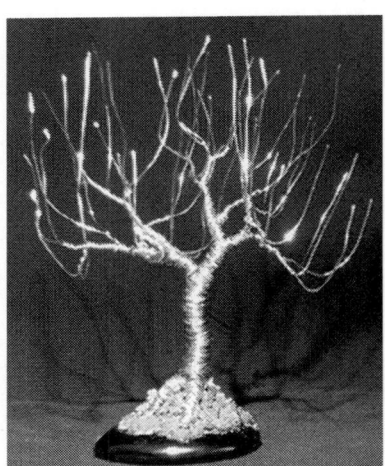

Upright Willow
Page 40
The same as the Weeping Willow, but with turned up branches and twigs.

Oak Tree
Page 44
This tree requires bending, twisting, re-shaping and cutting of all the branches and twigs.

Bonsai with Leaves
Page 47
Similar to creating the Oak tree, but the ends of the twigs are hammered flat to look like thin leaves.

To see completed pieces in Full Color, visit my website: www.salvillano.com

Making the Jig to Create a Tree Sculpture
Choosing Wood or Metal

You may or may not know what a jig is, so I'll explain what it is and what it is used for. A jig is a device that is used to aid, speed up or make more exact, the construction or assembly of something else. A jig is used to create the same object over and over again to the same standards. However, the jig itself is not part of the final product, but it is an important part of the process to create the final product. For the creation of wire trees, the jig is used to control the size and total amount of wire needed for the basic tree structure you will be creating. After you make your jig, you should save it for future use. The jig can then be altered, as can the amount of wire wraps used to create larger and different varieties of tree sculpture.

THE WOOD JIG

This jig is very easy to construct using a piece of wood, (it can of course be scrap wood), cut the wood to the sizes indicated in the illustration. You will also need three or four 2.5" or 3" finishing nails. Finishing nails are the type of nails that have small heads. The small heads of the nails will help when you need to slip the wire off the nails. ***Fig. 1/22*** To facilitate easier removal you can also cut the small heads of the nail off using your large wire cutters. The nails should be driven into the wood about 1/2 to 3/4 inch before you cut off the nail head. After you drive the nails into the wood as shown, loosen one of the nails in its hole. This is done so that you can remove this loosened nail after you have wrapped the wire which will allow you to more easily remove the finished wrapped wire. If you like, you can, as an alternate way of inserting the nails, drill a hole that is larger than the hole the nail would make. This will allow the nail to be more easily removed. Notice that the overall size of the jig is given, however the position of the holes will be given in the instructions as you prepare to create each tree sculpture. ***Fig. 2/22*** Once you have cut the wood jig to size, be sure you sand all the edges to avoid getting splinters. You may also want to clamp the wood jig to a table or workbench which will make wrapping the wire easier.

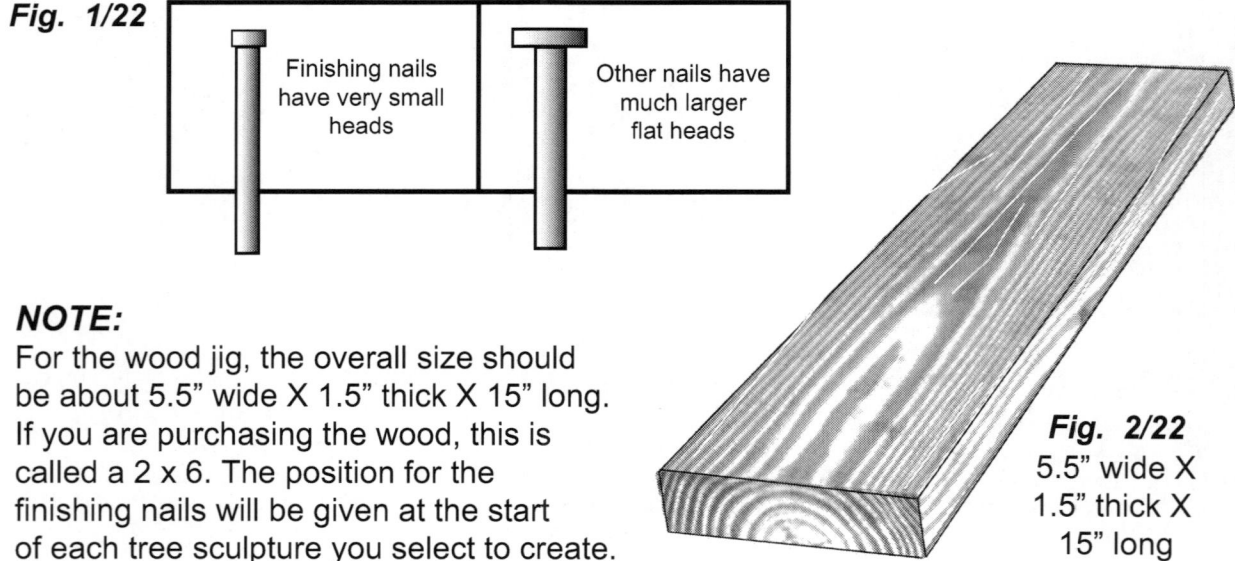

Fig. 1/22

Finishing nails have very small heads

Other nails have much larger flat heads

NOTE:
For the wood jig, the overall size should be about 5.5" wide X 1.5" thick X 15" long. If you are purchasing the wood, this is called a 2 x 6. The position for the finishing nails will be given at the start of each tree sculpture you select to create.

Fig. 2/22
5.5" wide X
1.5" thick X
15" long

The Metal Jig

If you think you may be creating several different types and sizes of tree sculptures, I would suggest that you use a more permanent and durable type of jig. I have been using this type of metal jig for many years and have found it is effective, durable and very versatile. I have created 2 inch to 20 inch tree sculptures using this type of metal jig. The metal jig is a little more involved to construct than the wood jig, but it will last indefinitely. You will need the following materials to create this jig:

1. 24 inch length of angle iron, with holes. This is a standard piece of building material and is available at most large or small hardware stores. 24" long x 1.5" x 1.5" **Fig. 1/23**

2. 2 each of 2.5" threaded bolts, wing nuts or hex nuts, flat washers, lock washers. Be sure the bolts fit through all the holes of the angle iron. **Fig. 3/23**

3. Open end wrench that fits the head of the bolt and the nut, if used.

4. Two spring clamps to hold the jig firmly onto a table or work bench.

5. Use marker or labels to number the holes in the angle iron, to keep a record of the placement of the bolts, so you can create a similar tree sculpture if you want. **Fig. 2/23**

6. When positioning the bolt in the angle iron, put at least one of the bolts through the end of an oval shaped hole. This will make it easier when you remove the wire from the bolt. **Fig. 2/23**

7. Fig. 4/23 Is the final set up for the metal jig. You will be given the final placement of the bolts into the holes angle iron to create your tree sculpture.

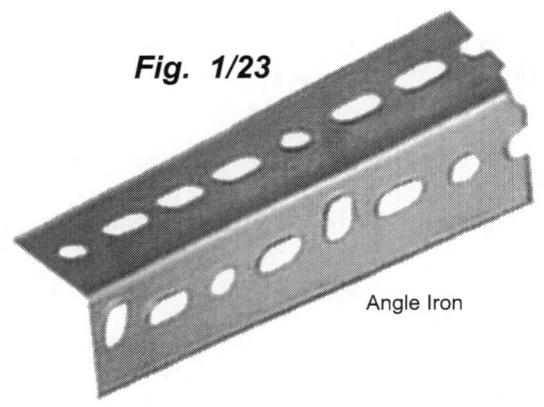
Angle Iron

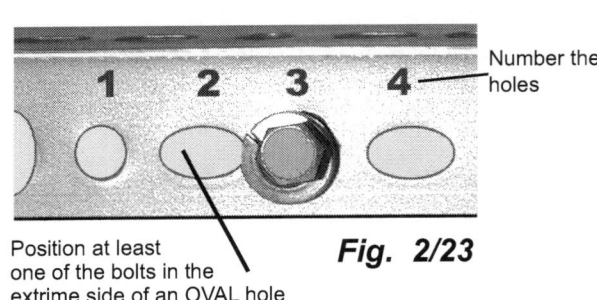
Number the holes
Position at least one of the bolts in the extrime side of an OVAL hole
Fig. 2/23

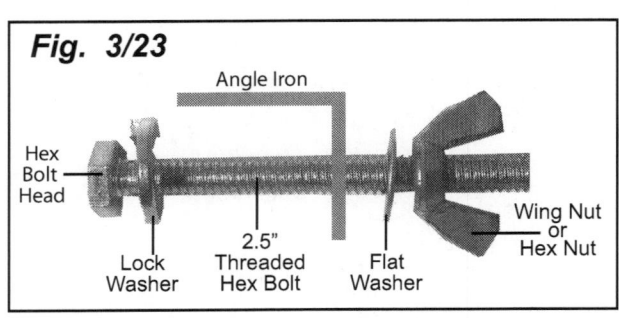
Fig. 3/23
Angle Iron
Hex Bolt Head
Lock Washer
2.5" Threaded Hex Bolt
Flat Washer
Wing Nut or Hex Nut

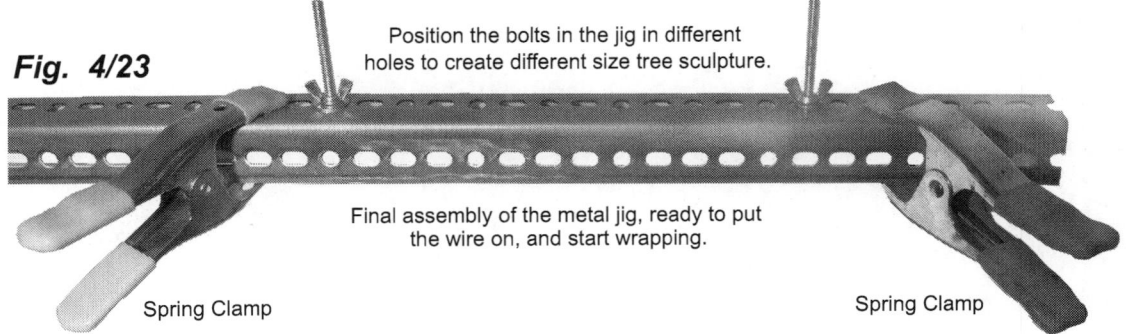
Fig. 4/23
Position the bolts in the jig in different holes to create different size tree sculpture.
Final assembly of the metal jig, ready to put the wire on, and start wrapping.
Spring Clamp — Spring Clamp

Wrapping the Wire to Create a Mini Tree Sculpture

I will show and explain how to create the mini trees using the wood jig. *See page 22* You can also use the metal jig. *See page 23.* If you choose to use the metal jig to create these trees, place the bolts 6 inches apart and follow the same steps.

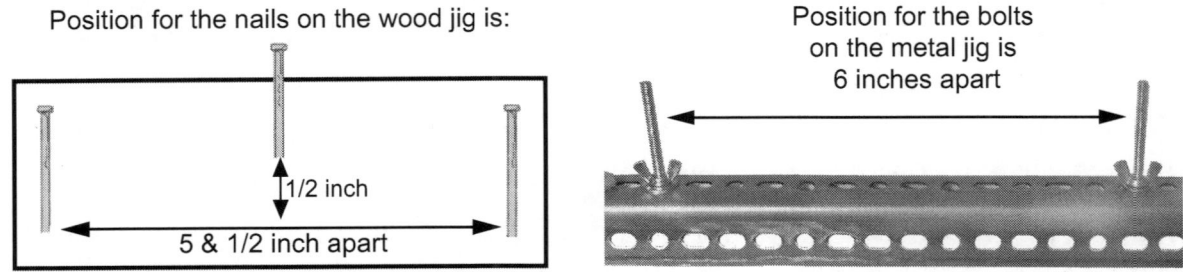

Position for the nails on the wood jig is: 1/2 inch, 5 & 1/2 inch apart

Position for the bolts on the metal jig is 6 inches apart

NOTE: Use 26 gauge wire, (any color you choose), as the SOURCE WIRE for all the following Mini Tree Sculptures.

1. Using the source wire create a small loop around any of the nails hammered into the wood. *Fig. 1/24* This loop will anchor the wire so it does not slip off the nails while you are wrapping the rest of the wire for the start of the tree. Do not try to hold the source wire in your hand while you are wrapping. Unwrap about 3 feet of wire before you start the wrapping. This will make the wrapping process much easier. You may find in the process of wrapping that the wire may sometimes get tangled or twisted. When this happens, twirl or twist the wire in the opposite direction of the tangle, this will remove the kinks.

2. Wrap the wire 35 times around the outside of all three of the finishing nails. *Fig. 2/24* Do not wrap the wire too tight. Remember, you will need to slip the wire off the nails when you have finished the wrapping. One wrap is completed when you are back at the point where you started. It does not matter where you start the wrapping or in which direction you proceed. Be sure you keep count of the wraps and end at 35. While you are wrapping, keep the wire bundle as close to the base of the nails as possible, this will prevent the wire from slipping off the tops of the nails as you wrap.

3. When the wrapping is completed, use the small wire cutters, and carefully cut the source wire about 2" away from the nail where you completed the 35th wrap. Gently slip the wrapped wire bundle off the nails. The wire bundle should look like a triangle with a straight wire at one end and a coiled wire at the other end. Uncoil the small section of wire that was used to hold the wire on the nail when you started. *Fig. 3/24*

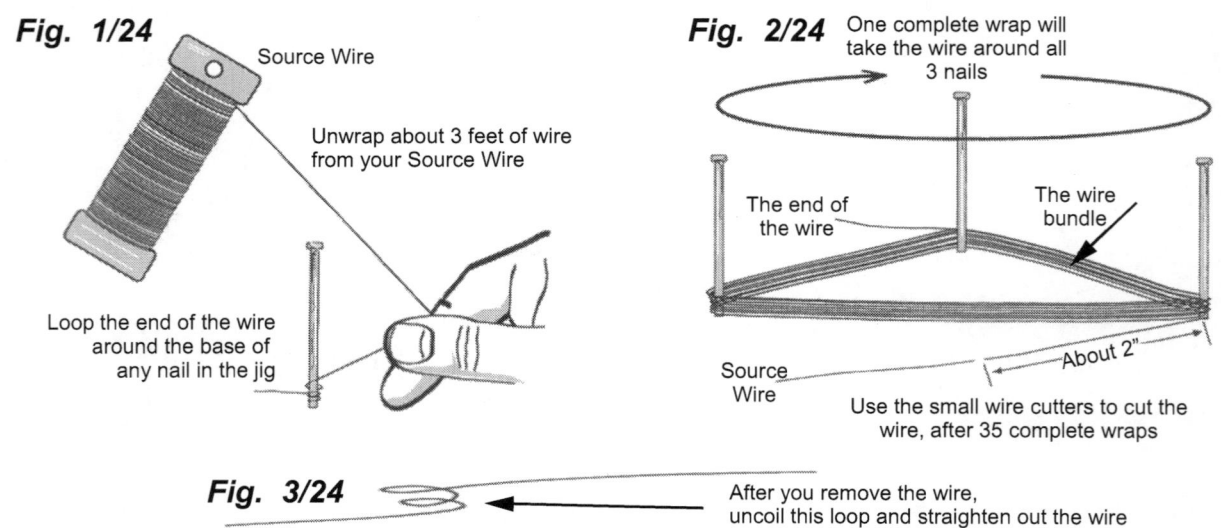

Fig. 1/24 Source Wire — Unwrap about 3 feet of wire from your Source Wire. Loop the end of the wire around the base of any nail in the jig.

Fig. 2/24 One complete wrap will take the wire around all 3 nails. The end of the wire. The wire bundle. Source Wire. About 2". Use the small wire cutters to cut the wire, after 35 complete wraps.

Fig. 3/24 After you remove the wire, uncoil this loop and straighten out the wire.

4. Hold the completed bundle of wire in both hands and shape it into an oval. ***Fig. 1/25*** Unbend, as much as possible, the corners of the wire bundle that were shaped by being wrapped around the nails or bolts. Leave both ends of the wire extended out of the bundle. Unwrap one end of the extended wire until it is about 2" long.

5. Firmly hold the wire bundle about 1/3 the distance in from the curved end of the bundle. ***Fig. 2/25***

6. While holding the wire bundle firmly in one hand, use your other hand to bend up the 2" end piece of the wire. ***Fig. 3/25***

7. Wrap the 2" piece of wire around the wire bundle as shown. Keep a firm grip on the wire bundle as you wrap, and wrap the wire as tightly as you can. Also wrap the other loose end of the wire onto the wire bundle. The first wrappings are important for two reasons. It is this wrap that will hold the bundle together as you work on the tree, and it will also give you a feel for how the wrapping is done. ***Fig. 4/25***

8. Using the medium wire cutters, cut through the entire wire bundle about 1" from the curve closest to the wire coil. It may take a few attempts to cut all the wire, but be sure all the wire is completely cut. ***Fig. 5/25***

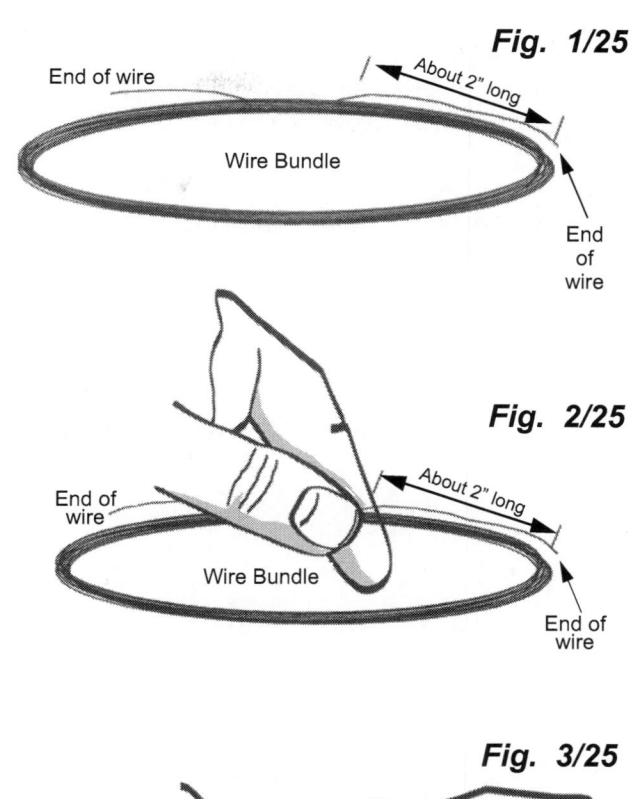

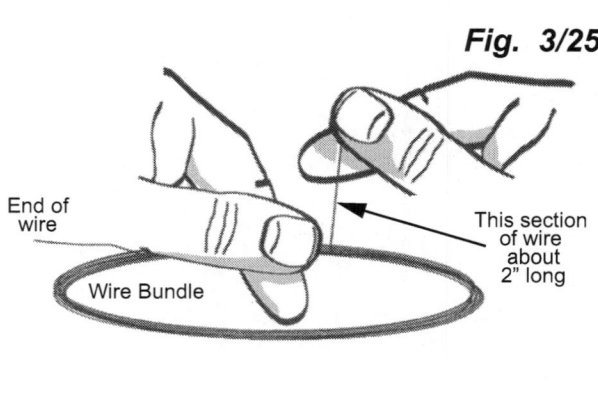

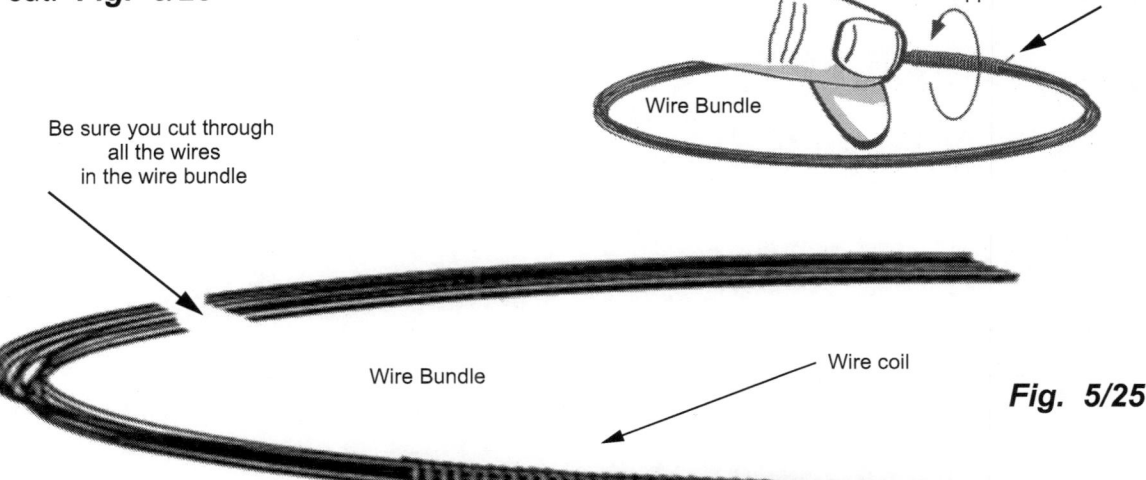

9. After all the wire in the bundle is cut, **Fig. 1/26** unbend both curves in the bundle. You should be left with one straight bundle of wire held together by the wire coil near the end of the wire. **Fig. 2/26**

10. At this point the wire bundle structure should look like **Fig. 2/26** The measurements indicated on the illustration do not have to be exactly as stated, however they should be as close as you can get them.

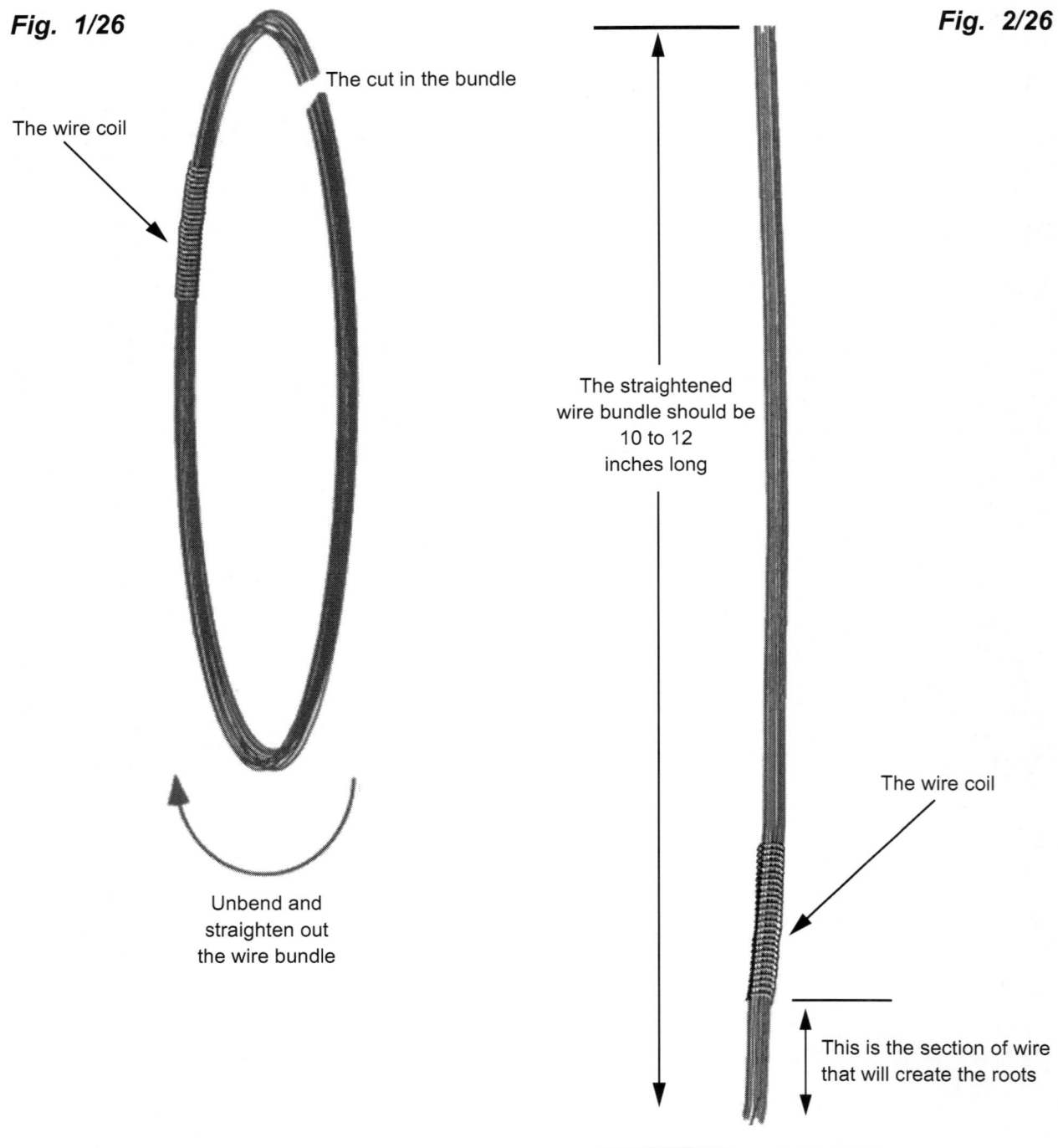

Fig. 1/26
The cut in the bundle
The wire coil
Unbend and straighten out the wire bundle

Fig. 2/26
The straightened wire bundle should be 10 to 12 inches long
The wire coil
This is the section of wire that will create the roots

Creating a Root System for a Mini Tree Sculpture

I find the root systems of trees very interesting. As with all elements in nature, each tree has a unique character all its own. Some trees have deep roots that show very little detail on the surface, with most of the root system buried deep into the earth. Other trees have roots that appear to be only on the surface of the soil and offering an exciting visual of how they support the structure of the tree. It is the trees that offer this unique view that I find the most interesting.

When you are creating the root system of your tree, do not try to follow exactly what I have illustrated in these pages. Use the techniques shown only as a guide and try to create a root system that is yours. When creating the root system do not be concerned about counting the wraps or if you are coiling the wire too tight. If the roots you create are a little larger or smaller than I show, it is really not important to the final look of your sculpture. The goal you should strive for is to create a root system that appears to be capable of supporting the tree. When you look at the roots, and they appear to be solid, stable and strong, you have created an effective root system.

The roots I will show you how to create will be partially buried in the "root mound" to help support the tree, therefore it is better to create the roots larger rather than smaller. (I will describe in detail the function and importance of the root mound in the upcoming chapters).

I have found through my years of observing the root systems of trees that in many instances the roots usually grow from the base of the tree in odd numbers at various angles and with many twists, turns and bumps.

You are now ready to start wrapping and creating the roots and the rest of the tree. You will be working from the same wire source for the entire tree. This wire will not be cut until the tree sculpture is completely finished.

1. Holding the wire bundle firmly in the area where the wire coil is, separate the lower part of the root wires into approximately 3 equal sections. *Fig. 1/27* Do not be concerned if the three sections are not equal. In fact, the root system will look more natural and interesting if the sections are of different sizes and shapes.

2. You are now going to start to wrap the rest of the tree with the wire. Using the source wire, wrap wire tightly up the wire coil toward the top of the tree. *Fig. 2/27* This first wire wrapping is used to hold all the wire together, so you only need enough to hold the rest of the wire in place as you wrap. This support wire will eventually be wired completely over when you start to add more volume and thickness to the entire tree trunk.

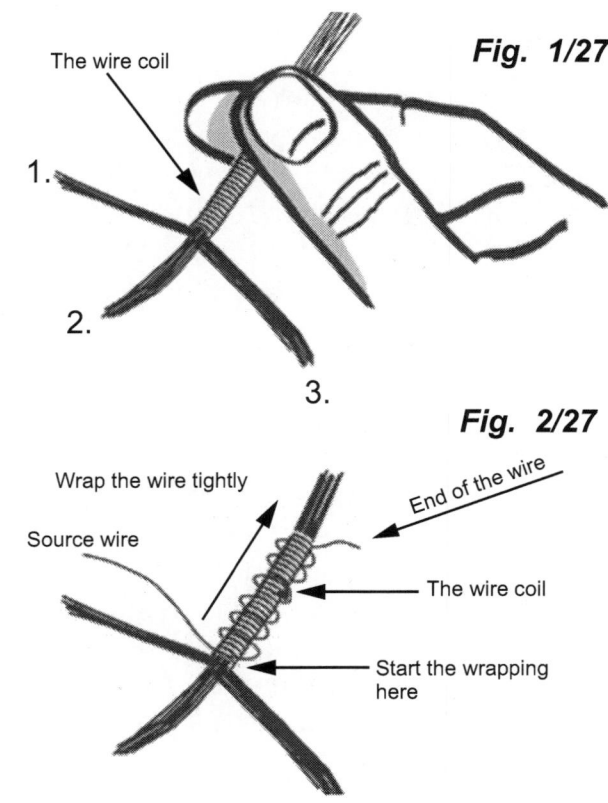

3. Using the source wire, start circular wrapping any one of the root sections beginning at the base of the trunk and wrapping out toward the end of the root. Wrap the wire half way down the root section, then stop. At the point where you stopped wrapping, separate the remaining root sections into 2 or more approximately equal root groups. Loop the wire through the "V" section of the root, then begin wrapping back toward the base of the trunk where you started. *Fig. 1/28*

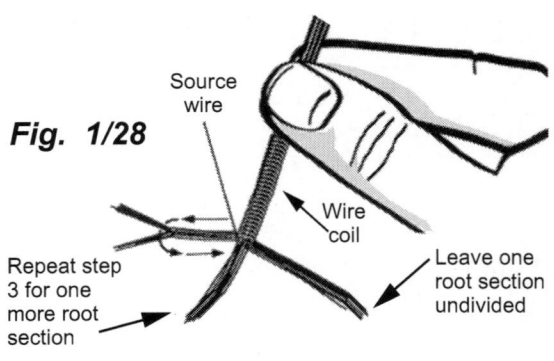
Fig. 1/28

4. Repeat step **3,** for one more of the root sections. The last root section will be created as one large root to add more interest and variation to the entire root system.

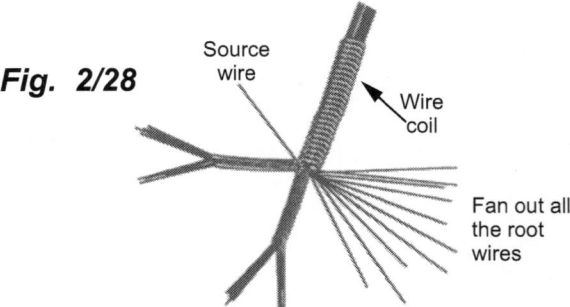
Fig. 2/28

5. Separate and fan out all the individual root wires of the final root section. *Fig. 2/28* This will be the largest of the three root sections. Keep this in mind as you create this section.

6. Starting with the longest of the root wires, and using the small wire clippers, snip off the ends of each strand of wire progressively and slightly smaller than the one before. *Fig. 3/28* Remember, you can always clip off more wire if needed, but you can't "grow" any of the root wire back!

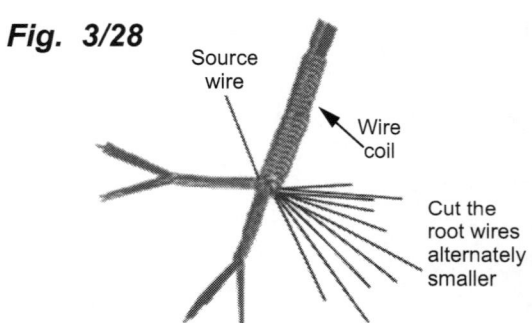
Fig. 3/28

7. Repeat steps 5 & 6 for the other smaller root sections.

8. Working with one root section at a time, squeeze the root wires together to create a total of five root point ends. The root section will have a slight taper. This tapering will give the root section a much more realistic look. *Fig. 4/28*

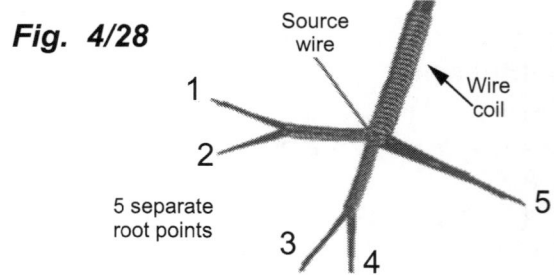
Fig. 4/28

9. Using the source wire, slowly and carefully wrap the wire on to each root section. This time, wrap the wire all the way to the end of the root then back to the trunk, then onto the next root section. *Fig. 5/28* You should end the wrapping of these sections with the source wire at the bottom of the trunk. Do not try to keep the wire equally spaced or neatly wrapped. Allow the wire to create irregular shapes and little interesting bumps wherever they happen.

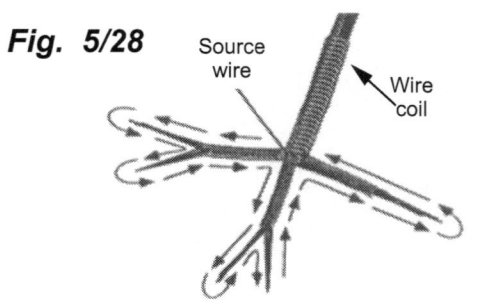
Fig. 5/28

Wiring the Trunk and Branches for a Mini Tree Sculpture

Wiring the trunk and branches requires the same basic techniques as you used to wire the root system, except now you will need to do much more wiring and over wiring. You should by now be proficient in the process of wiring the tree sculpture. If you feel you are not yet proficient in the process you may want to practice on some scrap wire to create a root system, trunk and branches. Once again, as you are wiring the branches and trunk do not try to keep the wiring equally spaced or smooth. The subtle differences and irregularities in the process of wiring are necessary to give the piece a varied surface texture. You may even want to double back over an area that was previously wired and overwire it for a small section. This doubling back technique will create the little bumps and stubs that are common on so many tree branches and trunks. If you do choose to do some overwiring, only do so for three to five wraps within a small area.

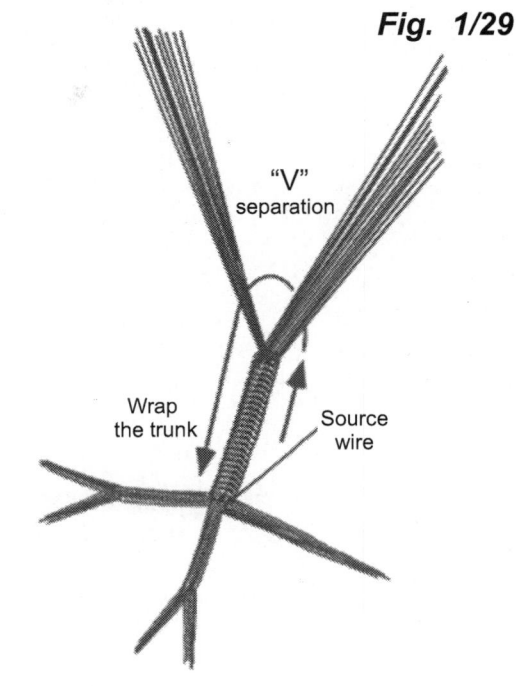

Fig. 1/29

1. Separate the top section of the tree into two equal parts. (They don't need to be exactly equal). *Fig. 1/29* Start the separation at the top of the trunk.

2. Wrap the wire up the trunk to the "V" separation in the branches, then back down the entire trunk to the roots. Repeat this wrapping two or three times, ending the wrapping at the base of the trunk. *Fig. 1/29*

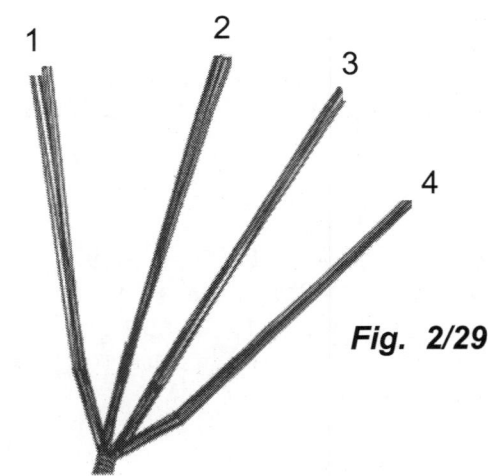

Fig. 2/29

3. Separate the two main branches into two more equal parts. This will create a total of four branches. *Fig. 2/29*

4. Wrap the wire up the trunk then onto any one of the four branches you just created. Stop wrapping about one inch up the branch. Separate the wires of this branch into two parts. Pass the wire through the "V" in this branch then continue wiring this branch until you reach the top of the trunk. Repeat this process for all the remaining branches. *Fig. 3/29* After you have finished all the wiring you will have created a total of eight branches.

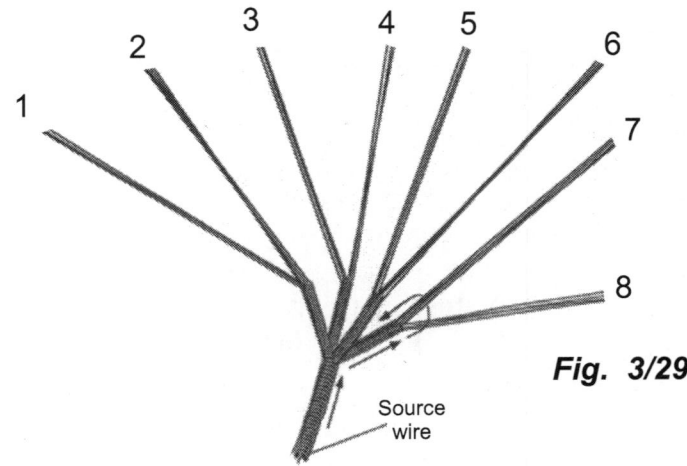

Fig. 3/29

Forming a Mini Tree Sculpture

See Fig. 1/30, for steps 1, 2, 3, & 4, on this page.

1.
Spread out the three root sections of the tree to form a tripod. Though the tree sculpture is not yet complete and may be thin, it should be able to stand on the root base you created.

2.
Twist two of the branches together at their base to form one larger branch with the two smaller branches "growing" out of the larger one.

3.
Gently bend the top section of the three root sections in toward the trunk to create a section that looks like a step.

4.
Gently bend all three roots at varied irregular angles. None of the roots should be straight. At this point you should also create a slight bend in the trunk.

5.
Wrap the wire down the trunk and onto each of the root sections. Do not wrap the wire to the tip of each root, but stop the wrapping and return to the trunk when you are about half way to the tip of the root. Wrap all the tops of the root sections that are closest to the trunk. This will create a trunk base that is the thickest part of the tree and it will look very realistic. End the wrapping at the top of the trunk. *Fig. 2/30*

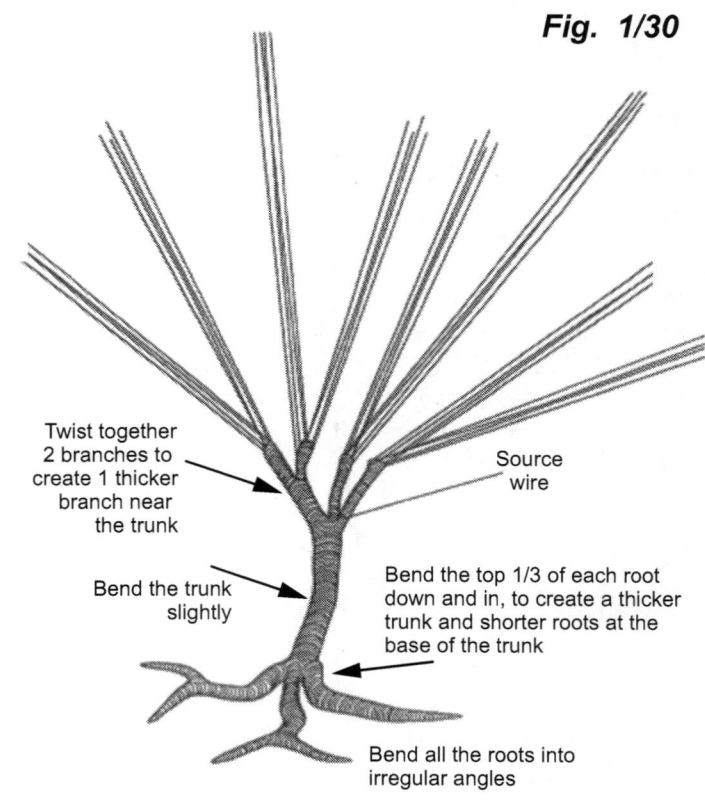

Fig. 1/30

Twist together 2 branches to create 1 thicker branch near the trunk

Source wire

Bend the trunk slightly

Bend the top 1/3 of each root down and in, to create a thicker trunk and shorter roots at the base of the trunk

Bend all the roots into irregular angles

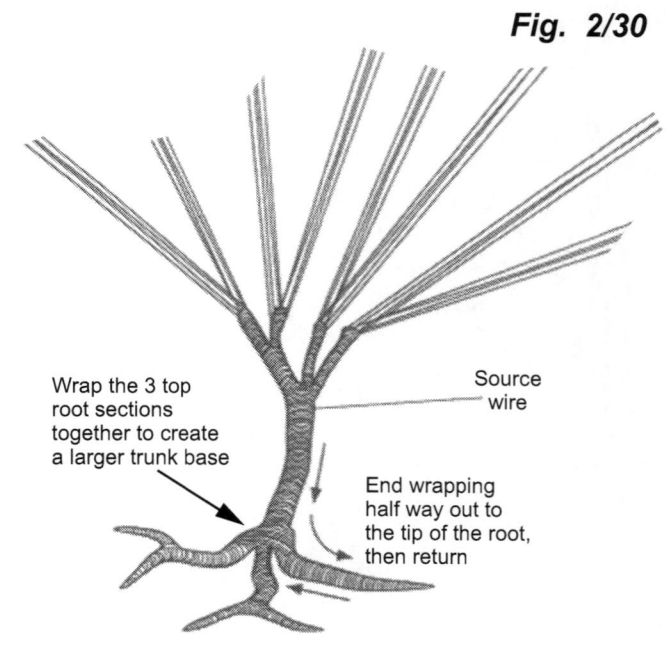

Fig. 2/30

Wrap the 3 top root sections together to create a larger trunk base

Source wire

End wrapping half way out to the tip of the root, then return

Thickening a Mini Tree Sculpture

See Fig. 1/31, for steps 1, 2, & 3 on this page.

1.
Continue wrapping the tree to thicken the trunk and roots. Do not wrap the wire all the way to the tip of the roots, but stop and return to different points along the way. This will make the finished tree much more interesting.

2.
Wrap the base of the trunk and the area where the roots enter the trunk several more times so they are thicker in these areas. You should continue to wrap the tree until you feel it is thick enough and looks good to you. Once the tree is fully wrapped, if you should feel it needs more thickness, you can always go back and add more wire.

3.
Apply the same procedure for the branches as you did for the roots. However, this time wire all the way to the end of the thicker branch coil, then return. Repeat this wrapping process for all the branches. As you are wrapping the tree you should stop for a moment and look at your work. In general the mini trees look much better if they are thick rather than thin.

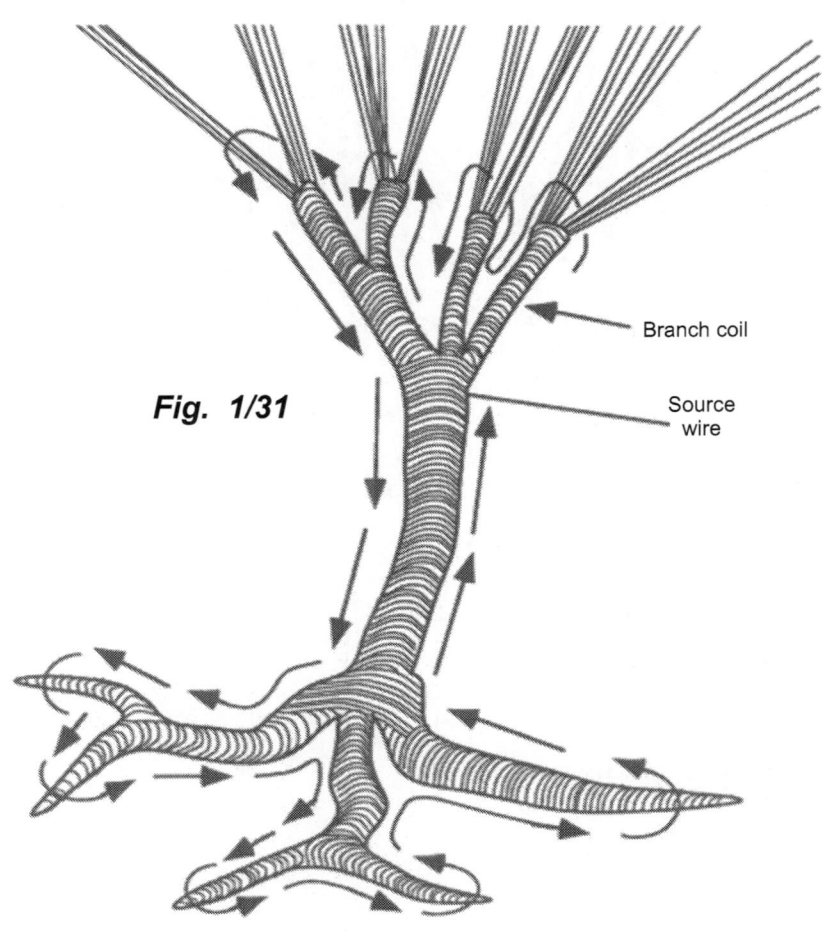

Fig. 1/31

The Final Branching of a Mini Tree Sculpture

See Fig. 1/32, for steps 1, 2, & 3 on this page.

1.
Separate the remaining wire of each branch into two approximately equal amounts. You will find that some of the remaining branches will have even amounts and some will have odd amounts. This is not a problem and will be addressed in later steps.

2.
Twist, as tightly as you can, each separate group of wire together to create an entirely new thicker branch. Twist the wire until the new branch you are creating is about one inch long. After you complete this step, you should have about sixteen branches in your tree.

3.
The final strands of wire are not wrapped. They are all left loose, as single strands of wire and will be used to create more detail to the different types of tree sculpture which will be explained later in the book. You will then be able to create 6 very different types of mini tree sculptures using this basic structure. *See page 21*

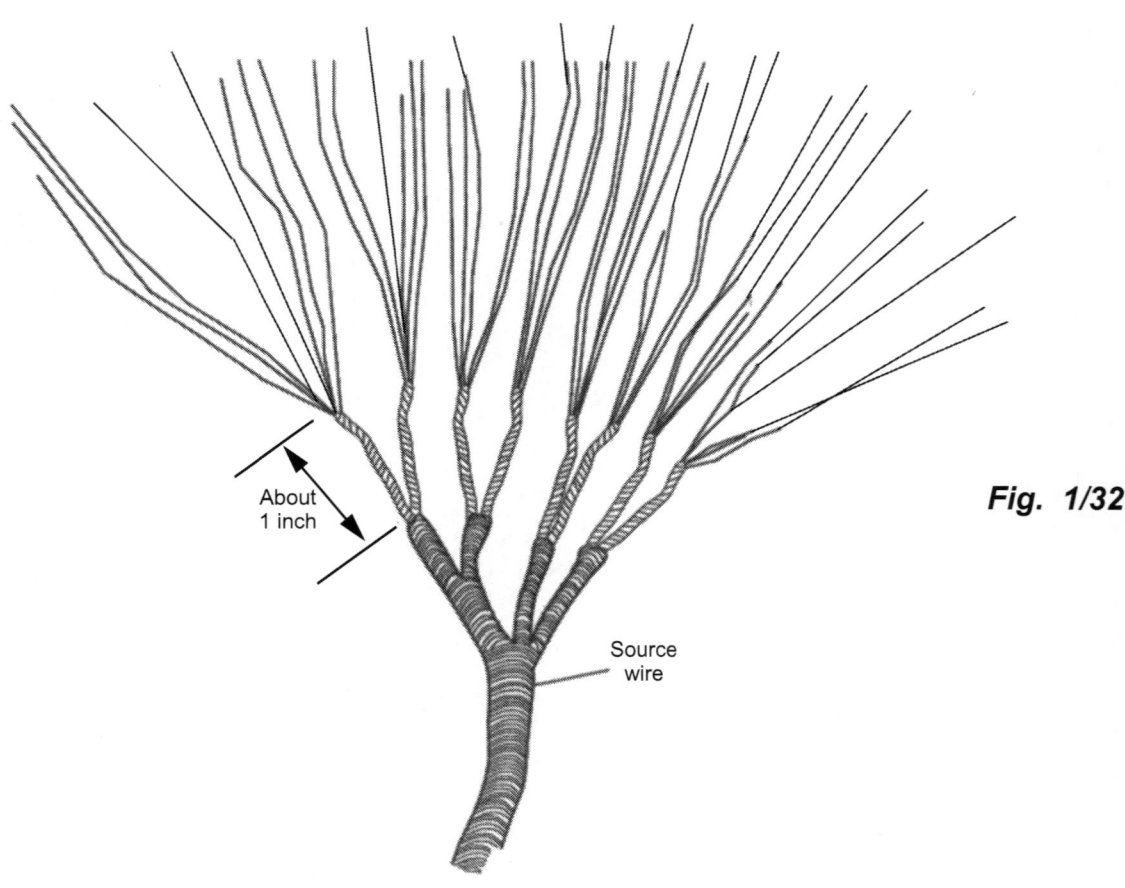

About 1 inch

Source wire

Fig. 1/32

Creating the Root Anchors for a Mini Tree Sculpture

The final use of the source wire is to create an anchor that will hold the tree onto the base material. This anchor will not be seen when the tree sculpture is completed.

1. Wrap the wire down the trunk and half way onto any root. Keep in mind that this wrap will be seen, so try to keep it consistent with the look of the trunk. Do not try to wrap too quickly to get to the base. *Fig. 1/33*

2. Twist the double loops together to create one thick loop. Repeat this process for the other root anchor wires. Be sure to twist the wires as tightly as you can so it is wrapped close to the bottom of the root. *Fig. 2/33*

3. Twist both double anchor wires together about half way up their distances. This will create one large root anchor that will be bonded into the root mound. This root anchor will not be visible when the tree is completed. *Fig. 3/33*

At this stage your creation, with all its twists, bends, bumps and curves, should actually start to look like a tree. *Fig. 2/33* As you look at your tree, If you feel the trunk, branches, or roots are too thin or not in the correct proportion, it is not too late to go back and add thickness or form to where you think it is needed. Simply get the end of the source wire, twist a small piece onto the main root anchor and if you want to work on the roots or trunk, wrap as needed. To add onto the branches, once again twist a small piece onto one of the twigs, and wrap as needed. This is the final use of the Source Wire.

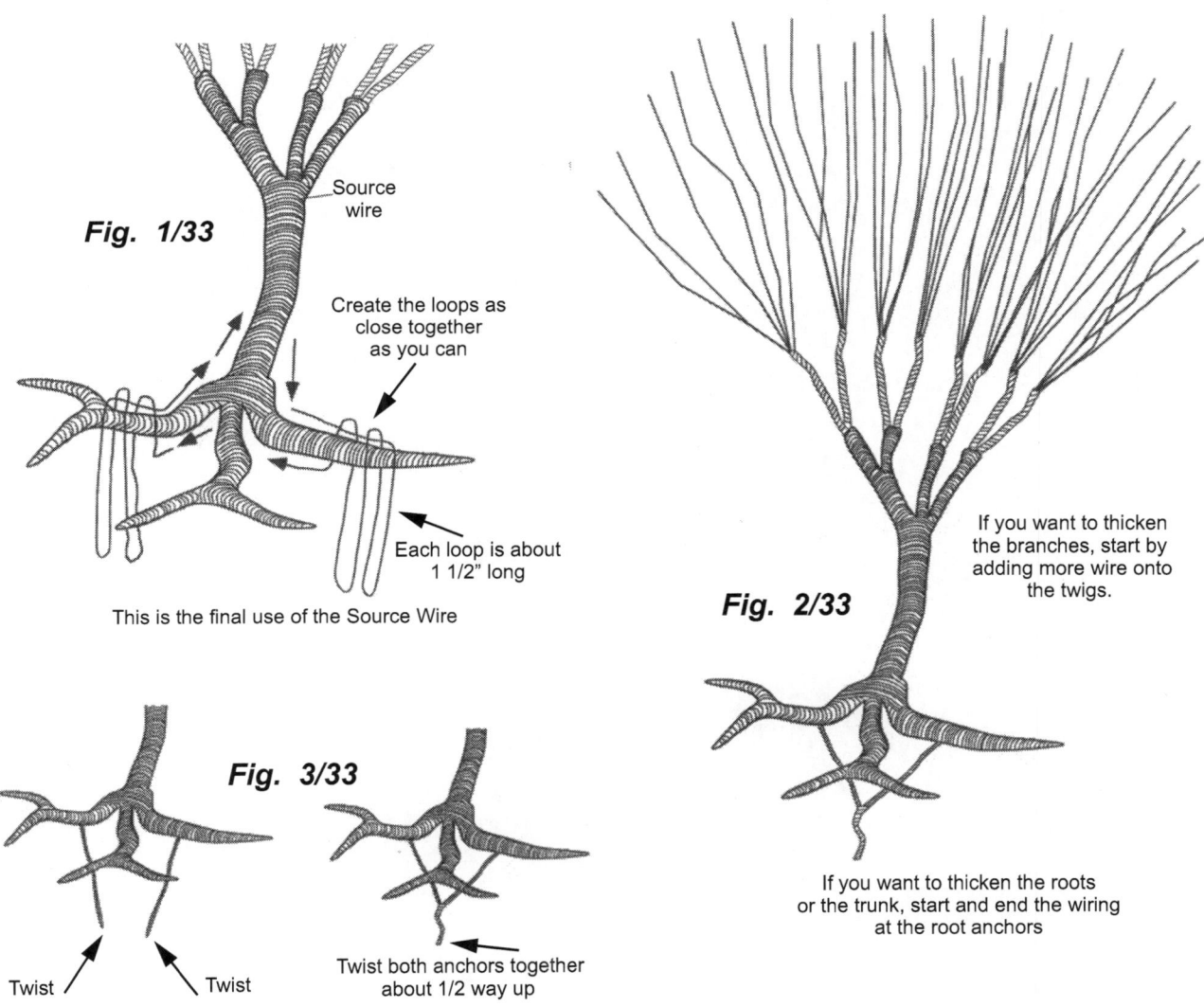

Fig. 1/33 — Source wire; Create the loops as close together as you can; Each loop is about 1 1/2" long. This is the final use of the Source Wire

Fig. 3/33 — Twist / Twist; Twist both anchors together about 1/2 way up

Fig. 2/33 — If you want to thicken the branches, start by adding more wire onto the twigs. If you want to thicken the roots or the trunk, start and end the wiring at the root anchors

Preparing a Mini Tree Sculpture for Mounting

Your mini tree is now ready to be mounted onto the base of your choice. There are many different types of bases that will work very well for this size tree. **See page 12** for base selections. I think this size tree looks best on a small free formed glass base or on a small flat rock. I have found it is much easier to mount the tree onto the base before you shape the branches and twigs into the style of tree sculpture you want. Your 6 choices, shown in this book are: BEADED **See page 41**, WIND SWEPT **See page 46**, WEEPING WILLOW **See page 39**, UPRIGHT WILLOW **See page 40**, OAK **See page 44,** and, BONSAI with LEAVES, **See page 47**. Or, you can create a mini tree sculpture of your own design.

1.
Hold the tree firmly by the trunk as shown, then gather all of the branches together. Next, point all the branches upward. This will help to keep the branches out of the way as you work on the mounting of the tree. *Fig. 1/34*

2.
Still holding the tree firmly, gather the roots together and point them down. Tuck the anchor wires into the center of the roots. The tree is now ready to be mounted onto the base. Finally, place the tree aside as the following pages show you how to prepare the base and create the root mound that will support the tree.

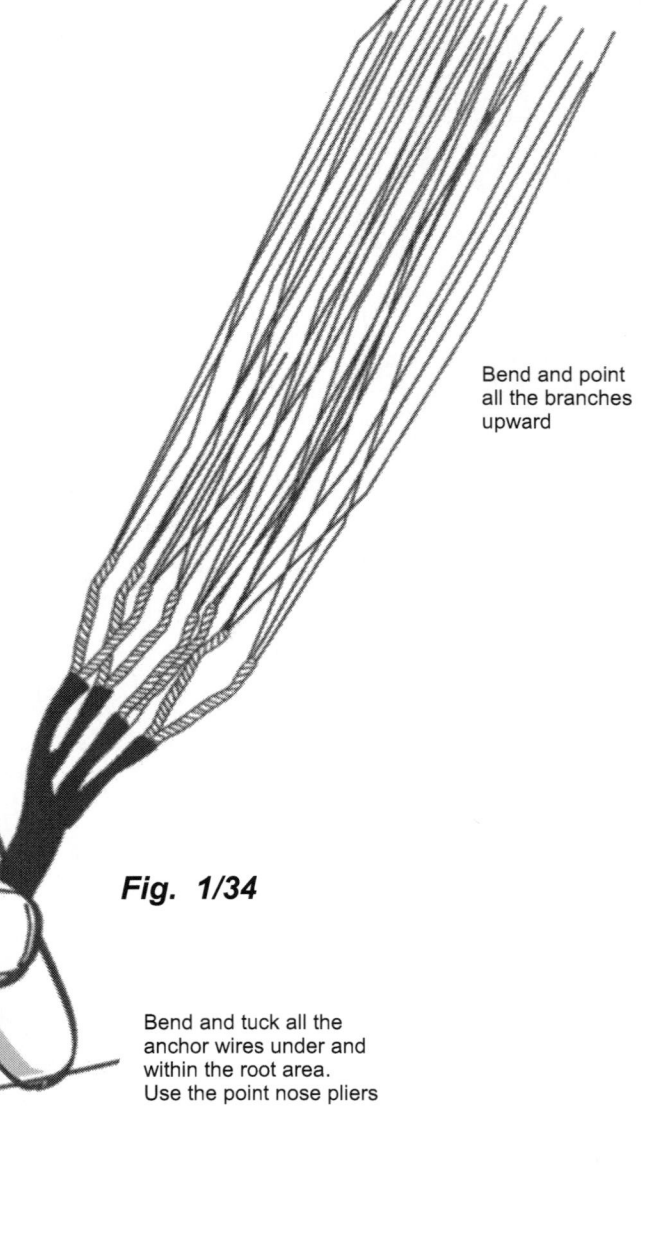

Bend and point all the branches upward

Fig. 1/34

Bend and tuck all the anchor wires under and within the root area. Use the point nose pliers

Bend and point all the roots downward

Mounting a Mini Tree Sculpture Onto a Base

After you selected the base you want, be sure the surface of the base is made of material that the white craft glue will adhere to. The tree will be bound onto the base in several steps. The first few steps will bond the tree to the mound, the remaining steps will create an interesting support structure from which the roots will appear to be growing. It is very important to let the white craft glue dry throughly each time you apply a layer of the glue and sand mixture. For the best results, let the piece dry overnight. If you want to speed up the drying process you can place the piece under a light to create heat which will help to speed up the drying.

1. Apply a piece of double stick tape, or a piece of masking tape that is folded over, to the bottom of the base piece to help hold it in place as you apply the layers of white glue and sand mixture. *Fig. 1/35*

2. Place the base in a small tray with sides, or a shallow dish, that will confine the sand you will be adding. *Fig. 1/35*

3. Spread the three root sections slightly apart. At about the half way point of each root section bend the root upward so it will support the tree, use the point nose pliers to do this. Gently but firmly push the tree down on the base so that the three main root sections begin to spread out. Be sure the anchor wire is tucked under the root area. Try to spread the root sections equally. The root sections should be optically spaced. *Fig. 1/35*

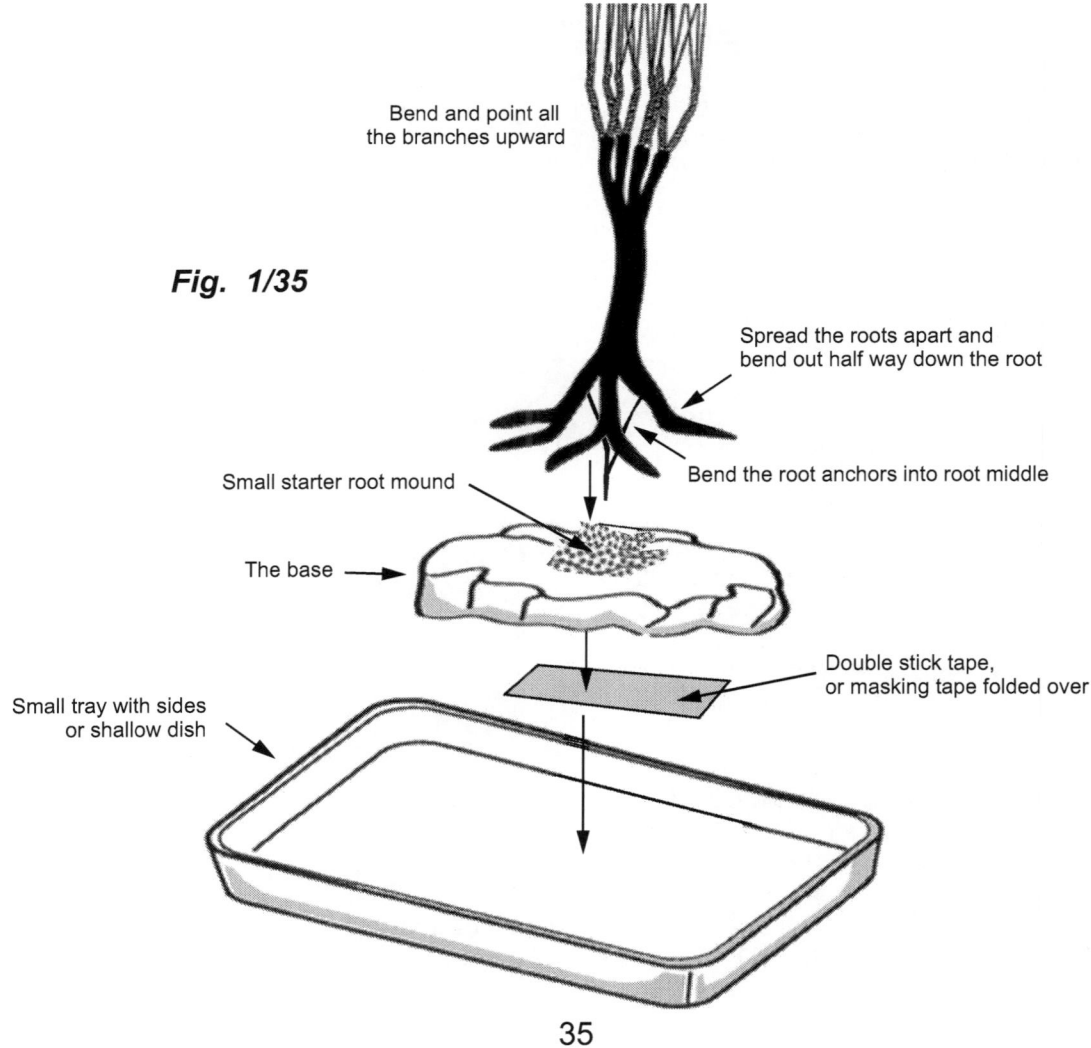

Fig. 1/35

The root mound is very important to the overall appearance of the tree sculpture. The structural purpose of the root mound is of course, to hold the tree onto the base. The visual purpose of it is to create the appearance that the tree is growing out of the center of the mound. To these ends, it is much better to have less root mound rather than more. All the roots of the tree will look much more realistic if they are only slightly imbedded in the mound, not covered by it. The top third of each root section, as a minimum, should be visible. To ensure the strength of the structure it is very important that each application of the sand and glue mixture is completely dry and solid before you start the next step. Remember, if you want to speed up the drying you can place the piece under a lamp with a regular 60 watt bulb in it. Place the piece as close to the bulb as you can. However do not allow the bulb to actually touch or rest on the tree sculpture. Doing this will cut the drying time in about half.

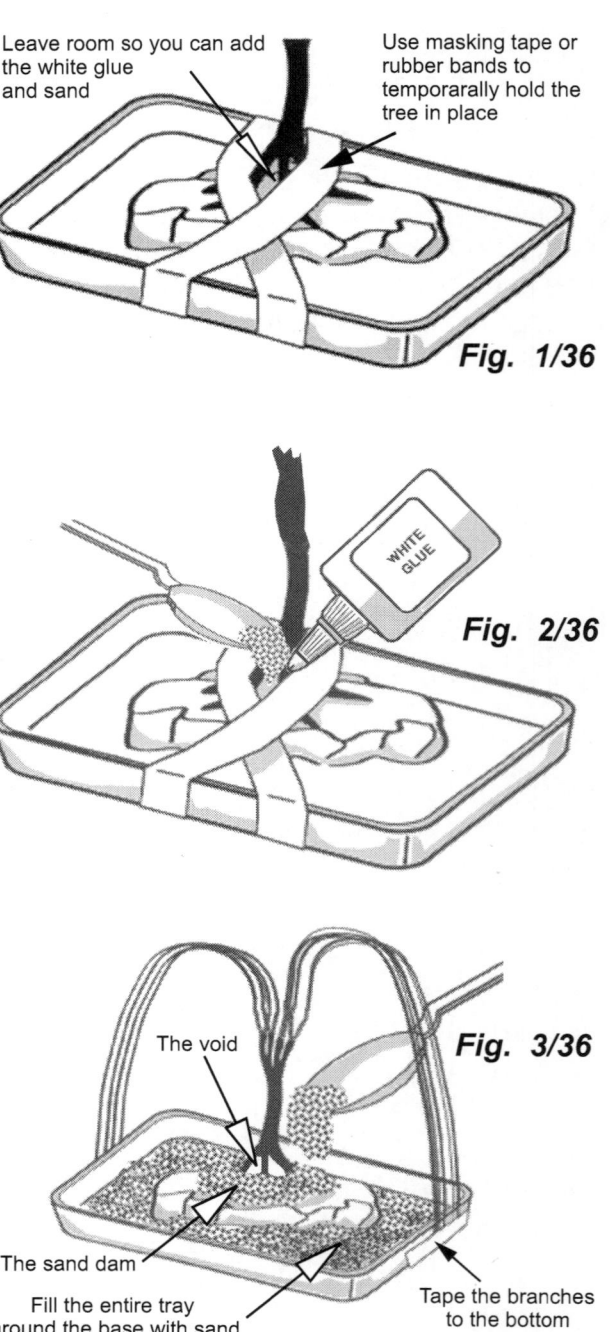

Fig. 1/36

Fig. 2/36

Fig. 3/36

4. After the roots are spread out, using masking tape, or several rubber bands, temporarily secure the tree to the base. Be sure to leave room around the small solid sand mound so you will be able to add the glue and sand to the top of the mound you created. *Fig. 1/36*

5. When you are sure the tree is securely fastened to the base, add several drops of white glue then a spoon full of sand to the top of the root mound. Be sure the glue and sand are intertwined into the anchors. Do not add too much glue and try not to get any glue on the tape or rubber bands. This is an important first step in the mounting the tree onto the base. *Fig. 2/36*

6. When you are sure the glue and sand mix are thoroughly dry and solid, remove the tape or rubber bands.

7. Construct a "sand dam" around the entire base of the trees root system. The tips of the roots should be entirely buried in the sand, but the center of the tree, directly under the trunk must not have any sand on it. This void will be filled with the sand and glue mixture. After you create the sand dam you should be able to see the original small glue and sand mound you first created. If you find you have used too much sand to create the sand dam, carefully dump out all the sand and start again. You can, for added support for the tree sculpture, bend all the branches down and tape them onto the bottom of the tray. You can also fill the entire tray around the base with sand, which will help keep the base from moving. *Fig. 3/36*

8. Apply about 15 to 20 drops of the white craft glue directly into the center of the sand dam. ***Fig. 1/37*** Be very careful not to apply too much glue. You can always add more, but it is very difficult to remove the glue. The total amount of glue should fill the void in the center only about half way. The sand dam will hold the glue in place as you proceed to the next step. This is where most people run into difficultly. Proceed slowly during these steps. It is much better to apply too little glue than too much. Keep in mind that the root mound will be created in layers not as one huge mound!

9. Slowly add additional sand to the rim of the sand dam until the entire center of the root area is covered. Get the sand from your source, not from the sand you created the root mound with, or the tray. Add the sand to the glue from the outer edge toward the center of the tree as you proceed around. As you are adding the sand you will see that it is being absorbed with the glue. Add the sand slowly and carefully and only a very little at a time. Do not move the tree as you are adding the sand. When you are finished adding the sand, you should not be able to see any of the root structure. ***Fig. 2/37***

10. After you are sure the sand mound is completely dry, gently brush away all the loose sand from around the roots and inside the root area into the tray. Save all this sand, you can use it again. Since the tree is now securely fastened to the root mound and to the tray you can dump out the extra sand, as you hold onto the tree, base and tray.

11. Build another sand dam as you did before. This time construct the dam so that when you fill it with the glue and sand mixture it will reach to the bottom of the trunk area. Again, if you find you have too much sand for the dam, dump it out and start again.

12. For this layer add about 10 to 15 drops of glue onto the center of the root mound and cover the entire sand dam with sand. Be sure to let it dry completely before you proceed to the next steps.

13. If you see any voids or spaces in the root mound that you would like to fill in, add 1 or 2 drops of glue in the void, then add the sand and cover the entire area as you did before. If any of the voids are large enough to require more than a few drops of glue, fill these in one layer at a time. As an alternative to filling the larger voids with just sand, you can also place small pebbles or sea shells in the void and glue them in place using the white craft glue and sand mixture.

14. After you are satisfied with the way the roots and the root mound look, you can carefully remove all the tape and take the tree sculpture off the tray. If you should find any areas on the root mound that are not dry and have some wet glue on them, simply sprinkle more sand over that area and let it dry.

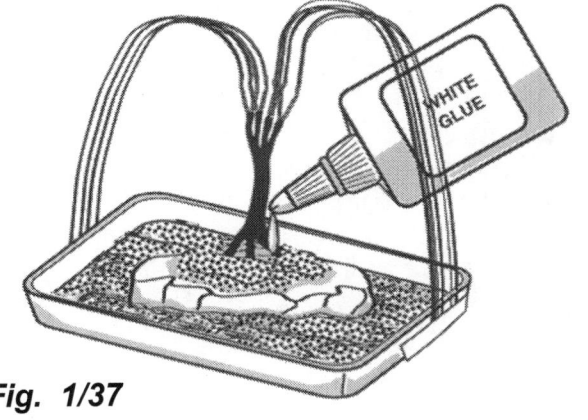

Fig. 1/37

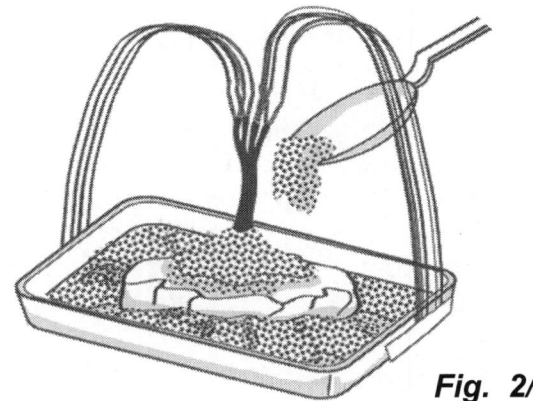

Fig. 2/37

Adding Color to the Root Mound

1. You are now ready to decide whether you want to leave the root mound as a natural sand mound, or have the sand look like moss covered earth. If you wish to keep the root mound natural, with no color, skip steps 1 through 6, and proceed to the next page.

2. To add color that will look like moss covered earth, you will need yellow, green and white India ink. Any brand of colored ink will due. Just be sure it is ink, not paint! I have found that ink is the best medium to use on the root mound. The ink will soak into the sand and it will keep its bright color for years. The ink is also very opaque and the colors will not run into each other as long as you follow my technique for applying the ink. This ink will not come out in the wash, so don't get it on your clothing. Please do not use water colors acrylics or oil paint for the root mound. I have tried them all and they just don't work for this application. You will use very little ink for each tree, so buy the smallest amount you can. You will also need a small, soft inexpensive artists or crafters brush. Size "1" will do fine. After you have finished using your brush wash it off with warm water and a bit of soap, rinse in clean water and let it dry thoroughly before you go on to the next color.

3. Before you start the coloring of the root mound, carefully bend all of the branches straight up, as you did before. This will keep all the wire out of your way as you work.

4. Starting with the green ink and the small brush, apply the color onto the root mound. You will notice that the sand of the mound will actually draw the ink out of the brush and into the sand. Do not attempt to "paint" the sand. Let the ink be absorbed into the sand. Color only about 3/4 of the overall area of the mound with green. And also keep in mind that you will be leaving about 10% of the mound with no color on it at all. This effect will give the root mound a very natural appearance. Try not to get any of the ink on any part of the actual tree, if you do, wipe it off as soon as you can. If the sand you are using is a mixture of items like small pebbles, shells, pieces of wood or glass, try to leave these items uncolored and natural. This subtle contrast in color and texture will add to the realism of the piece and give it much more depth. Proceed slowly, once the ink is on it is very difficult to remove. If you should get any color on the tree itself, you will need to scrape it off with a razor blade or some other sharp tool. It is much better not to get any on any of the tree or the base. Again, as soon as you finish using the brush wash it.

5. After the green color is dry, and your brush is dry, usually about 3 hours, apply the yellow color. Use the same absorption technique as you did for the green color. Apply only about 1/4 the amount of yellow as you did green. This will make the green the dominate color on the root mound.

6. After the yellow and your brush is dry you will be applying the final color, white. The white is used only as a highlight so you need only apply a small amount to get the desired effect. Apply the white using only the tip of the brush. Use only enough white to cover about 10% of the total area of the root mound. You will be amazed how bright and white this ink is and how little you need to create the desired effect. When you finish adding the white let the piece dry. If you feel you need to add more of any color you can still do so. Since these colors are opaque you will be able to add any color over an other color. Do not add or apply any other coating or protective spray to the root mound, you will just be dulling the colors. If, in a few years you see the colors have dulled due to dust or dirt, you can clean the piece with a damp cloth and apply fresh ink colors.

To see completed Root Mounds in Full Color, visit my website: www.salvillano.com

Creating the Style of Mini Tree Sculpture You Want

Your tree sculpture is now ready for the final steps. Using the basic tree shape you just created you can form and change the trunk, branches and twigs into any of the following 6 different tree styles. If this is your first attempt at creating wire tree sculpture, I would suggest that you start with the Weeping Willow or the Upright Willow.

Weeping Willow
The easiest of all the trees to form it requires very little additional cutting and shaping.

Beaded
This decorative tree is created by adding glass fringe beads to the Weeping Willow tree.

Wind Swept
To create the Wind Swept you will need to re-shape the trunk, branches and trim some of the branches and twigs.

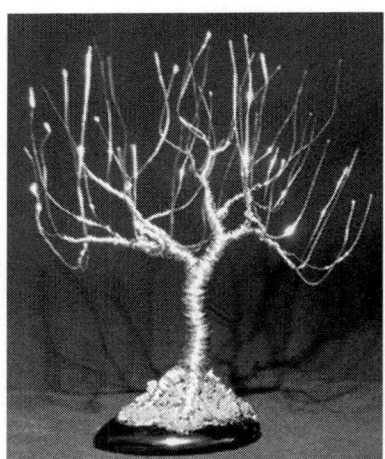

Upright Willow
The same as the Weeping Willow, but with turned up branches and twigs.

Oak Tree
This tree requires bending, twisting, re-shaping and cutting of all the branches and twigs.

Bonsai with Leaves
Similar to creating the Oak tree, but the ends of the twigs are hammered flat to look like leaves.

Creating the Weeping Willow Mini Tree Sculpture

The Weeping Willow is by far the easiest to create. It requires little cutting and shaping. Creating the Weeping Willow will give you a feel for working with the wire and the tools.

1. Hold the tree firmly by the trunk. This is the best way to hold the tree securely as you work on it. This grip will allow you to turn and view it from different angles.

2. Spread out the branches so they look like a fan. At this point the tree will look flat, we will create the roundness and fullness later on. ***See page 40, Fig. 1/40***

3. Hold the tree firmly at the top section of the trunk with one hand. With your other hand grip any two outermost branches at the "V" section. Twist the branches toward you half a turn. ***See page 40, Fig. 1/40*** This action will result in the two branches you have twisted becoming perpendicular to the branches next to them. The tree is now more rounded.

4. Holding the tree at the point where the branches start to extend out of the trunk, place your index finger about half way up the branch. Start bending the twig wires over the top roundness of your index finger until all the twig end of the branches point directly down. As you are bending the wires, try not to bend all the wire at the same point. Move your finger to a place on the next branch that was different than the previous one. This will create a much more realistic grouping of branches. For more of a variety, bend the wires one at a time. *Fig. 3/40* After bending all the wires, if you are not happy with the look, you can very easily unbend all or part of the wire and start again.

5. As you are bending the branches, stop for a moment to look at the tree from above looking directly down at it. *Fig. 4/40* The tree should have a rounded shape. If you think your tree looks flat, pull the branches away from each other to create the desired round or oval shape.

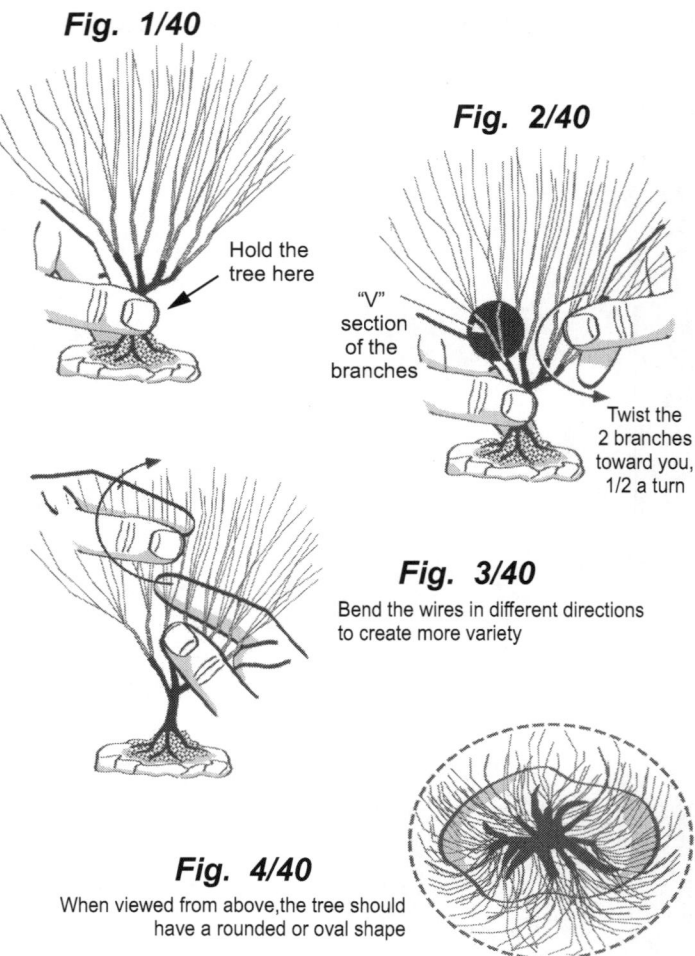

Fig. 1/40 — Hold the tree here

Fig. 2/40 — "V" section of the branches — Twist the 2 branches toward you, 1/2 a turn

Fig. 3/40 Bend the wires in different directions to create more variety

Fig. 4/40 When viewed from above, the tree should have a rounded or oval shape

Creating the Upright Willow Mini Tree Sculpture

The Upright Willow tree sculpture follows the exact steps as the Weeping Willow. The only difference is that when you get to the instructions about bending the branches, you bend them **UP** instead of **DOWN**. All the other instruction remain the same.

Bend all the branches **DOWN** for the Weeping Willow

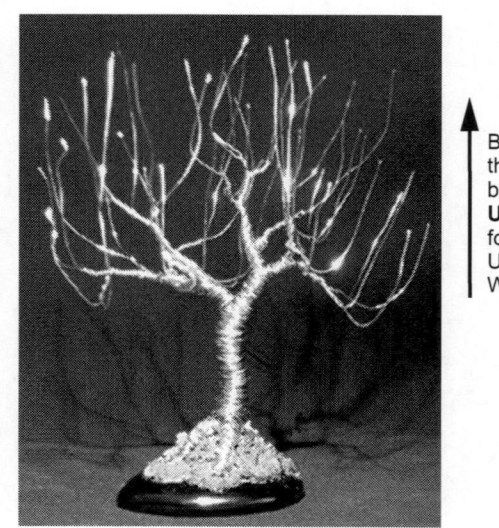

Bend all the branches **UP** for the Upright Willow

To see completed pieces in Full Color, visit my website: www.salvillano.com

Creating the Beaded Mini Tree Sculpture

THE BASIC BEADED MINI TREE
The beaded tree sculpture is created by first making the Weeping Willow tree, as shown on *page 39*, then adding the beads to the twig end wires. Since the weeping willow tree is very easy to create, this tree is also easy to create.

BEAD VARIETIES
Although you can use any type of small bead that will slide onto the wire, the type of beads that I think look the best are called "Fringe Beads" They are so named because the hole in the bead is in the top part of the bead, not in the center as most beads.

I chose to use this type of bead because it hangs from the twigs, rather than having the twig pass through the bead. I feel this gives the beads on the tree a more natural look. The fringe beads I use are made of glass. They are manufactured in a very wide variety of colors. And each color is offered in several different finishes, including: solid, rainbow, clear matte, and gunmetal. I like the "clear rainbow" color because these beads catch and reflect the light very dramatically. When this type of bead is used and the tree sculpture is displayed in direct sunlight or a very bright light, the beads will seem to glisten and glow. Even if you use the same color beads for the entire piece, the light will bounce and reflect off each bead at a different angle creating a kaleidoscope of color. And, since the beads are hanging loose from the wire, they are free to move slightly in a gentle breeze or the least vibration, adding more color and variation to the creation.

I will sometimes use all of one color beads for the entire tree or mix several colors together to get a specific effect. For example, I will use all clear beads on a tree made of silver colored wire mounted on a glass base. The combination of glass and silver gives the effect of a tree in a winter setting with ice clinging to its branches and snow covering the ground. I have also created beaded trees using several different shades of green beads producing a summer tree in full bloom.

If you wish, you can also use beads that are named "Seed Beads" These are beads that have the holes in the center of the bead, not on the edge like the fringe beads. Seed beads also are available in a very large variety of colors and shapes. Please be sure that no matter what type of bead you are using, the hole in the bead is large enough to accommodate the wire gauge you are using.

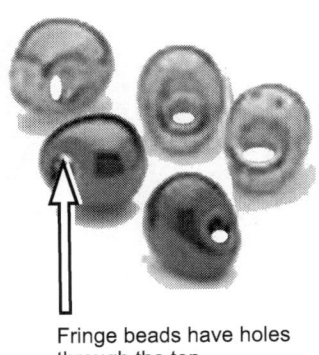
Fringe beads have holes through the top

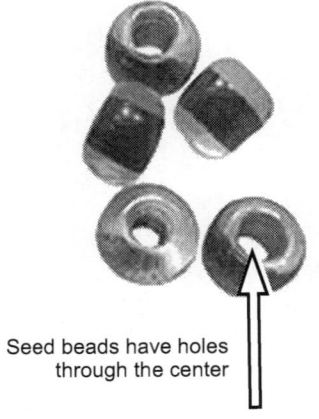
Seed beads have holes through the center

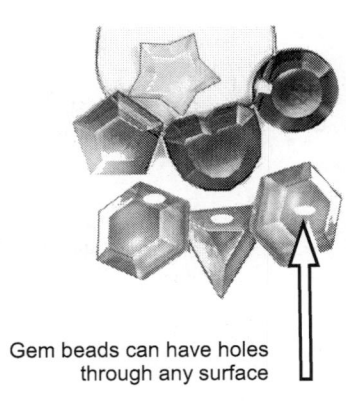
Gem beads can have holes through any surface

THE WIRE Any type or color wire can be used with the fringe beads. The only restriction is the size (gauge) of the wire. Remember, the thickness or gauge of wire is given in numbers. However, THE SMALLER THE NUMBER, THE THICKER THE WIRE. For example, 24 gauge is thicker than 26 gauge. The best thickness of wire to use is 26 gauge for the tree sculpture shown here. 24 gauge can also be used but it is not as easy to work with. The fringe beads will not fit on any wire larger than 24 gauge. Of course, if you wish you can use a thinner gauge wire or larger beads. *See page 125*

SELECTION OF THE BEADS Begin by selecting the type of beads and colors you wish to use. If you choose to use a variety of colored beads on the same tree, mix all the colors before you start. Do not try to mix them as you go along. I usually mix all the different colored beads in a saucer or other wide flat dish. This makes it much easier to randomly pick up one bead at a time. Do not try to add the beads onto the tree in any set pattern or order. Doing so will create an uninteresting use of color and as in nature, the best creations are random. Do not be concerned if you find that as you are adding beads to the tree you have several beads of the same color all next to each other. This will actually look very nice when all the beads are in place. The number of beads needed for your tree will of course depend on the size of the tree and how closely you space the beads. The fringe beads are usually sold in small plastic bags of one hundred beads per bag. The fringe beads are inexpensive, I would suggest you place your first order of five hundred to one thousand. If after you finish your beaded tree sculpture, and you have extra beads you would like to use, you can use E6000 jewelers glue, or any glue that's clear and will bond glass to glass, to bond the extra beads onto the base of the tree, giving the appearance of falling leaves or fruit. You can also use any type of bead for your piece, or even mix different types of beads together. The combinations are almost endless.

This is the final look of the mini beaded tree sculpture. This piece was created on a flat base. You can also put this tree into a small bonsai base. ***See page 12 for more bases.***

To see completed pieces in Full Color, visit my website: www.salvillano.com

Adding Beads to a Tree Sculpture

1. Start by opening the twig ends to create a "V" shape. This is where you will slide each bead onto the wire. *Fig. 1/43*

2. Slide one fringe bead onto the single wires. Move the bead all the way to the double twisted wires. *Fig. 2/43*

3. Hold the bead in place tight against the double twisted wire using your thumb and index finger. Then, twist one end of the single wire over the top of the other single wire. Now, twist the wire an additional three to five times. This will lock the bead in place and create the necessary space to add the next bead.

4. All the remaining beads are added to all the remaining twigs in the same way as described above. Some twigs will have more or less beads than others. But each twig should have at least 2 beads.

5. As you add beads toward the end of the twig, try to leave enough wire after the last bead on the branch so you can create a small "V". This will give the twigs a very nice finished effect. *Fig. 3/43*

6. After all the beads have been added to all the twigs, shape the tree as explained on *page 40.* If you find you have a single strand of wire without a second wire on which to add a bead, just trim the single wire smaller and it will look like a twig.

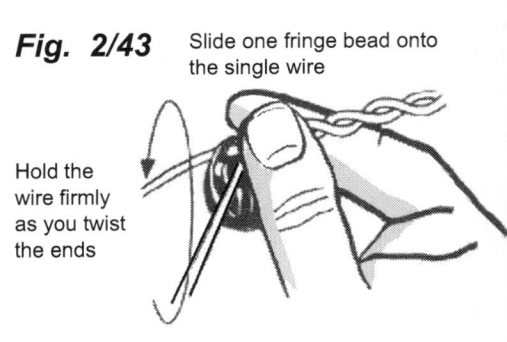

Fig. 1/43 — Open the twig ends to create a "V"

Fig. 2/43 — Slide one fringe bead onto the single wire. Hold the wire firmly as you twist the ends

Fig. 3/43 — The final look

Fig. 4/43, is the final look for beading a tree. This method can be applied to any size tree. If you feel your beading does not look like what is shown below, you can unbend the wire and try again. The wire is very resilient and may be reworked maney times.

Fig. 4/43

To see completed pieces in Full Color, visit my website: www.salvillano.com

Creating the Oak Mini Tree Sculpture

The Oak tree is a little more difficult to create than the other mini trees. This tree will require more work on the creation of the branches and twigs. It will also involve some cutting of the longer twigs. This is also the basic form of the tree structure that will be used to create the "Mini Bonsai with Leaves" **See page 47**

1. Hold the tree firmly on the trunk **See page 40, Fig. 1/40**

2. Spread out all the branches and twigs so they look like a fan. **See page 40, Fig. 1/40**

3. The following steps illustrate how to create different size branches and twigs for this tree. The look of the oak tree requires a varied amount and size of the branches and twigs. I think you will understand the procedures better after starting. In the following steps you will be cutting the wires to create the branches and twigs. So, it is important that you are sure of the cut you are making before you make the cut. If you feel you may have some difficulty creating the branches and twigs, I would suggest using some scrap wire to practice. Simply twist two pieces of wire together to create a practice branch.

4. Gripping any outer branch at its base closest to the trunk, loop one single wire over the wire next to it to create an oval. **Fig. 1/44** The oval size should be about the circumference of your index finger. This first oval should be created about 1/4" to 3/8" from the thicker part of the branch closest to the trunk.

5. Hold the loop you just created and the other loose wires firmly and twist them in the opposite direction about four or five complete twists. **Fig. 2/44**

6. Repeat step 5, use the longer section of the loose wires to create the next loop. Repeat step 5 to create as many loops you can with each section of wire. **Fig. 3/44** You should be able to create two to four loops per pair of wires. Do not be concerned if the loops you created are different sizes, this will actually add more interest to the piece. Repeat the above on all the remaining pairs of wires. Should you come across a branch with an extra wire that you cannot pair with another, just leave it as a single wire. All extra wires will be trimmed in the following steps.

7. After you have created all the loops on the tree, you are now ready to cut the loops to create the final smallest twigs. Use the small wire cutters for this step. Whenever you make a cut in the wire, try to keep the cut perpendicular to the wire. This will create blunter ends in the wire rather than "knife blades". I have found it is much better to work slow when handling the cut ends of wire. I have also tried working with gloves on but I find it too restricting. However, if you find you can work in gloves you should do it!

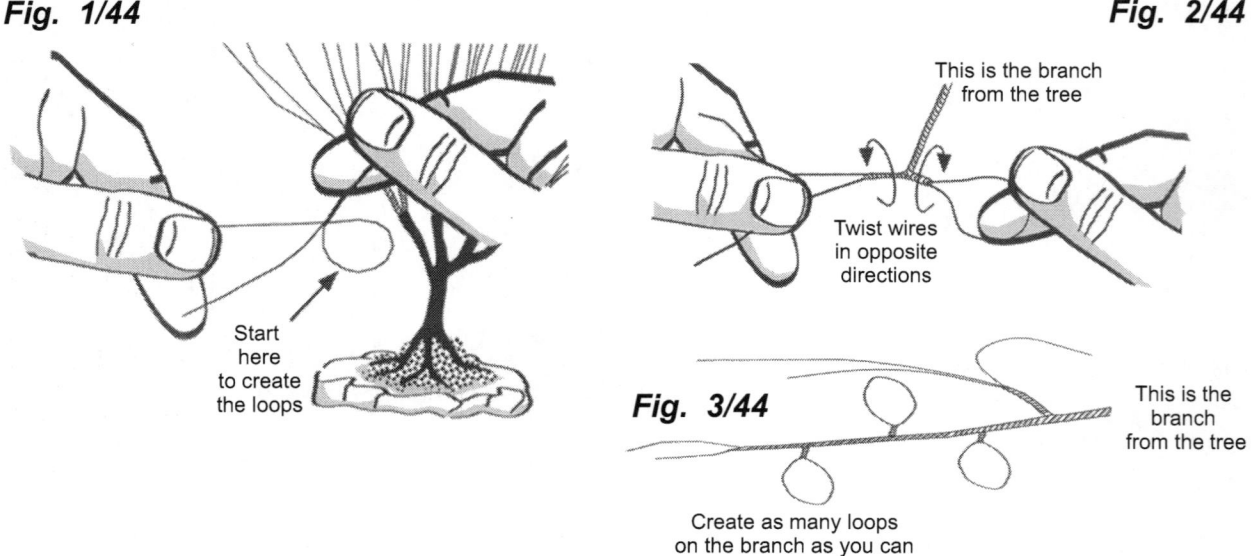

Fig. 1/44 — Start here to create the loops

Fig. 2/44 — This is the branch from the tree. Twist wires in opposite directions

Fig. 3/44 — Create as many loops on the branch as you can. This is the branch from the tree

8. Cut each loop once. This will create two twigs growing from a branch. Do not cut the loops exactly in the center. Cut each loop in a slightly different location. After you cut the loop and create the twigs, grip the end of each twig and gently pull on it so it is straighter. Try to remove most of the round shape from each twig and make it more angular. Trim any of the end wires that are too long. *Fig. 1/45*

9. This next section is perhaps the most difficult part, Upon completion of the following steps, if you do not like the resulting look of your tree sculpture, you can very easily repeat the final steps. The wire you are working with is very workable and can be bent and re-shaped many times.

10. Push all the branches and twigs straight up, and flatten the sections that are closest to the top of the trunk. Spread out and separate the main branches. *Fig. 2/45*

11. You are now ready to begin to style and shape the outermost twigs of the tree. *Fig. 3/45* If you have ever looked closely at the twigs of an oak tree, or almost any tree, you will have noticed that the twigs seem to go in every conceivable direction with no particular rhyme or reason. The twigs are never evenly spaced nor are they bunched together.

12. Hold the tree from the top section of the trunk and bend each of the branches in the opposite direction of the branch next to it. You will notice that this action will start to create a more rounded and full appearance of the tree. *Fig. 4/45*

13. As you are bending the twigs, stop for a moment to look at the tree from directly above. The tree should have a rounded or oval shape. *See page 40, Fig. 4/40*

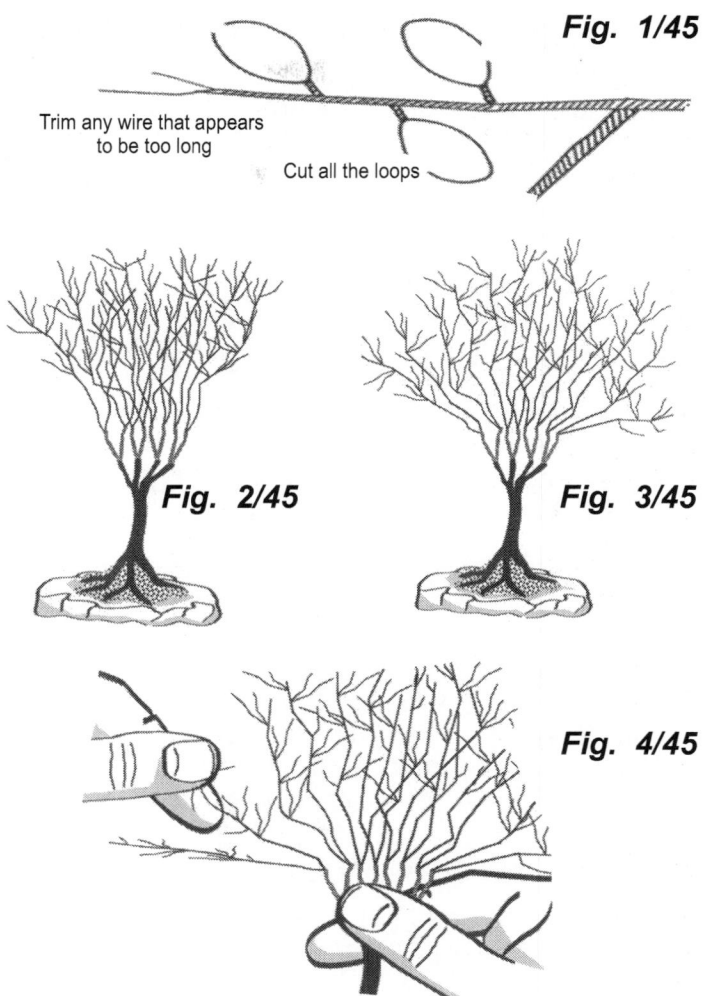

Fig. 1/45

Trim any wire that appears to be too long
Cut all the loops

Fig. 2/45 *Fig. 3/45*

Fig. 4/45

This piece was created on a flat glass base. You can use other types of bases. ***See page 12 for different base selections.***

To see completed pieces in Full Color, visit my website: www.salvillano.com

Creating the Wind Swept Mini Tree Sculpture

Of all the trees I have created, the Wind Swept receives the most comments. Perhaps people relate to the movement they see in it, or they admire the tenacity of the tree holding fast to the earth against the force of a mighty wind storm.

1. Hold the tree firmly on the trunk.

2. Spread out all the branches and twigs so they look like a fan. *See page 40, Fig. 1/40*

3. Hold the tree firmly at the top section of the trunk with one hand. With your other hand grip any two outermost branches at their "V" section. *See page 40, Fig. 1/40*

4. Hold the base of the sculpture in one hand and place the thumb of your other hand about half way up the trunk. Slowly bend the top half of the trunk over the top of your thumb as if you were trying to bend the tree in half. Continue bending the top half of the trunk until it appears to be about half way down the distance toward the roots. Do not be concerned about the trunk snapping, it is very flexible and can be easily formed. *Fig. 1/46*

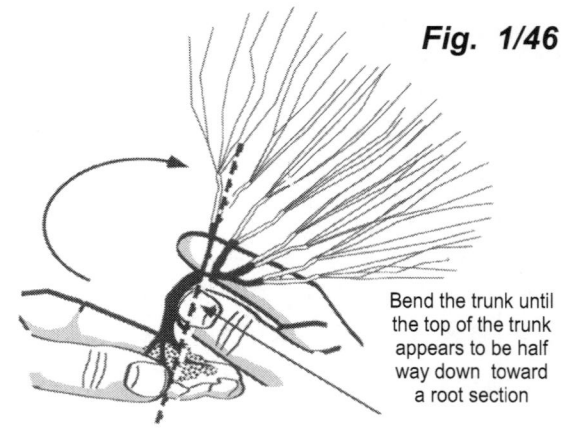

Fig. 1/46

Bend the trunk until the top of the trunk appears to be half way down toward a root section

5. Hold the tree firmly at the top of the trunk and bend a group of the branches in the opposite direction from which the trunk is bent. *Fig. 2/46* Do not try to bend too many branches at one time. This opposite bending action is the action that will give the tree the appearance of bending, yet resisting the force of the wind. As you bend the branches, also separate any branches that appear to be too close together. Move some of the branches down and some of the branches up. For the most part the branches should all be almost parallel to each other yet not exactly parallel. After all the bending is completed, if you feel any of the branches are too long you can either bend them into an "S" shape to use up some of the length of the wire or you can simply trim them using the small wire cutters.

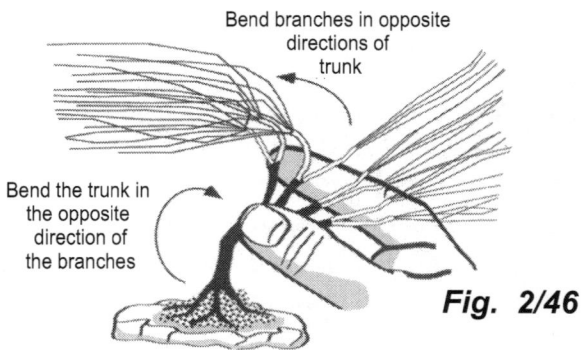

Bend branches in opposite directions of trunk

Bend the trunk in the opposite direction of the branches

Fig. 2/46

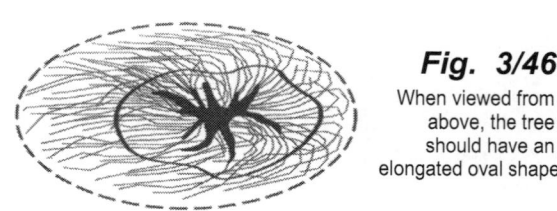

Fig. 3/46
When viewed from above, the tree should have an elongated oval shape

6. As you are bending the branches, look at the tree from directly above. *Fig. 3/46* The tree should have an oval and elongated shape. If you tree looks flat, pull the branches apart to create the elongated shape.

This piece was created on a flat glass base. You can use other types of bases. *See page 12 for more selections.*

To see completed pieces in Full Color, visit my website: www.salvillano.com

Creating the Bonsai with Leaves Mini Tree Sculpture

The Bonsai with Leaves mini tree is created from an Oak mini tree. **See page 44** Create the oak mini tree first, then continue here.

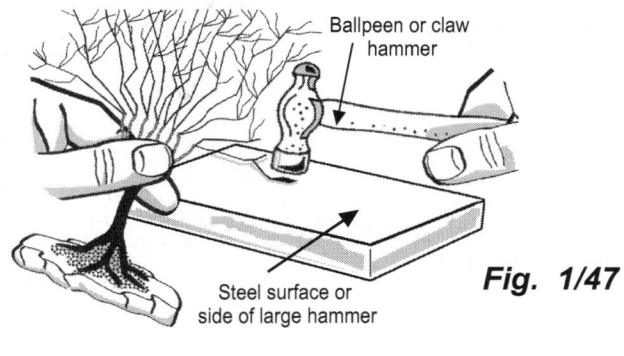
Fig. 1/47

1. Spread out the branches one at a time so it looks like a opened fan. Keep the twigs on a flat plane. Bend any twigs out of the way so you will be able to hammer the twigs one at a time. This will make it easier to hammer the ends of the twigs when you place them on the hard metal hammering surface. **Fig. 1/47**

2. It is a very good idea to practice creating the leaves using some scrap wire.

3. Hold the trunk firmly and place the end of one twig on the hammering surface. Hammer the end of the twig no more than 4 or 5 times until it is flat. The leaf you create should be about 1/2" long. Do not over hammer the leaf, this will weaken the stem which holds the leaf to the branch. Do not try to make all the leaves look alike. It is better if they don't. Repeat this step to create the remaining leaves.

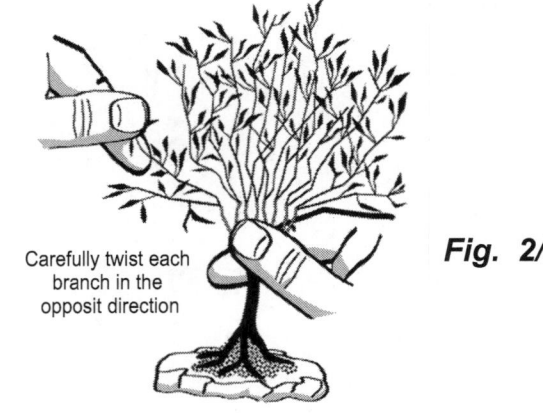
Fig. 2/47

4. Try not to over bend the leaf at the place where it meets the branch, this is its weakest point. No matter how careful you are some of the leaves will be broken, simply leave the remaining twig as is.

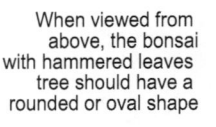
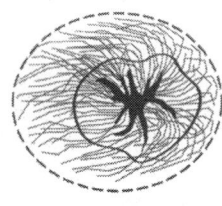
Fig. 3/47

5. You are now ready to shape the tree. Hold the tree firmly from the top part of the trunk. Twist each of the branches in the opposite direction of the branch next to it. This will give the tree a rounded shape and a natural look. **Fig. 2/47**

6. As you bend the branches, stop and look at the tree from directly above. The tree should have a round or oval shape. If your tree looks flat, pull some of the branches away from each other, this will create a more rounded shape. **Fig. 3/47**

7. For the final step, bend some of the leaves downward. Keep some of the leaves flat then give them a slight twist. Be very careful as you are bending the leaves.

This piece was created on a flat glass base. You can use other types of bases. **See page 12 for more base selections.**

To see completed pieces in Full Color, visit my website: www.salvillano.com

Creating a Bird Nest with Pearl Eggs

I have only illustrated the material and tools I feel need to be shown. The obvious items are only listed, such as, "assorted bare wire". If you want to see the photos of the actual items used, *See pages 9 & 10* for a complete list.

Once again, I must state, to get the best results when creating any piece in this book I would strongly suggest that you read all the steps before you start. It is also a good idea to have all the tools and material on hand.

**FINISHED BIRD NEST
WITH PEARL EGGS**

MATERIAL NEEDED

Window Screening.
Cut a 2 inch square of metal screening. This screening can be very easily cut using regular scissors a utility knife or a single edge razor blade. Be sure the screen you use is metal, not nylon or plastic. It must be metal so it holds its shape as you work on it to form the basic shape of the nest and add the various pieces of wire to it. *Fig. 1/48*

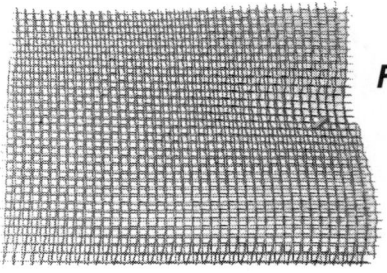

Fig. 1/48

Assorted Pieces of Bare Wire.
You will need about 30 to 40 pieces of 2 to 4 inch various types and gauges of bare wire. The gauge should range from 30 gauge (the thinnest) to 24 gauge (the thickest). You should also try to use as many different colors of wire as you can, such as; copper, brass, aluminium, galvanized and non-galvanized steel and even green floral wire. This wire can be scrap wire you have saved from other projects or you can cut the necessary pieces you need from your spool. In order to create an authentic looking nest you should use as much of a variety of wire as possible. Keep in mind that the birds who create nests will use whatever material that will help to construct the nest.

To see completed pieces in Full Color, visit my website: www.salvillano.com

Pearls with Stringing Holes.

You will need as many pearls as you wish to place in your nest. Some of the nests I have created were used as gifts, with each of the pearls representing a child in the family. For the nest shown here I have used 2 pearls. The size of the pearls I used is 1/4 inch round (6.35 mm). You can use any size you like. Just be sure you have thin enough wire to fit through the hole in the pearls. I also add a few drops of E6000 jewelers glue under the pearls before I permanently wire them in place. This glue dries clear so it will not be seen. If you do not want to use pearls, you can use any type of gem or stone you like. I have also created nests with birthstones. Just be sure the stone you use has a hole in it to accept the wire. I do not recommend using the glue as the only way to fix the stones into the nest. **Fig. 1/49**

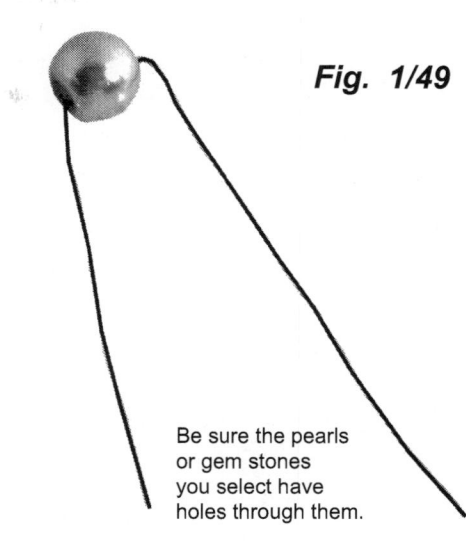

Fig. 1/49

Be sure the pearls or gem stones you select have holes through them.

TOOLS NEEDED

Scissors or Utility Knife or Single Edge Razor Blade. - To cut the screening.
Ball Peen or Small Claw Hammer - To shape the nest.
Medium and Small Wire Cutters - To cut the wire.
Point Nose Pliers - To pull the wire through the nest.
Spring Clamps - To hold the hammer in place as you work on shaping the nest.
Gloves - The edges of the screen are very small and very sharp.
Bent Nose Pliers - To bend the ends of the wire.

PROCEDURE

You may want to work on a white piece of board or a white cloth as your backdrop. This will make it much easier to see all the wires and the nest as you proceed.

1. Using your scissors, or a single edge razor blade, or a utility knife, carefully cut off the four corners of the 2 inch screening to create an approximate circle. If you are using a single edge razor blade or a utility knife, hold the screen in the center. And be sure you are cutting on a proper surface. The finished cut piece does not need to be a perfect circle. This size circle will create a one inch round nest. If you should ever want to create a larger nest, just increase the size of the square used to create the circle and also increase the amount and size of the wire you will be using. **Fig. 2/49**

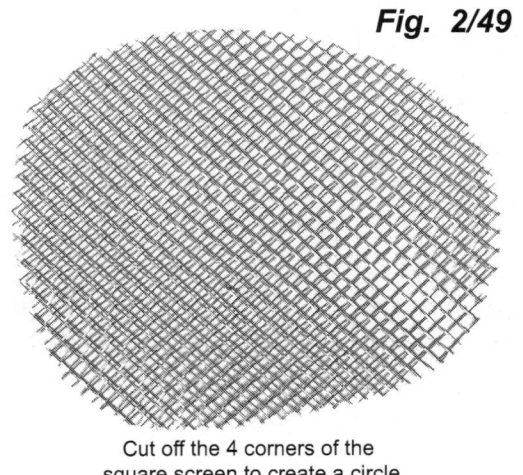

Fig. 2/49

Cut off the 4 corners of the square screen to create a circle

2. Before you start to work on the screen, set up the ball peen hammer and clamp as shown in *Fig. 1/50* This will make it much easier to shape the nest. Then after putting on your gloves, (you will be working with the very fine sharp edges of the screening so you will need them on). Place the circular piece of screening over the round end of the hammer. Force the screening down onto the round shaped end of the hammer. *Fig. 2/50* This will create the basic shape and size of the nest. If you want to create a larger nest, you will need to use a larger ball peen hammer or some other type of hard round object.

Fig. 1/50

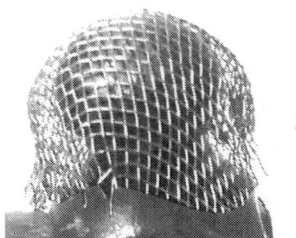

Fig. 2/50

Force the screen down onto the round end of the ball peen hammer

3. Keeping your gloves on, start weaving the assorted pieces of wire in and out of the holes in the screening. This is similar to weaving a basket. For the first several pieces of wire, weave it in horizontally, *Fig. 3/50* then weave it in all directions. This method will help the nest keep its round shape. *Fig. 4/50* Try to use a variety of types and colors of wire. The more variety of wire you use, the more realistic your nest will be.

Fig. 3/50

Weave the wire horizontally, for the first several pieces

As you weave more and more wire into the nest you may see that some of the ends of the wires are protruding out through the nest. Simply bend any of these wires toward the center of the nest. You may need to use the point nose pliers to do this. It will take quite a lot of wire to build the nest and get the look you are seeking. You will also find that the nest may lose its round shape as you are adding, pulling and bending the wire into it. If this should happen, simply put the nest back onto the round end of the hammer and re-shape it. The nest will now be strong enough that you will even be able to use another hammer to shape and round the nest. *Fig. 5/50*

Fig. 4/50

Weave the remaining wire pieces in all directions

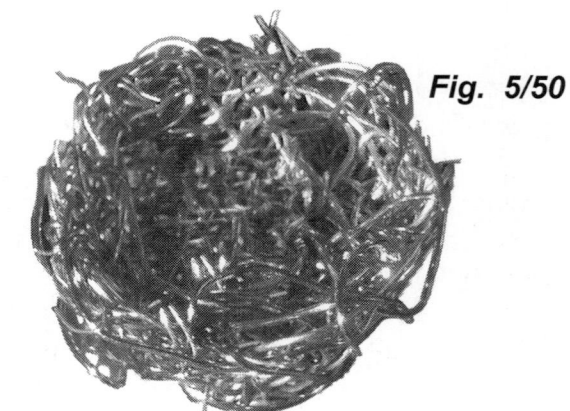

Fig. 5/50

Bend any loose ends back into the nest or over the top of the nest

4. After you are satisfied with the look and shape of your nest, you are now ready to add the pearl eggs. Start by cutting a 4 inch piece of wire for each pearl that you will use to thread through the pearl. Use a gauge of wire that will slip easily into the pearl. Thread the wire through the pearl and bend each of the ends of the wire down. This will create two, 2 inch "legs" protruding from the pearl. These wire legs will be used to hold the eggs into the nest. **Fig. 1/51**

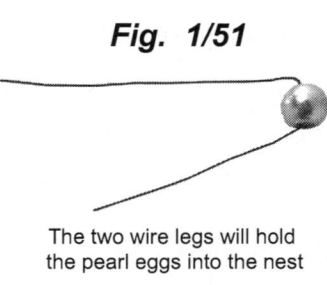

Fig. 1/51

The two wire legs will hold the pearl eggs into the nest

Your selection of the wire for the legs through the pearls does not matter, since for the most part, the wire will blend in with the wire that makes up the nest. Repeat the above instructions for each of the pearl eggs you want in the nest. For the size of the nest you just created, you can put up to 8 or 9 eggs. Next, thread each of the pearl legs straight down through the bottom of the nest. **Fig. 2/51** Try to keep the legs as close together as you can. Pull the 2 legs of each pearl tightly through the nest, getting the pearl to sit securely on the bottom of the nest. If you are using more than one pearl. Get them as close together as possible. The finished piece will look much more realistic if the pearls are touching. Once the pearls are where you want them, lift them up slightly and add a few drops of glue under them. I use *E6000, medium viscosity, clear glue.* You can certainly use any glue you may have on hand, as long as it will bond the pearls to the metal nest. Be sure to follow the directions on the label. After you have glued the pearls to the nest, and the glue has dried, using the point nose pliers, twist the two legs of each pearl tightly so the pearls are firmly locked into the nest. **Fig. 3/51**

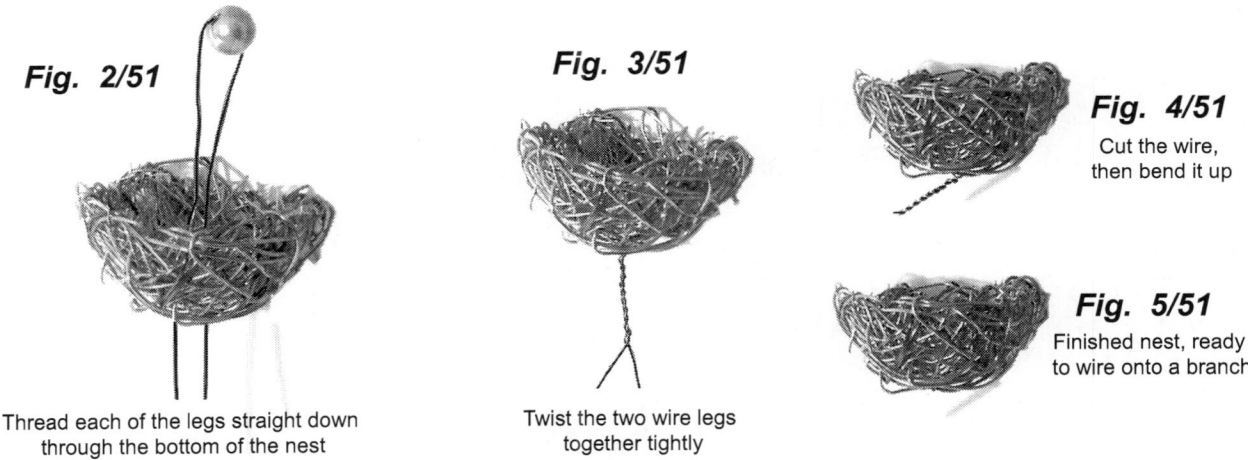

Fig. 2/51

Thread each of the legs straight down through the bottom of the nest

Fig. 3/51

Twist the two wire legs together tightly

Fig. 4/51

Cut the wire, then bend it up

Fig. 5/51

Finished nest, ready to wire onto a branch

5. Using the medium wire cutters cut off the excess wire leaving about 1/2 inch of wire that you will then fold up to the bottom contour of the nest. **Fig. 4/51** The nest is now ready to be placed onto the branches of your tree sculpture or, onto a free standing branch. **Fig. 5/51** To secure the nest onto the branch you will need to create more "legs" through the nest. Add two more pieces of 6 inch wire through the nest, as you did to secure the pearls to the nest. The wire you select as these legs should be the same color wire as the branch on which it will sit. This will hide the wire that is holding the nest onto the branch. **See page 52, Fig. 1/52** Each of the legs will be about three inches long. These are the wires that you will use to fix the nest to the branch. Now, position the four wire legs over the branch in the tree you selected for the nest. Try to select a part of the branch that intersects with another branch. This a very strong place on the branch to wire the nest onto. **See page 52, Fig. 1/52**

6. I would suggest you try placing the nest in different places in the branches until you find the one you like. Sometimes I place the nest in a very obvious position, like at the end of the branch, or on one of the top branches. And other times I try to hide the nest deep within the tree so that the viewers are delighted when they discover that there is a nest in the tree, and it has eggs in it.

Once you have found a position you are happy with, you can begin to wire the nest onto the selected branch. It is very important that you wire the nest onto the branch so it is as level as possible. To do this you should wire one set of legs at a time. Tighten one side, then the other, creating the level position for the nest. After you have wired the nest onto the branch by securely twisting the wire, you should have some excess wire at the end of the legs. Cut off what appears to be any excess wire, then bend the ends of the remaining wire up toward the nest. This will effectively hide the wires that are holding the nest onto the branch. **Fig. 1/52** Remember, you do not need to use pearls as eggs in your nest. I have also used other gems and stones as eggs. Just try to use a gem or stone that will contrast the wire of the nest so they will be easily seen. You may want to consider using all the same color wire, instead of different color wire to create the nest. The different color wire works well using the pearls as eggs because the pearls are white and will contrast almost any color wire. To be sure that the color of the gem or stone will look the way you want, you should look at it next to the wire you have chosen for the nest, before you start.

I have also created a commissioned piece out of steel wire which I then had gold plated. To this nest I added two real pearls. This was given as an anniversary gift to a wife and mother, from her husband. The two pearls represented their two children. Although this was expensive, the resulting piece was beautiful and unusual. This type of piece can also be created, less expensively while looking equally as well, by using metal screening that has been spray painted with several layers of gold paint. Then following the weaving instructions using medium soft, gold plated wire for the entire nest.

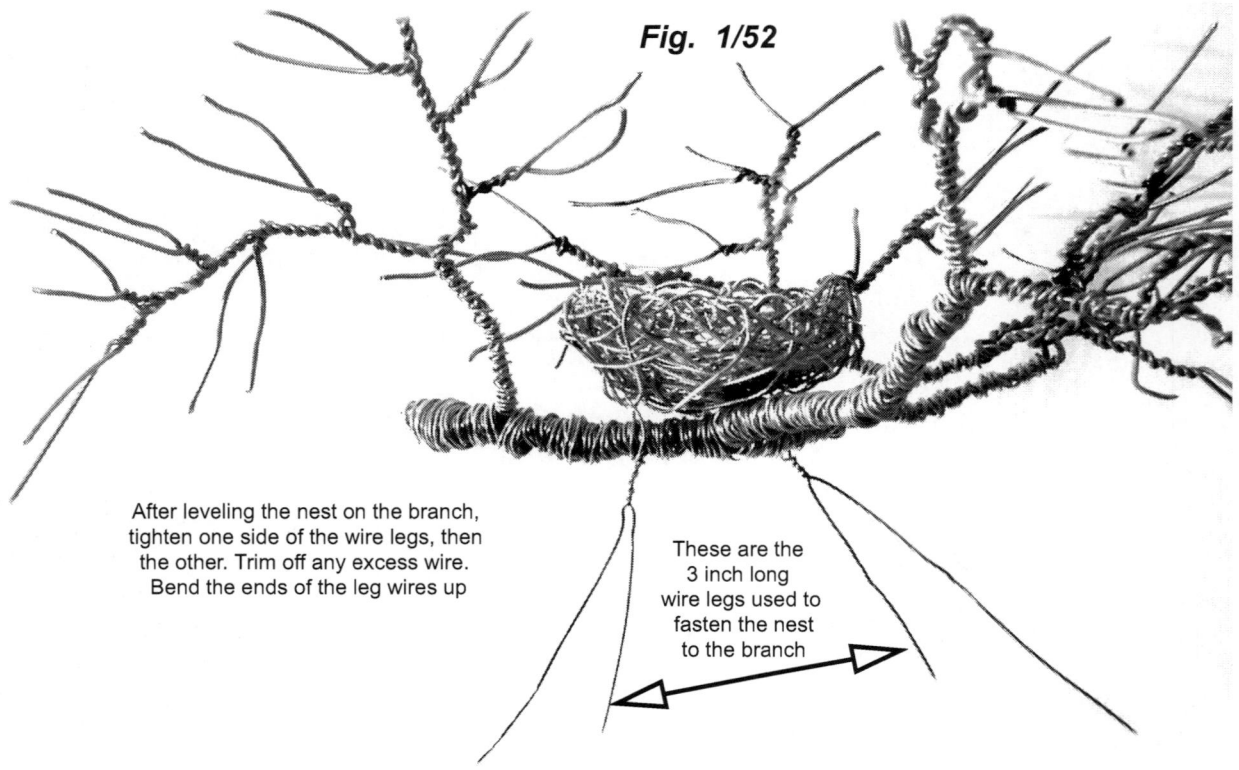

Fig. 1/52

After leveling the nest on the branch, tighten one side of the wire legs, then the other. Trim off any excess wire. Bend the ends of the leg wires up

These are the 3 inch long wire legs used to fasten the nest to the branch

To see completed pieces in Full Color, visit my website: www.salvillano.com

Creating Jade Leaves for a Tree Sculptures

The jade leaf trees I create are generally made with either gold color or copper wire. Either type of wire looks very dramatic and will emphasize the dark green color of the jade leaves. The jade trees are created in three stages. First I create the tree, then all the leaves, one at a time, and finally I assemble and wire all the parts together. You can use any size tree you wish and transform it into a jade tree. I have created trees from 6 inches to 24 inches. Since you can use almost any tree as the basic tree, I will show you how to create the leaves and assemble them onto the tree.

This tree sculpture with jade leaves is only 6" and has 51 leaves on it.

This tree sculpture is 22" and has 218 jade leaves.

Fig. 1/53

Be sure the leaves have a notch in the bottom

The leaves I use do not have holes through them as other gems do. **Fig. 1/53** I feel the leaves without holes look more natural and "leaflike" when wired onto the tree. The size of the leaves are 6mm X 8mm (about 1/4" X 5/16") These leaves also have a small notch at the base. This notch is an important part of the way I wire the leaf. You will need a simple jig made of wood and two nails. Both nails are hammered completely through the wood base, then the base is turned upside down. File the sharp points of the nails to blunt them, Use either 26 or 28 gauge wire only. Any other size is either too thick or too thin. **See page 54** for exact sizes and details to create the jig.

To see completed pieces in Full Color, visit my website: www.salvillano.com

Making the Jig to Create the Jade Leaves

The jig is used to simplify adding the wire to the leaves. Start with a wood base, the size is: 7" x 5.5" x 3/4". Cover the entire top surface of the base with white tape or paint it white, this is done so you can see the work more easily. Drill small pilot holes through the wood base, before you drive the nails. This will help prevent the wood from splitting. Or covering the wood with white tape, before you drive the nails, will also help to prevent splitting the wood. Follow **Fig. 1/54** for the positioning of the holes for the 2 nails.

1. Cut a length of the wire you are using 12 inches long and loop it over the larger nail **Fig. 2/54** (remember, the wire should be either 26 or 28 gauge).

2. Using the bent nose pliers, twist the wire until it is coiled up to the small nail, then coil the two loose ends all the way back to their ends. **Fig. 3/54**

3. Remove the coiled wire from the small nail, but leave it on the large nail. Turn the wire around so the end you just twisted is away from you. **Fig. 4/54**

4. Once again, as in step 2, twist this end of the wire until the small loop you create is about 1/16 inch away from the large nail. **Fig. 3/54** The loop must slip easily off the large nail or it will not fit on the leaf.

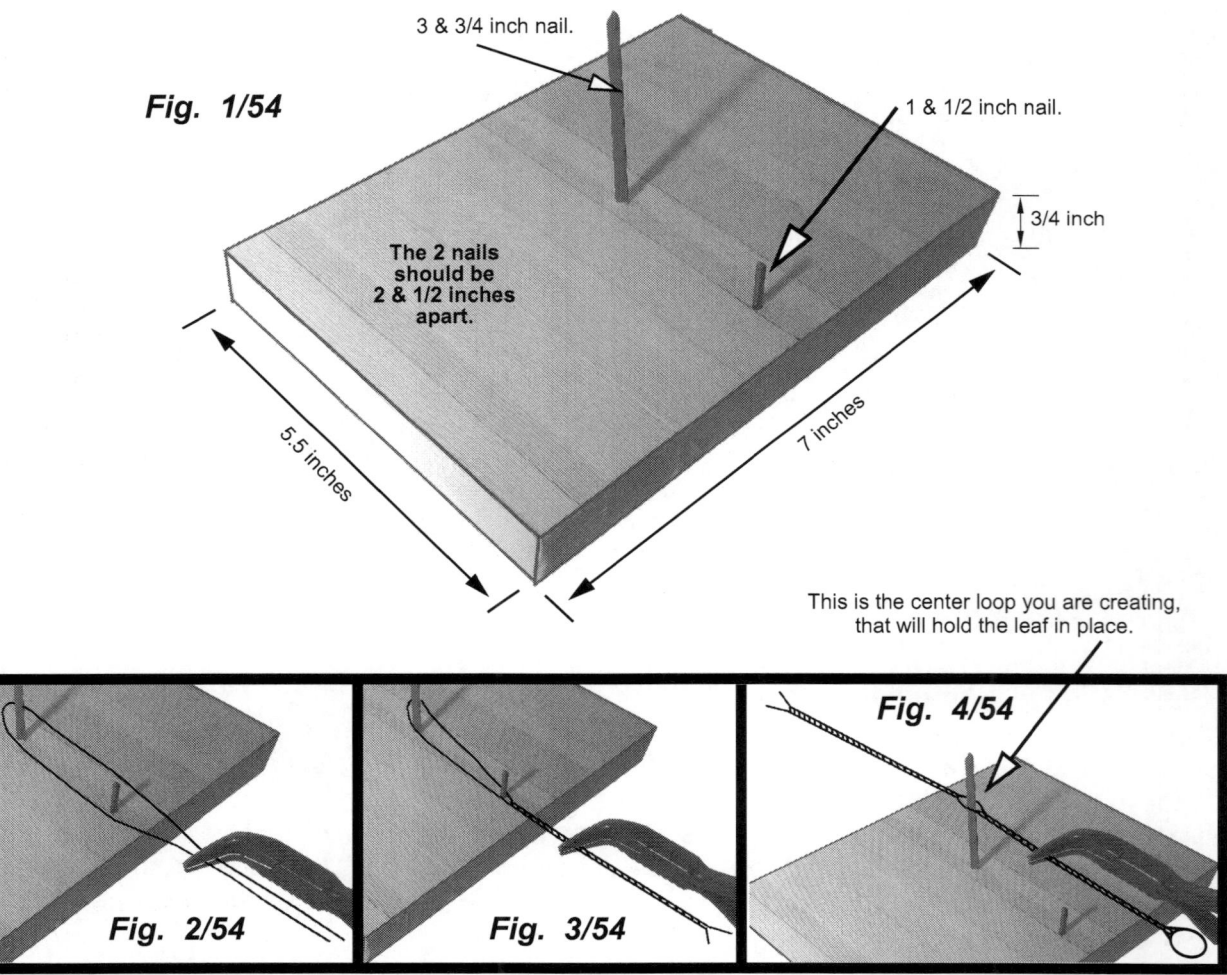

54

5. You will end up with a length of wire with a loop in the middle. **Fig. 1/55** This is the loop that will go around the top of the leaf and will hold the leaf in position.

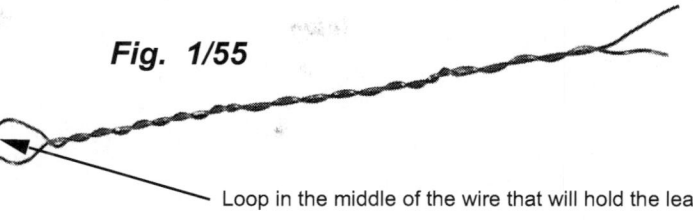

Fig. 1/55

Loop in the middle of the wire that will hold the leaf

6. Fold the wire up at the center of the loop creating a 90 degree angle. **Fig. 2/55**

7. Place the jade leaf into the new loop you have created. **Fig. 2/55**

8. Fold the perpendicular wire end down over the top side of the leaf, toward the notched side of the leaf. **Fig. 2/55**

9. Hold the leaf and the wire firmly and use the point nose pliers to twist the 2 legs of the wire toward the notch in the leaf. Be sure you twist the wire so that the last twist of the wire fits into the notch in the leaf. **Fig. 3/55**

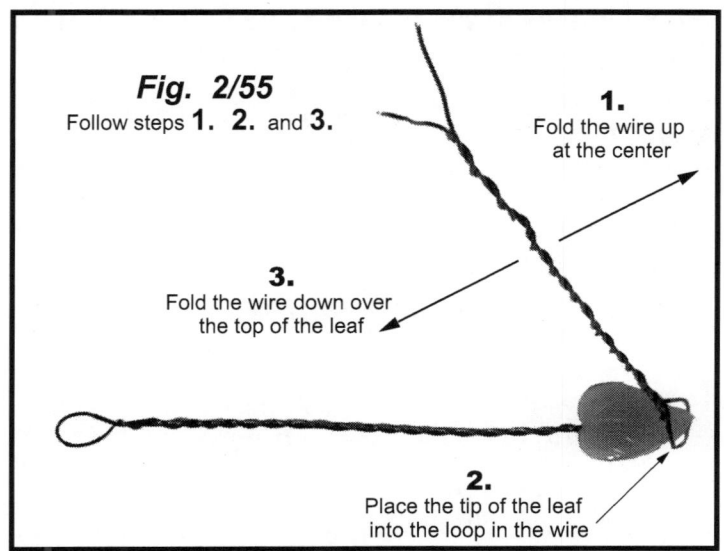

Fig. 2/55
Follow steps 1. 2. and 3.

1. Fold the wire up at the center

3. Fold the wire down over the top of the leaf

2. Place the tip of the leaf into the loop in the wire

10. Continue twisting the wire legs, until you have about 3/4 of an inch of both legs twisted together to create one stem for the leaf. The other two legs should about 1/2 inch long each. **Fig. 4/55** Be sure the twisted wire of the legs fits tightly into the groove of the jade leaf.

11. Use the wire cutters to snip off and even out the two legs of the leaf wires. The final wired leaf should look like **Fig. 4/55**

*See page 58
Attaching leaves
to the tree sculpture.*

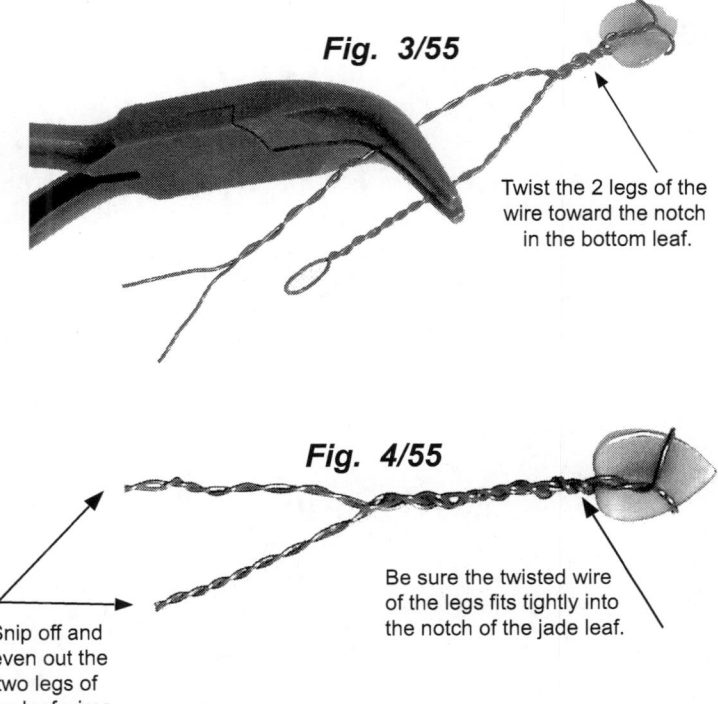

Fig. 3/55

Twist the 2 legs of the wire toward the notch in the bottom leaf.

Fig. 4/55

Snip off and even out the two legs of the leaf wires

Be sure the twisted wire of the legs fits tightly into the notch of the jade leaf.

Creating Multiple Leaves

As you can imagine, I need to create many leaves to use on my small and large jade leaf trees. I have created a way to very easily twist the wire necessary to hold the leaves. Twisting the wire by hand is not only slow but also is hard on your wrist. I use a battery powered screw driver. I have found the battery powered screwdriver turns the wire at the correct speed and is light weight. The only difference in creating the wire by this method, is that you need to create loops at both ends of the wire, not just the loop you create when you loop the wire over the large nail. **Fig. 2/56** Once you create the second loop, you create the wire for the leaves the same way you did by hand. *See page 54*

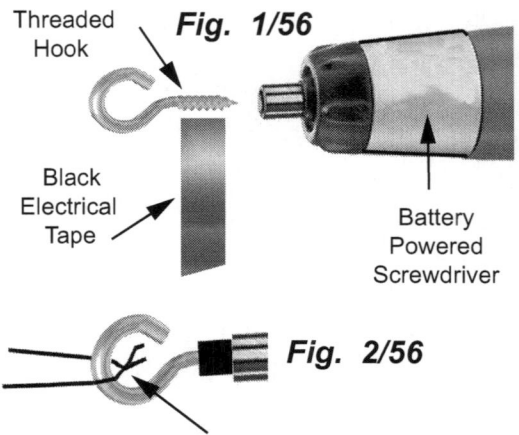

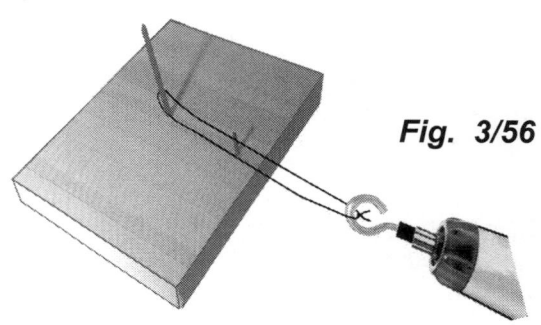

Create a loop with the two open legs of the wire. This loop is where the hook will fit.

1. Use a threaded hook, cover the threads with black electrical tape until it fits snugly into the battery screwdriver. **Fig. 1/56**

2. Insert the hook with the tape on it into the receiver of the battery screw driver. **Fig. 2/56**

4. Twist the two ends of the legs of the wire to create a loop to fit the hook into. **Fig. 2/56**

5. Use the same method as you did by hand, to create the wire that will hold the leaves. *See page 54*

After creating the two loops, proceed to create the wire loops as you did by hand.

Jade Leaves Mixed with Glass Beads

For some of my larger jade leaf trees I also add another dimension to the tree by adding glass beads onto the twigs next to the jade leaves. This creates a very interesting visual effect because the glass beads reflect the light and bounce it off the jade leaves. It is actually very easy to incorporate the glass beads with the jade leaves. It will take a bit longer to create this type of tree, but I think you will feel the time spent is well worth it.

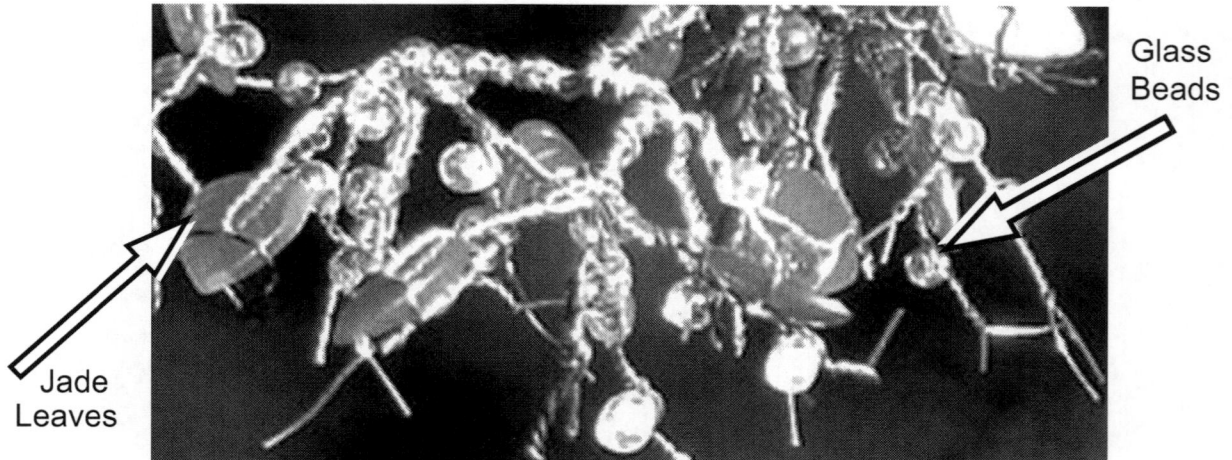

To see completed pieces in Full Color, visit my website: www.salvillano.com

Jade Leaves Mixed with Glass Beads

1. Use the same jig as described on **Page 54**

2. Cut a 12 inch length of 26 or 28 gauge wire, gold color or copper. Place the wire over the large nail on the jig as shown on **Page 54, Fig. 2/54**

3. Place the bent nose pliers half way up both of the legs of the wire, and coil the wire until it reaches the smaller nail, stop coiling when it does. **Fig. 1/57**

4. Remove the wire from the jig, it should look like this. **Fig. 2/57**

5. Wire three fringe beads, any color of your choice, onto the open legs of the wire. The fringe beads should be about 1/4 inch apart. **Fig. 3/57**

6. Place the large open loop back onto the large nail on the jig, and twist the wire until it is about 1/6 inch away from the large nail. **Fig. 5/57**

7. The wire should now look like this. **Fig. 4/57** and is now ready to accept the leaf into the small loop in the center of the wire.

8. Finally to complete the wiring of the jade leaves with beads, follow steps: 6,7,8,9,10, on **Page 55**

9. Your final jade leaf with glass fringe beads should look like **Fig. 6/57**

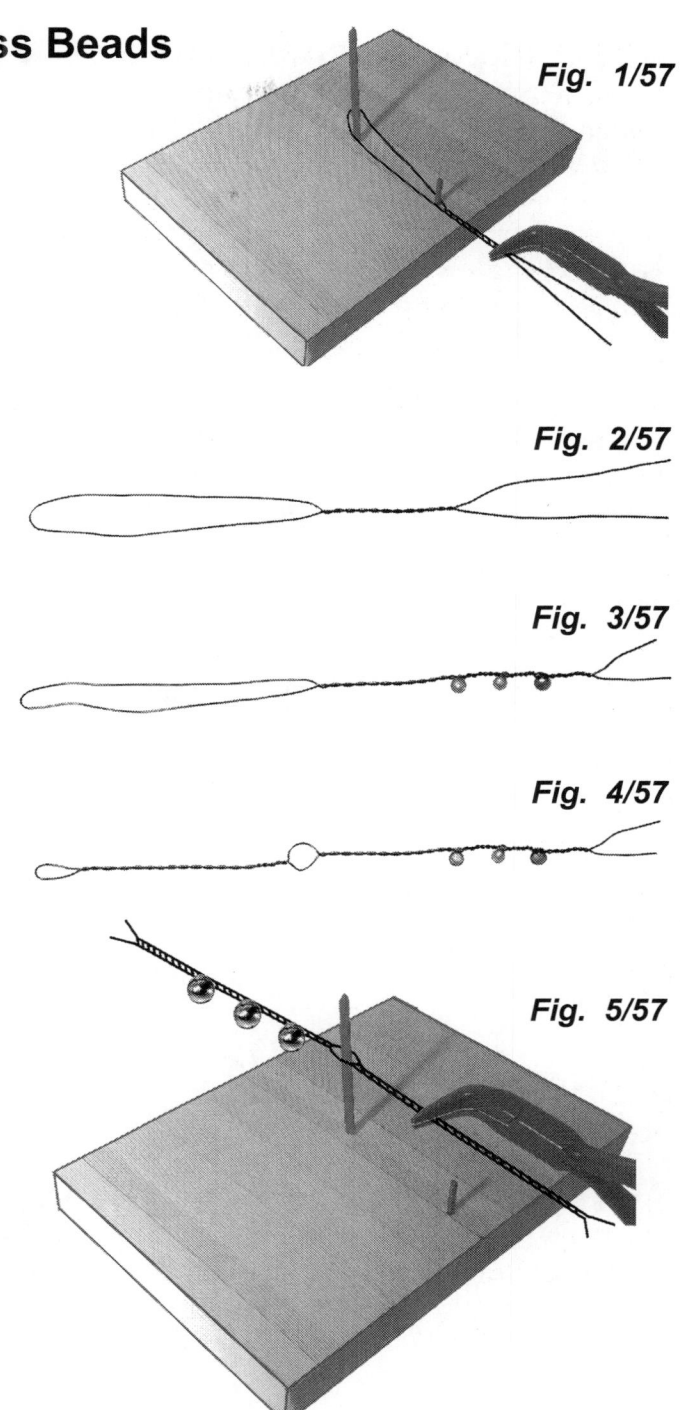

Fig. 1/57

Fig. 2/57

Fig. 3/57

Fig. 4/57

Fig. 5/57

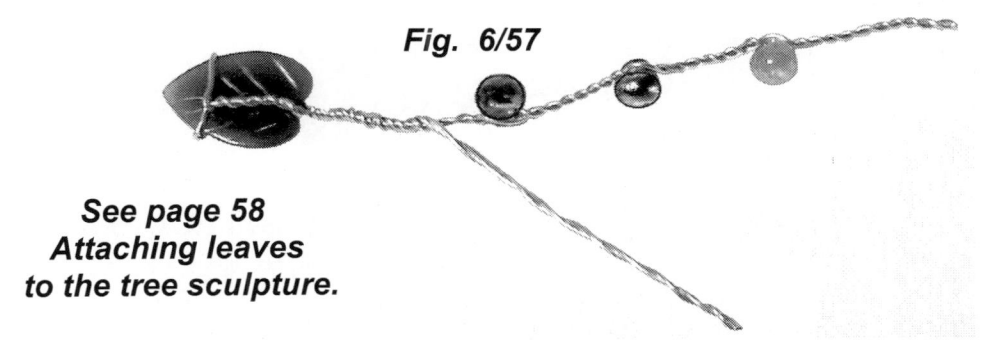

Fig. 6/57

See page 58
Attaching leaves
to the tree sculpture.

Attaching Jade Leaves to a Tree Sculpture

After you have created as many leaves as you want to put on your tree sculpture, it is very simple to attach them to the tree. The leaves can be attached either to the twigs or the branches. I think the best place to attach them is at the ends of the twigs or branches, not close to the trunk of the tree. This, of course, is your choice.

1. Spread out the 2 legs of the Jade leaf so that they are perpendicular to the wire that is holding the leaf in place. *Fig. 1/58*

2. Wrap the 2 legs around the twig or branch where you want to attach it. *Fig. 2/58*

3. Using a thinner gauge wire, that is the same color as the tree and the leaf wire, (this wire should be 26 or 24 gauge), twist this wire around the leaf legs and the twig or branch. Twist enough wire to hold the leaf leg securely in place. Wrapping once up and once down the leaf leg should be enough.

4. If you are adding the leaves to the smaller twig portion of the tree, you may need to trim off some of the leg.

5. If you are placing the leaves near each other you can proceed to the adding the next leaf, if the leaves are far apart you can cut the thinner wire before you add the next leaf.

6. After the leaves are securely mounted, bend the leaf stems in different directions and up and down. This will create a more natural leaf arrangement.

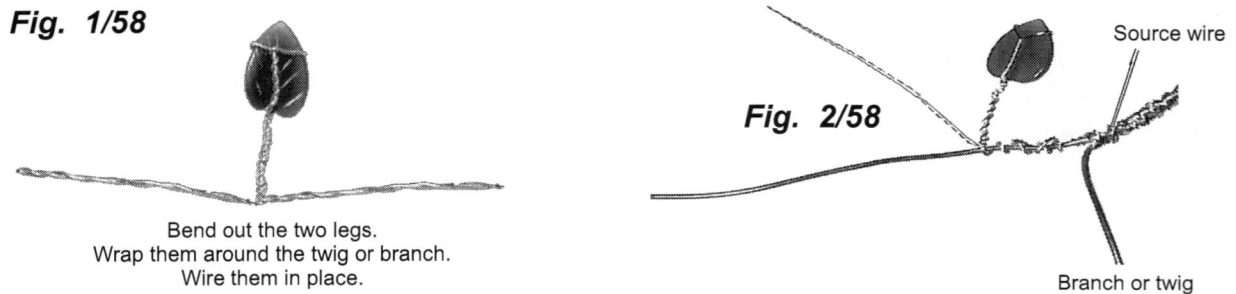

Fig. 1/58
Bend out the two legs.
Wrap them around the twig or branch.
Wire them in place.

Fig. 2/58
Source wire
Branch or twig

Attaching Jade and Glass Beads Leaves

To attach the Jade and Glass Bead leaves to the tree, use the same basic steps as stated above. The only difference is that the Jade and Glass Bead leaves only have one leg that you will attach to the twig or branch. The remaining instructions are the same *Fig. 3/58*

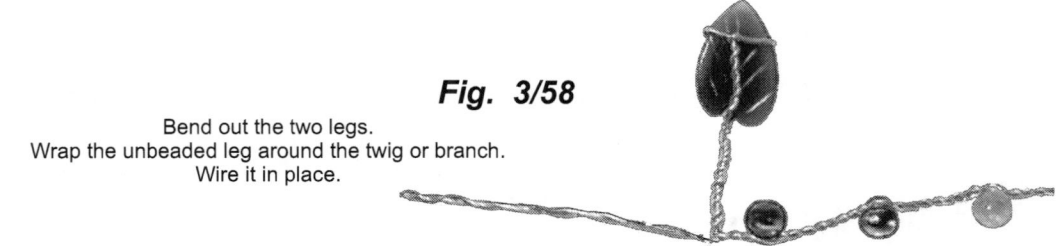

Fig. 3/58
Bend out the two legs.
Wrap the unbeaded leg around the twig or branch.
Wire it in place.

See page 79, Figs: 1/79, 2/79, 3/79 for additional information

To see completed leaves on the trees in Full Color, visit my website: www.salvillano.com

The Next Section Shows How to Create the Following

Cascade on Rock *Page 60*

Mini Jade Leaf Cascade *Page 76*

Wall Art Sculpture

Wind Swept
Page 81

Beaded
Page 81

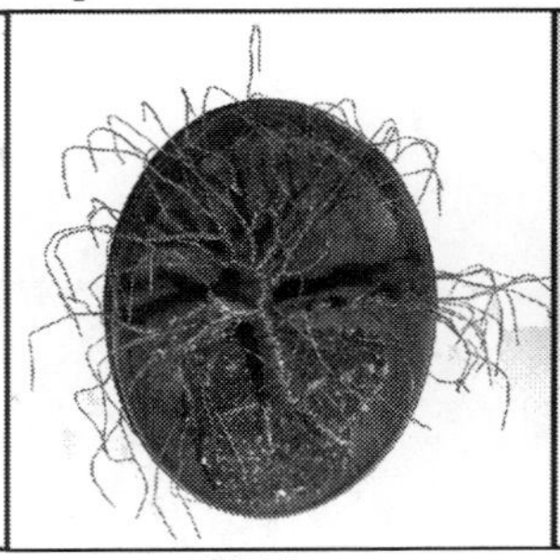

Oak
Page 81

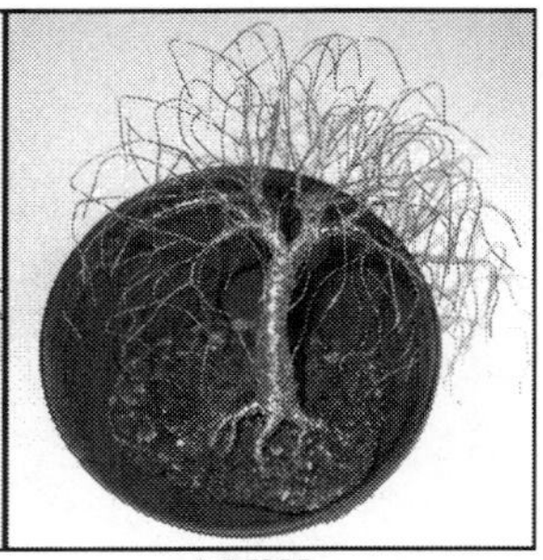

Willow
Page 81

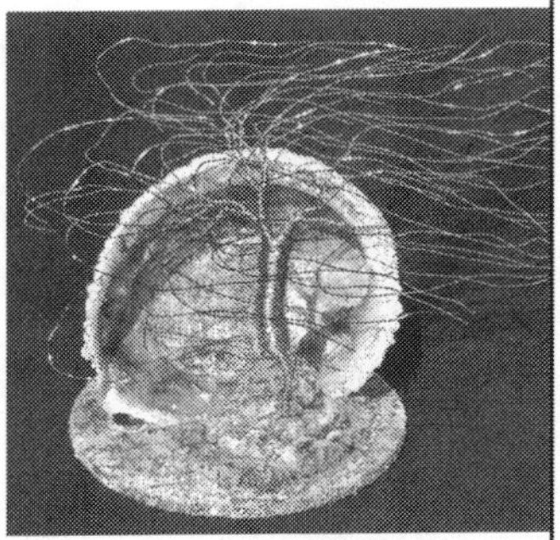

Tree on Sea Shell
Page 86

Glass Bonsai *Page 91*

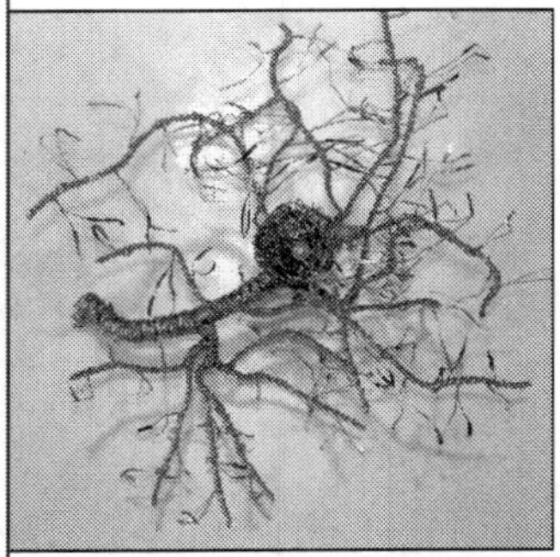

Bird Nest
Page 101

To see completed pieces in Full Color, visit my website: www.salvillano.com

Cascade on Rock Wire Tree Sculpture - *21"h X 18"w X 11"d*

Difficulty Scale:
(1 = easy, 10 = difficult) this is a **10**

MATERIAL CHECK LIST:
__ 26 gauge wire (900 ft.)
__ 22 gauge wire (800 ft.)
__ 18 gauge, 6 strand cable wire (60 ft.)
__ 2"x6"x18" piece of lumber
__ Base to plant tree into **See page 12**
__ Rock to support tree
__ Electrical or masking tape
__ Electrical staples or 2" nails, (6 each)
__ Electrical end caps (30 to 40)
__ White cloth or heavy white paper
__ India ink, green, yellow, white
__ Painting leaves **See pages 73 & 74**
__ White glue
__ Sand and pebble mixture

TOOLS CHECK LIST:
__ Protective eye wear
__ Gloves
__ Long sleeve shirt
__ Large & small wire cutters
__ Large pliers & regular pliers
__ Flat nose pliers
__ Spring clamps, 3
__ Ruler, 24 inch
__ #0, #1, & 1" brushes
__ Ballpeen, or small claw hammer
__ Steel plate or anvil

To see completed pieces in Full Color, visit my website: www.salvillano.com

This piece is called "Cascading" because it appears to flow from a high point on one side to a lower point on the other side, creating a cascading motion. I have placed this tree in a 9 inch round, 5 inch high rose wood stand, with legs. I have chosen this type of base so that the lower branches of the tree can cascade below the rim of the base. I have added a rock for an interesting effect and to add more weight to stabilize the piece. **See page 12** for more base suggestions.

Before you start to create the Cascade on a Rock, you should first create the base. This is done for two reasons. The first is that since a considerable amount of drying time is needed for the base, rock and sand mound to be bonded together, you can work on the rest of the piece while all the other elements are drying. It is important that all the parts of the base are dry and solid before you mount the tree. The second reason is, by completing the base first, you will be able to fit and make adjustments to the root system and have a very good idea how the final piece will look before you bond the roots to the base.

Creating the Tree

1. Use the large wire cutters to cut 17 pieces of the 6 strand 18 gauge cable to 21 inch lengths. Try to uncoil and straighten each length, as much as possible. This will make the cable easier to work with. *Fig. 1/61* If you want, you can put electrical end caps on the end of each cable to prevent the cable from cutting into your hands or wrists.

2. Group all the lengths of the cable together, pull out 11 pieces until each piece is about 3 to 4 inches longer than the remaining pieces. The extra length of these 11 pieces will be used to create the root system. After the root lengths are created, use masking or electrical tape tightly wrapped around all the cables, to hold all in place. You can leave this tape in place, since it will be well covered by the additional wire you will be adding. *Fig. 1/61*

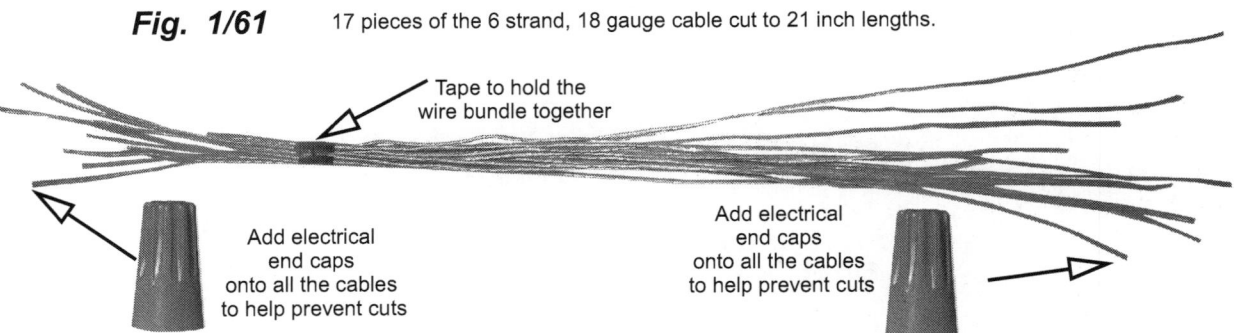

Fig. 1/61   17 pieces of the 6 strand, 18 gauge cable cut to 21 inch lengths.

3. Measure up about 4 inches from the longest of the pieces you pulled through to create the root structure. Mark the distance with tape and wrap the tape around 2 or 3 times to hold the wire bundle in place. **See page 62, Fig. 1/62** Next, measure up about 5 inches from the bottom of the tape you just wrapped and secure this part with 2 or 3 wraps of tape as you did before. You should now have created 3 wraps of tape that will hold the wire bundle in place as you proceed to the next steps.

The Wire Bundles

All the tape you use will by covered by additional wrapping of more wire.
(A) will be the root section.
(B) will be the trunk section.
(C) will be the branch section.
Fig. 1/62

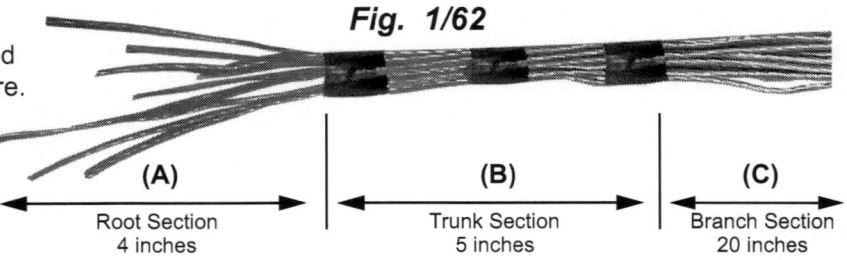

Fig. 1/62

Root Section 4 inches | Trunk Section 5 inches | Branch Section 20 inches

Making the Root System

1. Separate the cable wire into 4 different groups. 1 group of 4 cable wires (D), 2 groups of 3 cable wires (E) and (F), and 1 single cable wire that will be used to anchor the tree into the base (G). Once again use tape to hold the root cables in their groups. Place the tape as close to the trunk section (B) as you can get it. *Fig. 2/62* After you have taped the groups, spread them apart so that they are equally separated.

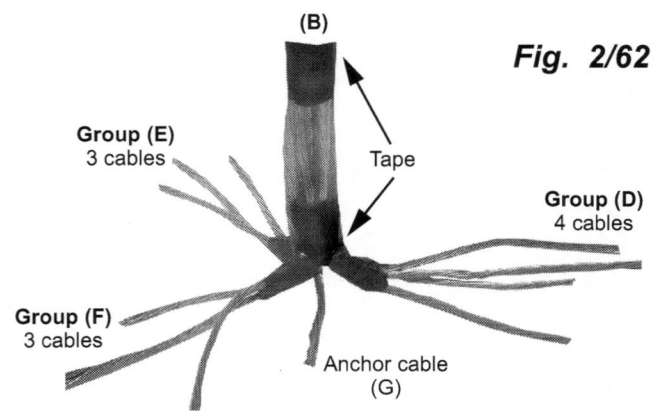

Fig. 2/62

2. Starting with the cable group (D), twist two of the four cables together for about 1 inch to create 2 smaller groups, (H) and (I). If you have trouble twisting the cable by hand, you may need to use the large wire cutters or large pliers. You should also be careful of the ends of the cable wires, they may be sharp. Twist cable groups (E) and (F) for 1 inch, creating a group with 2 cables. (J) and one single cable (K). Leave the anchor cable (G) as is. *Fig. 3/62*

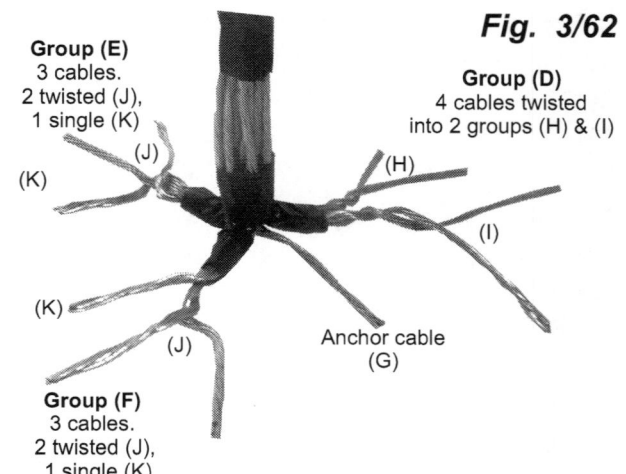

Fig. 3/62

Wrapping the Wire

1. The under-wrapping of the wire will start with 22 gauge steel galvanized wire, and will finish with 26 gauge steel galvanized wire for the final wrapping. Uncoil about 4 feet of the 22 gauge wire. let the source of the wire rest on the floor, this will make it easier for the source wire to unwind as you use it.

2. Starting with either group (E) or (F), twist the 22 gauge wire source around the single piece of the cable wire. This will secure the wire as you proceed. *Fig. 4/62* Hold the trunk of the tree firmly and begin to wrap the source wire around the entire root section. Wrap the wire over the tape and all the way to

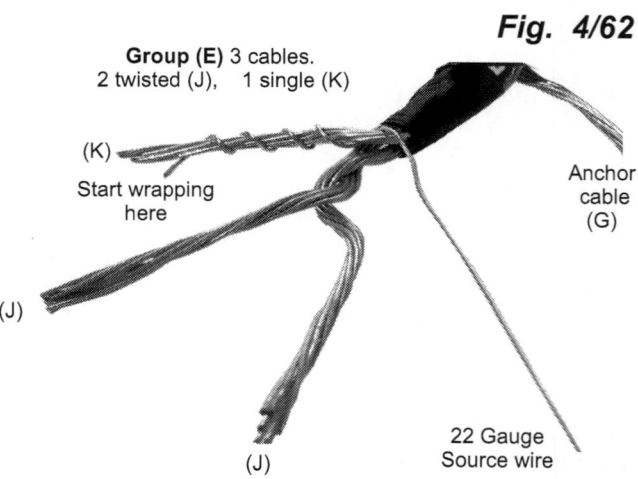

Fig. 4/62

the base of the trunk. ***Fig. 1/63*** Continue to wrap the wire until the entire root section is covered and you can no longer see the cable wire or the tape. Wrap the wire all the way to the tip of each root, then back. ***Fig. 2/63*** You will return to this and all other sections of the tree to add more wire which will create the actual tree shape. Repeat the above instructions to complete the other two root sections. ***Fig. 3/63***

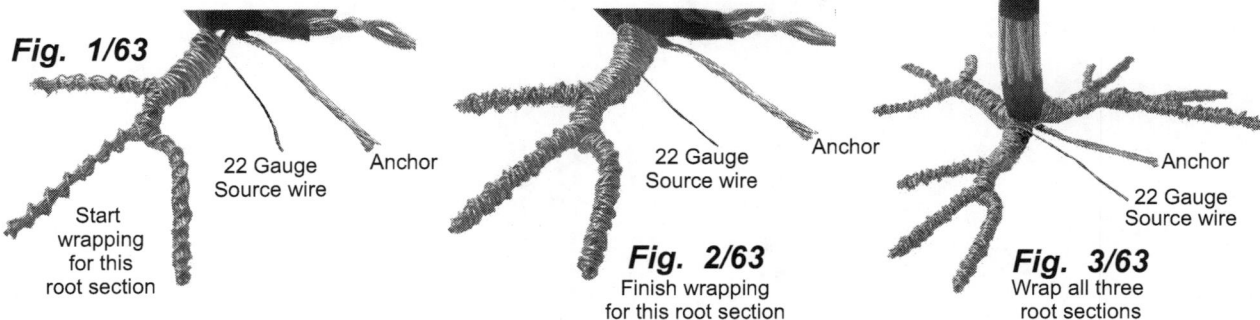

Fig. 1/63 Start wrapping for this root section — 22 Gauge Source wire — Anchor

Fig. 2/63 Finish wrapping for this root section — 22 Gauge Source wire — Anchor

Fig. 3/63 Wrap all three root sections — Anchor — 22 Gauge Source wire

Creating the Trunk

Before you start wrapping the trunk, hold the top of the trunk firmly and give the middle part a slight bend. If you are unable to bend the trunk by hand you can use pliers or you can bend the trunk on the edge of a table. Giving the trunk this slight bend will create a more natural and less rigid tree. Start wrapping the trunk at the bottom where you ended wrapping the root sections. Wrap the wire up and down the trunk 4 times ending the top wrap just above the tape. This time do not try to hide all the tape with the wire, the tape will all be covered in the final wrapping. ***Fig. 4/63***

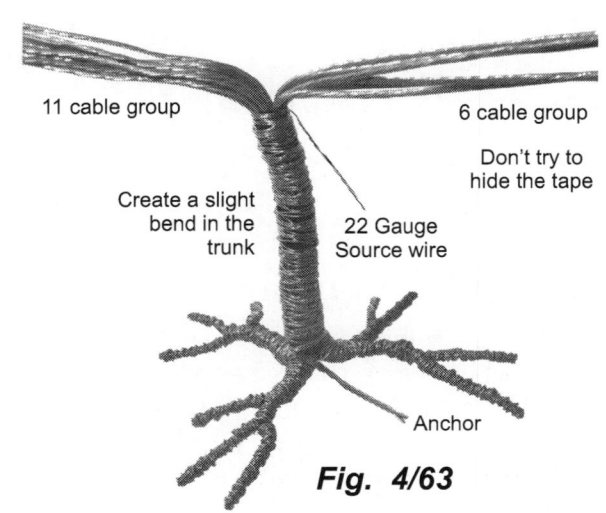

11 cable group — 6 cable group — Don't try to hide the tape — Create a slight bend in the trunk — 22 Gauge Source wire — Anchor

Fig. 4/63

Creating the Branches

Separate all the cable wire at the top of the trunk into two groups. One group with six cables and the other with the remaining eleven. For the next few steps, you will be wrapping the branches starting at the top of the trunk, wrapping the length of the branches, then returning to where you started. When you get to the section in the branch where you will start to return the wrapping, wrap the source wire through the "V" created by the cable wires. This will help to create a much stronger branch. Next, wrap the group containing the 6 cable wires 2 inches up, then divide this group into 4 cables and 2 cables and wrap these about 1 more inch up. Continue wrapping until you return to the top of the trunk where you started. Now, wrap the group of 11 cables about 2.5 inches up, then divide this group into one group of 6 and one group of 5. Divide the group of 6 into 1 group of 4 and one group of 2. The wrapping distance for these groups is about 1 inch as stated above. The group with the 5 cables is then divided into 2 groups of 2 and 1 single cable wire. After you have created all these groups, wrap the wire back to the starting point at the top of the trunk. The above steps may seem confusing when written, but I am sure you will see how this is done when you look at ***See page 64, Fig. 1/64*** I use this method that employs the use of 6 strand cable wire to create many of my larger tree sculptures. When completed, the strength of the tree, branches and twigs is amazing. In fact, the technique of wrapping wire around a cable is how many bridges are constructed.

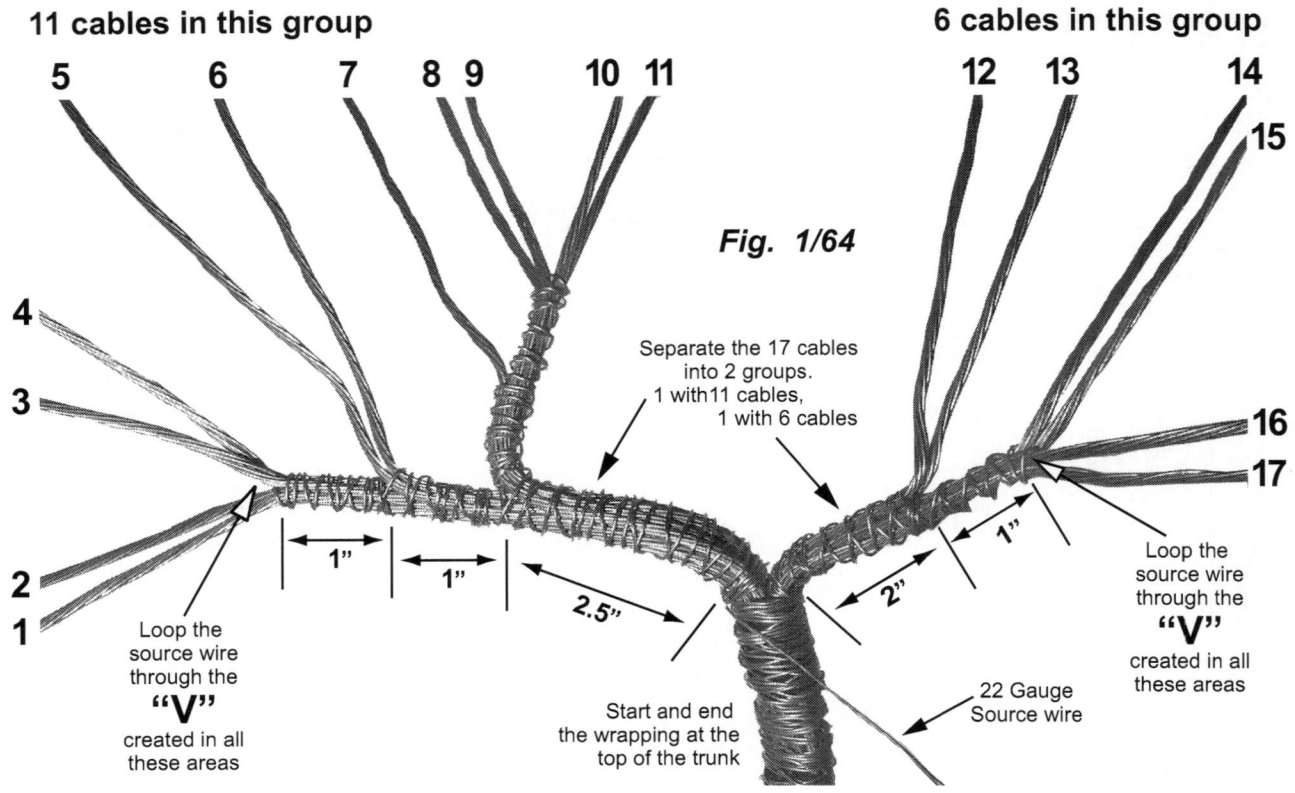

11 cables in this group — 5, 6, 7, 8, 9, 10, 11
6 cables in this group — 12, 13, 14, 15, 16, 17

Fig. 1/64

Separate the 17 cables into 2 groups. 1 with 11 cables, 1 with 6 cables

Loop the source wire through the **"V"** created in all these areas

Start and end the wrapping at the top of the trunk

22 Gauge Source wire

Wrapping the Branches

Holding the base of each pair of wire cables, twist the pair of wires for about 1 inch up. Repeat this for all of the 8 pairs of wires. To get a better grip, you may want to hold the cable wire with the standard pliers as you twist. Leave the one single cable wire as is. *Fig. 2/64*

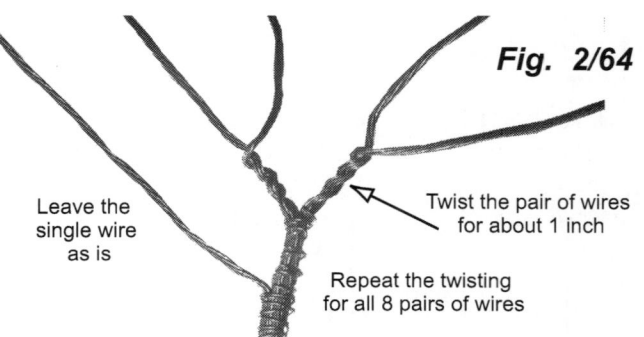

Fig. 2/64

Leave the single wire as is

Twist the pair of wires for about 1 inch

Repeat the twisting for all 8 pairs of wires

Wrapping the Tree

Use a few spring clamps attached to the root section to securely hold the tree in place as you work on it *Fig. 3/64* Once again, starting at the top of the trunk, wrap the source wire out toward the end of the cable branches. When you get to the "V", loop the source wire through the "V" in the new pairs of wires you just made. *Fig. 5/64* Wrap all the branches as described above, ending where you started. You can tape the branches after completed, to keep them out of your way. *Fig. 4/64*

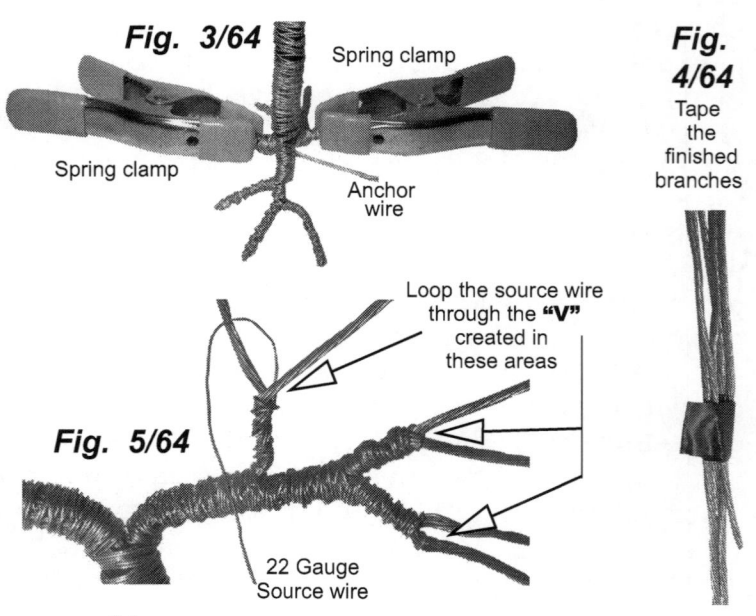

Fig. 3/64 Spring clamp — Spring clamp — Anchor wire

Fig. 4/64 Tape the finished branches

Fig. 5/64

Loop the source wire through the **"V"** created in these areas

22 Gauge Source wire

Wrapping the Trunk and Roots

Start at the top of the trunk and wire down to the base of the trunk and out to each root section. When you get to each individual root section, just wire the section half way out toward the tip, then back toward the base of the trunk. This will give the root sections a tapered look. Make one complete pass, wiring the entire trunk and all the roots, then ending at the top of the trunk. Rewire the trunk only, down and up 12 complete times, ending at the top of the trunk. Each time you end the wrapping at the top and bottom of the trunk, loop the wire through the "V" as you did with the branches. Do not wire the roots with this wiring. The roots are finished with the 22 gauge wire, but will still need to be wired with the 26 gauge wire. For the 13th wrapping of the trunk, wrap down to the base of the trunk, then about 3/4 of the way up the trunk, then back. Repeat this up and back wiring 4 times, ending at the base of the trunk. For the final wrapping of the trunk using the 22 gauge wire, starting again at the base of the trunk wrap about 1/2 the way up and then back 4 times, ending again at the base of the trunk. For the last wrap, start at the base of the trunk and wrap all the way to the top of it. ***Fig. 1/65***

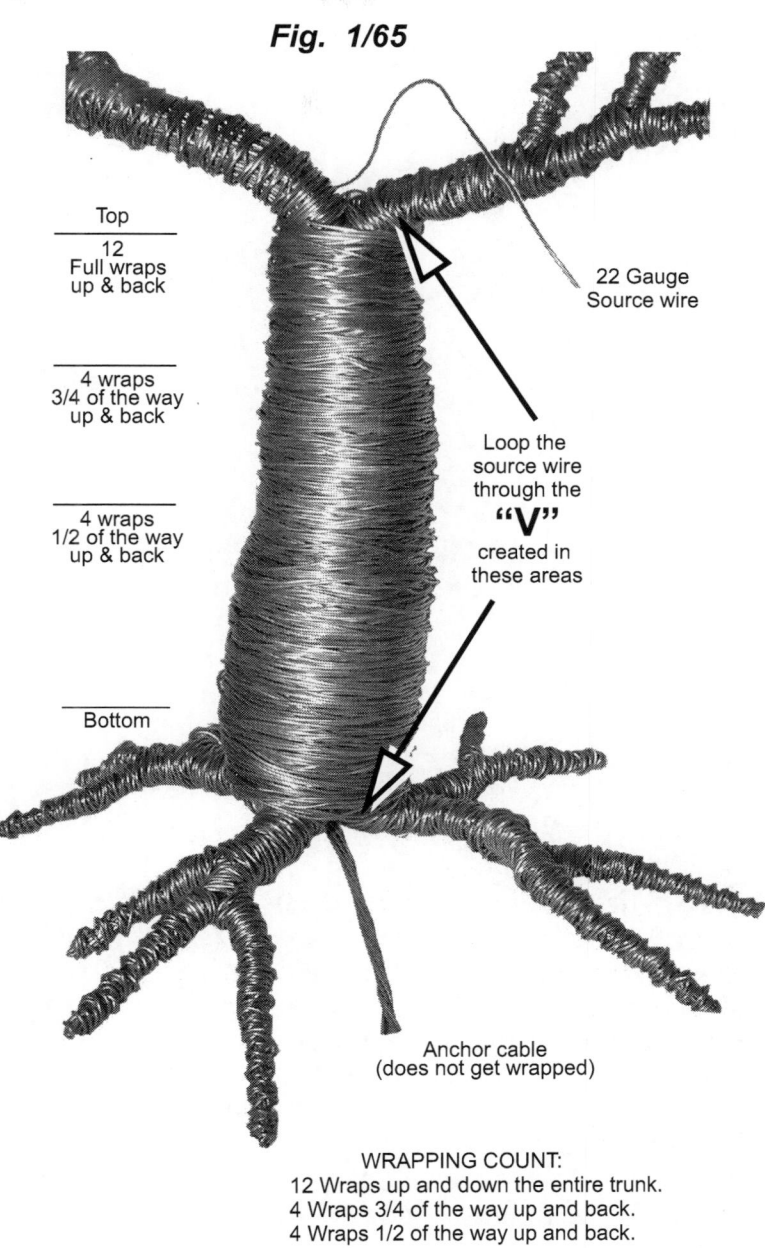

Fig. 1/65

WRAPPING COUNT:
12 Wraps up and down the entire trunk.
4 Wraps 3/4 of the way up and back.
4 Wraps 1/2 of the way up and back.

More Wrapping of the Branches

Use several spring clamps, attached to the roots to hold the tree in place as you work on it. ***See page 64, Fig. 3/64*** If you used any tape to group the branches together, remove it before you work on the branch section. Starting at the top of the trunk, wrap out toward the end of each branch. When you get to the "V" section of the branch, wrap out onto the cable wire for about 1/2 inch then back. Follow this same procedure for all of the cable branches. End the wrapping at the top of the trunk. Wrap from the top of the trunk out to where the first branch starts then back to the top of the trunk. Repeat this wrap 3 times, out and back, for both of the main branches, ending at the top of the trunk. ***Fig. 1/65***

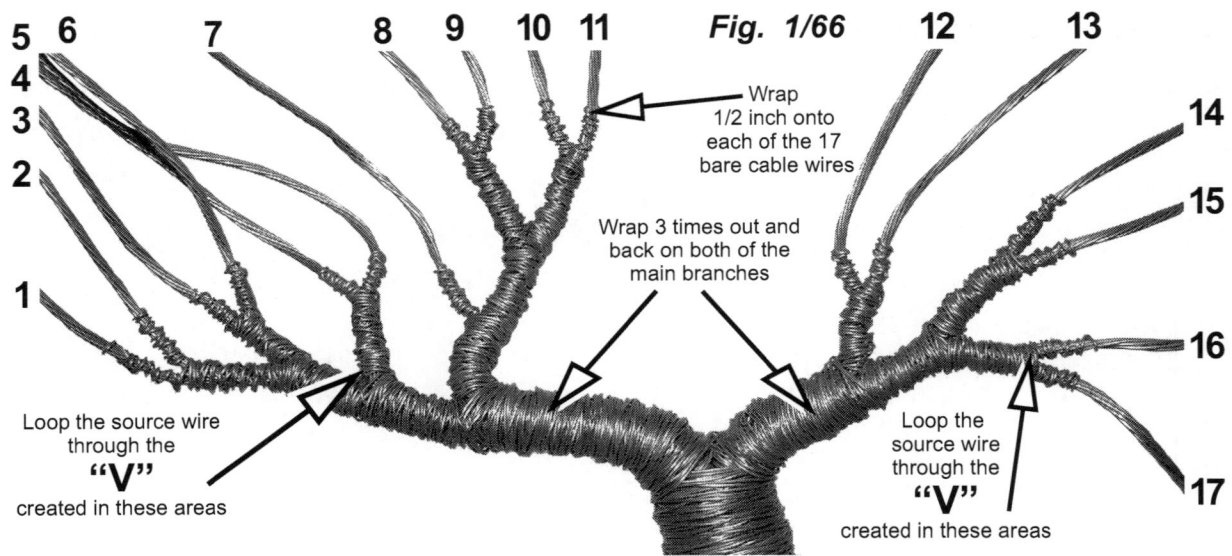

Fig. 1/66

- Wrap 1/2 inch onto each of the 17 bare cable wires
- Wrap 3 times out and back on both of the main branches
- Loop the source wire through the "V" created in these areas
- Loop the source wire through the "V" created in these areas

Final use of 22 Gauge Wire For the final wrap, using the 22 gauge wire as your source wire, wrap once down the trunk and onto the root anchor cable wire. Wrap the 22 gauge wire around the root anchor and cut it. This is also the location where you will start wrapping the tree sculpture using the 26 gauge wire as the source wire. *Fig. 2/66*

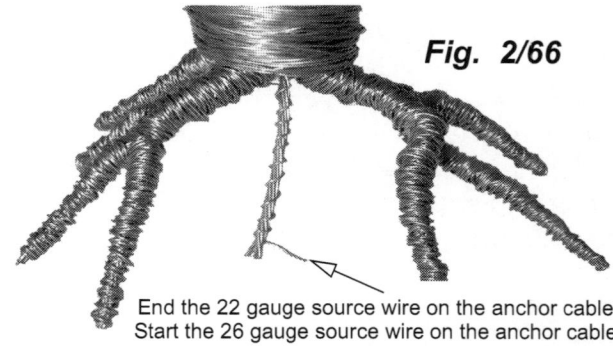

Fig. 2/66

End the 22 gauge source wire on the anchor cable
Start the 26 gauge source wire on the anchor cable

Wrapping the Roots and Branches The remaining wrapping for the roots and the rest of the tree sculpture will use the 26 gauge wire as the source wire. Start at the end of the anchor wire and wrap the source wire to the base of the trunk. Do not be concerned about how the root anchor looks, it is designed for support only and will be hidden in the root mound. Wrap the entire trunk top to bottom 3 times ending at the bottom of the trunk. Try to fit the 26 gauge source wire in between the 22 gauge wire whenever possible. Look at the three root sections and you will see that 2 of them have 3 final points and the last has 4 final points **See page 67, Fig. 4/67** Starting at the base of the trunk, wrap out to the end of any one of the 2 root sections with the 3 points. Wrap out and back all the way to the end 7 complete times, 3/4 of the way out and back 3 times, 1/2 of the way out and back 3 times, and finally 1/4 of the way out and back 3 times. Repeat the above steps for the other 3 point root section. For the 4 point root section, wrap out and back 2 complete times, ending at the base of the trunk. Wrap out and back only onto the longest of the root section 2 times all the way to the end and back, 3/4 of the way out and back 3 times, 1/2 of the way out and back 3 times, and 1/4 of the way out and back 3 times. As the final wrap for this root section, wrap out and back 4 times from the base of the trunk to the first "V" section in the root. Loop the wire through the "V" in the root section, as you did before. *Fig. 1/66* Wrap the entire tree with the 26 gauge wire. Start where you left off the wrapping of the root section and continue up and down the entire tree. Cover all the 22 gauge wire with the 26 gauge wire. This wrapping may take some time to complete, since you are wrapping a thinner wire over a thicker wire. Try to get the 26 gauge wire to fit in between the wraps of the 22 gauge wire. This will add texture and create a more natural surface. End the wrapping of all the branches at the base of any of the original 17 branches. *Fig. 1/66* This will be the point where you will be adding more branches.

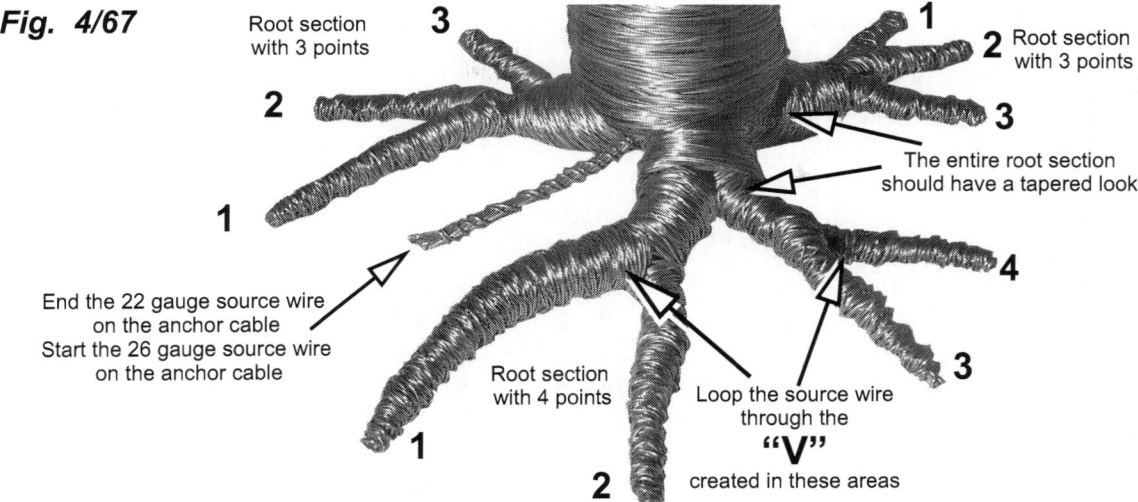

Fig. 4/67

Root section with 3 points — 3

Root section with 3 points — 1, 2

The entire root section should have a tapered look — 3

End the 22 gauge source wire on the anchor cable
Start the 26 gauge source wire on the anchor cable — 1

Root section with 4 points — 1, 2

Loop the source wire through the **"V"** created in these areas — 3, 4

Option for Holding Your Work in Place

Another way to hold you tree in place while you work on it, is to staple or nail the root system to a sturdy wood base. I use a scrap piece of 2x6 lumber, about 18 inches long. Flatten out the root system so that, if possible, the tree can stand on its own. Place the tree in the center of of the wood and secure it to the base. I use 3/4 inch electrical wire staples. **Fig. 1/67**, or you can also use nails that you hammer in a ways, then bend them over the roots. 3 or 4 staples or nails will hold the piece in place. **Fig. 2/67** I find this type of support works very well, especially on larger pieces. The support will not only hold the piece steady as you work on it, you are also able to turn the piece around as you work on it. You can also place a wedge on one side of the wood base which will allow you to tilt the entire piece on an angle. This step can be very helpful when you are working on the top of the tree. Once the piece is finished, simply pull out the stapels or the nails. If the wood you are using is dark in color, you may want to paint it white which will allow you to see the piece more clearly as you work on it. Or, you can place a piece of white cloth or heavy piece of white paper over the base **Fig. 3/67**

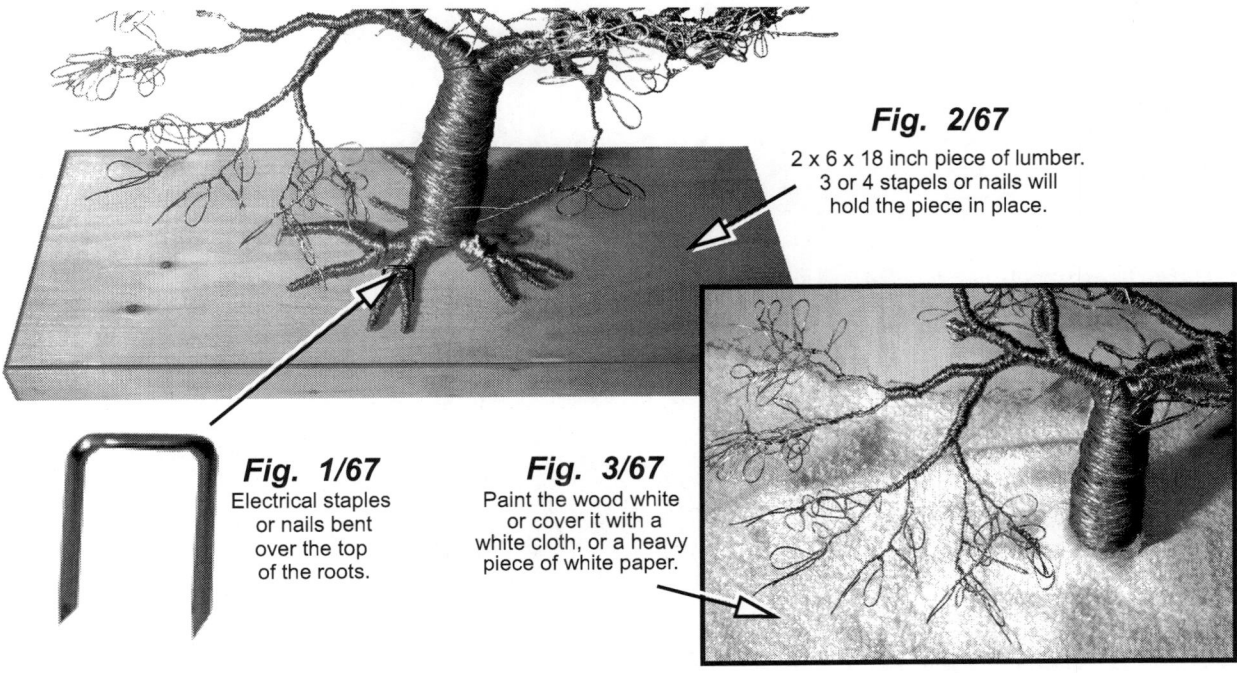

Fig. 2/67
2 x 6 x 18 inch piece of lumber. 3 or 4 stapels or nails will hold the piece in place.

Fig. 1/67
Electrical staples or nails bent over the top of the roots.

Fig. 3/67
Paint the wood white or cover it with a white cloth, or a heavy piece of white paper.

Adding More Branches

This step will add many more branches to the basic tree which will create a much denser, fuller and thicker twig and leaf area. Start by spreading out all the root sections so that they will support the tree upright, then attach a few spring clamps to the root section of the tree for support, or you can use the wood base option as shown on **Page 67** Either method will hold the tree in place as you work on it. Cut a length of the 6 strand, 18 gauge wire to approximately match the length of each of the 17 original branches. The length of each of the pieces you cut does not need to be the exact size of the matching branch. Variations in the size of the branches will create a more interesting final tree. Tape the new branch next to the base of the existing branch, using a piece of black electrical tape. (The tape will be covered by wire and will not show). Twist the 2 branches together for 1 or 2 twists. Since this is 6 strand, 18 gauge wire, you may find it difficult to twist these 2 pieces of wire using only your fingers. If you do find it difficult to twist the wires, use the large pliers to do the twisting. **Fig. 1/68** Repeat the above for all of the 17 branches on the original tree, creating a total of 34 branches. **Fig. 2/68**

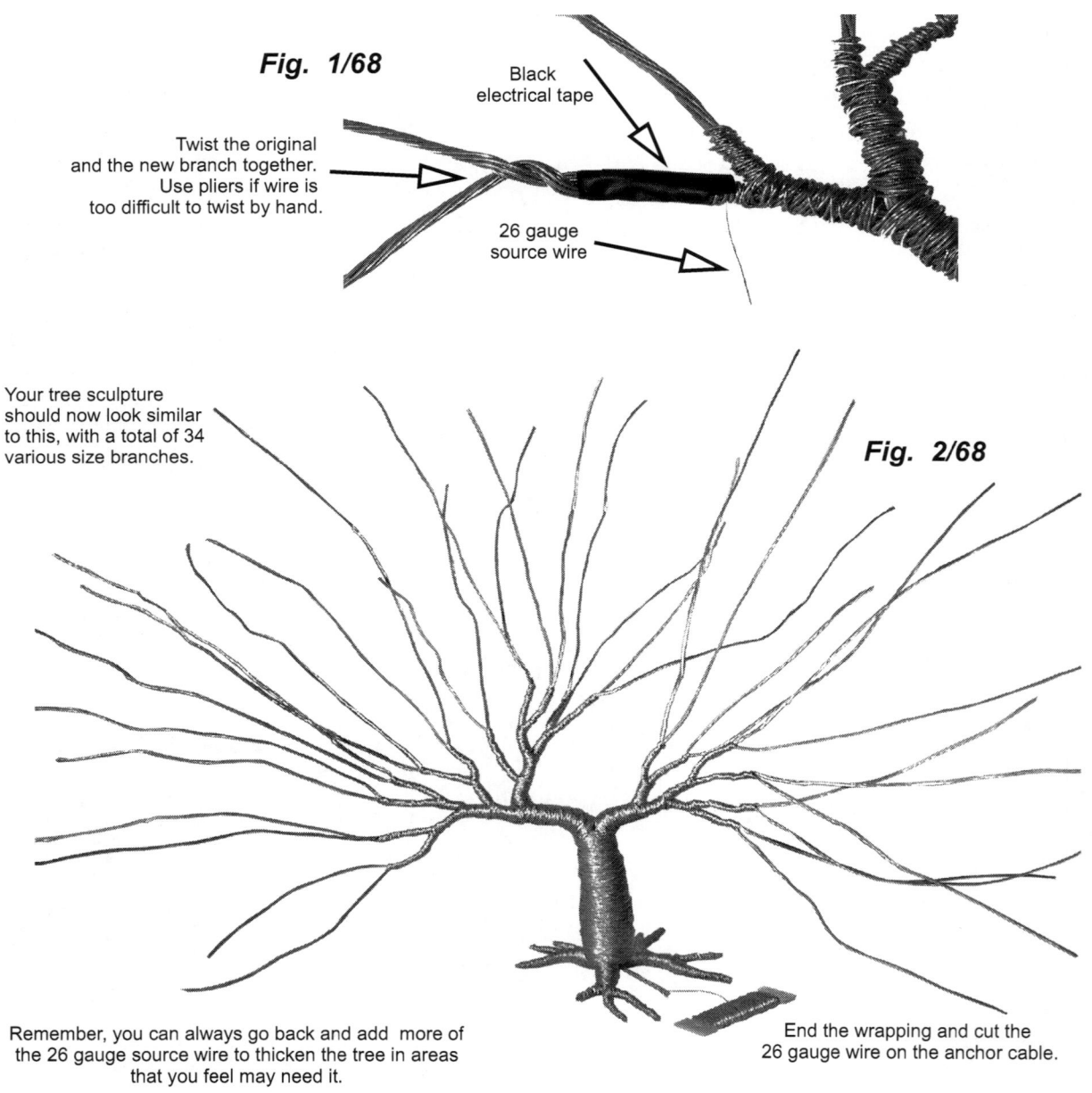

Fig. 1/68

Twist the original and the new branch together. Use pliers if wire is too difficult to twist by hand.

Black electrical tape

26 gauge source wire

Your tree sculpture should now look similar to this, with a total of 34 various size branches.

Fig. 2/68

Remember, you can always go back and add more of the 26 gauge source wire to thicken the tree in areas that you feel may need it.

End the wrapping and cut the 26 gauge wire on the anchor cable.

Creating the Twigs

1. Use the spring clamps or the wood base option to support the tree as you work on it. See page **Page 67** The following steps will show how to create the twigs at various points on the branches. Start by separating one of the 6 strand cables all the way back to the main branch that you have covered with the 26 gauge wire.
Fig. 1/69 Separate the 6 wires into two groups. One group with 2 wires and the other with 4 wires. Twist the group with 2 wires together for about 1/2 inch. Twist the group with the 4 wires together also for about 1/2 inch. Finally, twist the 2 pairs of wires in the 4 wire group together for about 1/4 inch. ***Fig. 2/69***

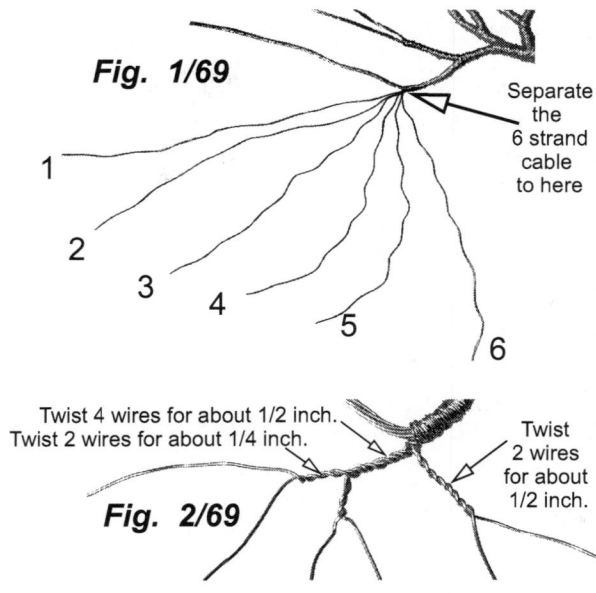

2. Bend one of the wires in the 2 wire group over the top of the other wire creating a 1 inch loop. Hold the loop firmly and twist it about 4 or 5 times. You can twist the loop by hand, or if it is too difficult for you to twist, use the pliers. Twist the two wire group to create a spacer twist about 1/4 inch long. Follow the same procedure as above to create another loop on the opposite side of the two wire group. This procedure will be repeated for all the branches on the tree. After you have created all the loops that will fit on the branch, you may have some pieces of the 6 strand wire that are too small to create another loop. Leave those as they are. If this is your first attempt at creating this type of tree, I would suggest that you practice creating the loops on a piece of scrap 6 strand wire, before you create the loops on the tree. After all the loops are created on the entire tree you will be cutting them to create the twigs. Do not cut the loops until all have been created, because if you cut the loops into twigs as you go along, you will most likely get small cuts on your hands or wrists from the cut wire. Creating all the loops will take some time but it is a very important step in creating the tree. ***Fig. 3/69*** For the remainder of the branches, once

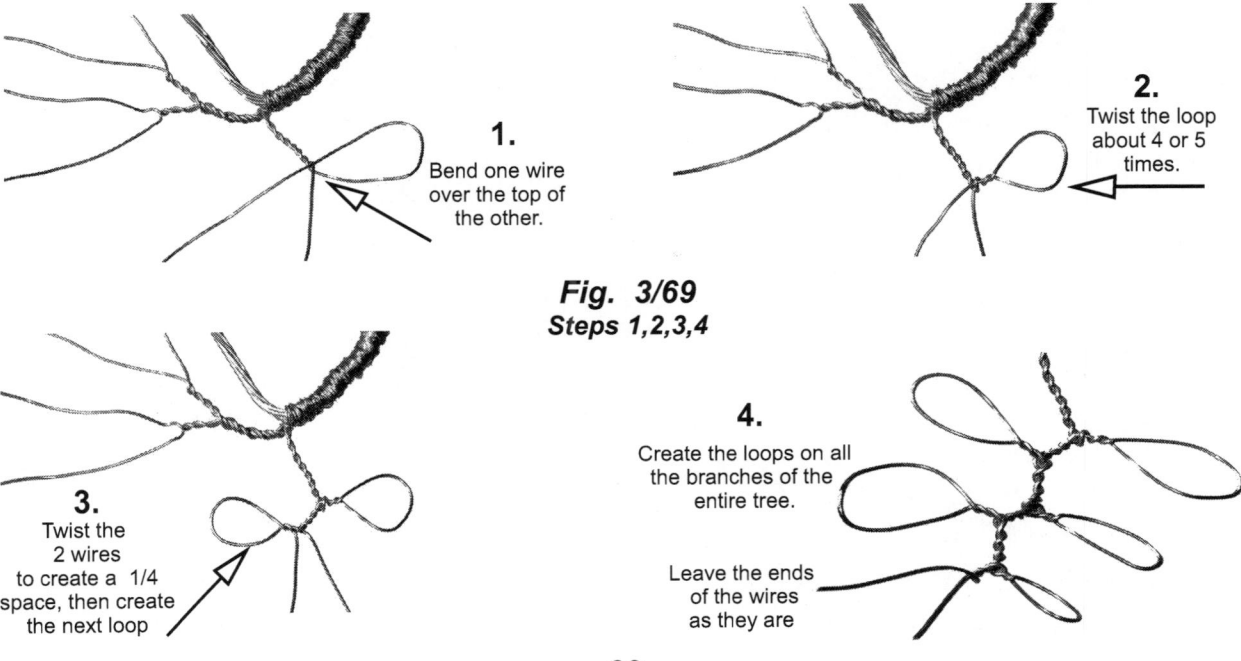

again, separate the 6 strand cable wire 2 groups as you did before. This time, instead of twisting these 2 groups separately, twist them together for about 1/2 inch, or if these wires are very long you can twist them for 2 or more inches. This will create another branch a little further out on the main branch. **Fig. 1/70** Proceed as you did before to create all the loops on the new branch. Carefully follow the preceding steps to create all the loops on the entire tree. This step will take some time, but is very important. The 6 strand cable wire is very durable, so you can bend any part of the unfinished or finished branches back or to the side, this will make it easier to work on the remaining branches.

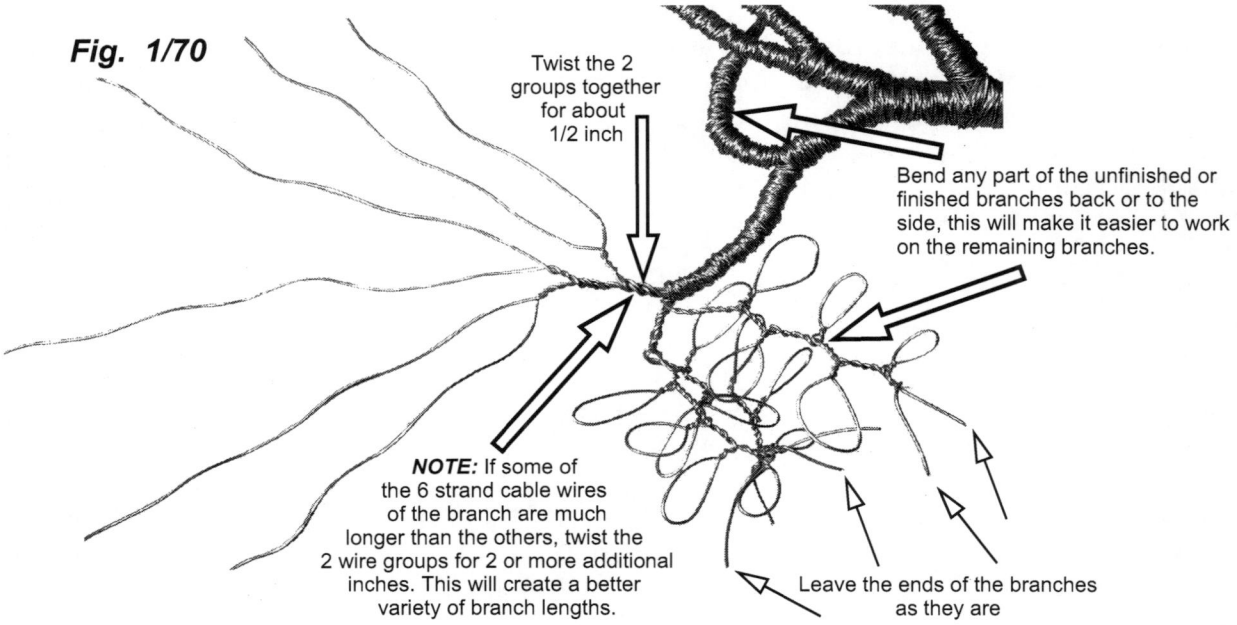

Option: *Fig.2/70* As an option to adding more detail to the transition of the larger branch ending and onto the beginning of the smaller branch, I sometimes wrap additional 26 gauge wire from the larger branch onto the smaller. I think it gives the tree a more natural look and is worth the effort. If you choose this option, follow these steps:

1. Start wrapping the 26 gauge wire at the point where the thinner branch starts, leave about 3 inches of extra wire that will later go onto the next branch. Wrap the branch you started on back and forth about 3 or 4 times ending where you started.

2. Wrap the next smaller branch as you did the first. Ending where you started on this branch and leaving about 3 inches of extra wire before you cut it.

3. When completed, you will have 2 pieces of the 26 gauge wire at the end of each smaller branch. Loop each wire through itself, pull it tight, cut the wire as close to the branch as possible. Bend down any small end of the wires, using the pliers.

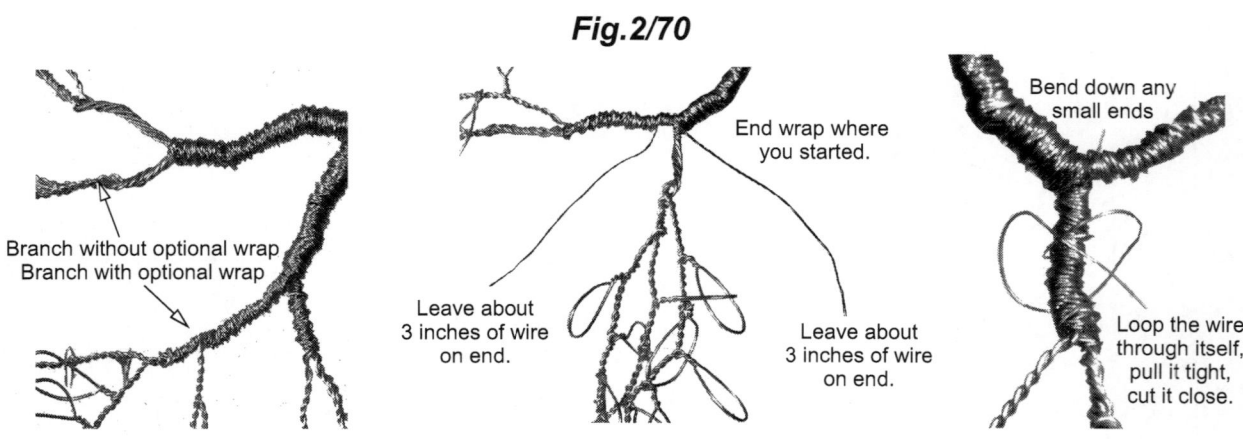

Fig.2/70

Mounting the Tree onto the Base

1. Paint a thin layer of white craft glue onto the base then cover all the glue with the sand and pebble mixture. Let this dry overnight, then dump off the excess sand and pebbles.

2. After you are sure the glue on the surface is dry, position the rock and glue it in place. The tree will be mounted onto the rock and the base before any additional work is done on the branches leaves and twigs. This is done so that the tree will be secure on the base as you work on it.

3. Hold the tree by the trunk and bend all the root sections toward the center, then position the tree on the top of the rock. Once you have decided where to place the tree on the rock, you will need to secure the tree as you bond the roots of the tree to the rock and base. I use black electrical tape to hold the tree in place. Try to position the root cable on the top and down the side of the rock. The root cable is one of the strong points binding the tree to the base. Tape the roots one at a time, with several wraps of the tape. I use tape because it will not mar the surface of the wood. The most important thing in this step is to be sure the tree does not move when you are applying the glue and sand mixture.

4. Place white craft glue around the base of any the roots that are touching the base sand. Then cover the glue and the root section with sand, or a sand and pebble mix.

5. Build a sand dam around the roots, fill it with white glue and cover it with the sand mix.

6. Cover the entire base of the tree with the sand and pebble mix. Let it dry overnight. After you are sure the glue and sand mixture is dry, brush off the loose sand and repeat this step until all the roots are securely bonded to the rock and the base. When completed. the tree will look like it is growing out of the sand.

Cover base with glue then add sand mix.

Glue rock in position.

Securely tape tree onto base.

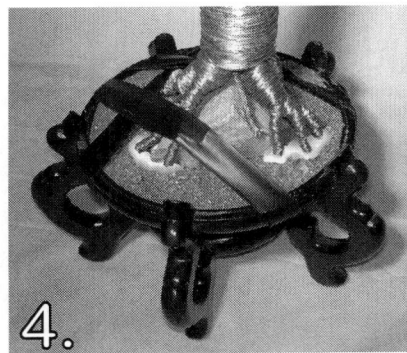
Glue and cover root tips with sand mix.

Glue and cover cable root with sand mix.

Cover all with sand mix, let dry, repeat until all roots are covered.

After you are sure the base of the tree is securely planted onto the base remove all the tape that was holding the tree to the base. You may find it necessary to add more of the glue and sand mixture in places near the roots that may need to be filled in. **Fig. 1/72** Try to allow some of the rock to show between the roots. Once you are satisfied with the root section you will be able to work on the branches, twigs and leaves.

Twigs and Leaves The next steps apply to all the loops you have created. I would suggest that you wear gloves, and a long sleeve shirt to protect your hands and arms from the sharp ends of the cut wire.

1. Use the small wire cutter to cut all the loops on one side Do not cut the loop directly in the center. By cutting the loop on one side, you will be creating a variety of twig lengths, rather than having all the twigs the same size. **Fig. 2/72**

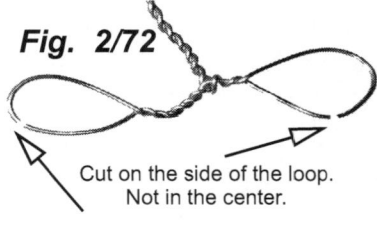

Cut on the side of the loop. Not in the center.

2. Use the flat nose pliers to straighten out the twigs. The twigs do not need to be perfectly straight. Irregularities in the shapes will add interest to the tree. **Fig. 3/72**

3. Repeat steps 1 and 2 for all the loops.

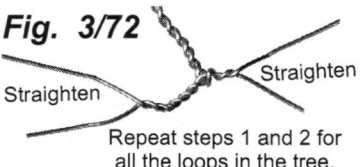

Repeat steps 1 and 2 for all the loops in the tree.

Chosing Twigs or Leaves for Your Tree

1. Leave all the twigs as they are which will create a tree with a "Winter Look".

2. Hammer the twigs into the shape of leaves, leave them Metallic. **Page 73**

3. Hammer the twigs into the shape of leaves, then paint them in various shades of green which will create a "Summer Tree". **Page 74**

4. Hammer the twigs into the shape of leaves, then paint them in yellows, reds, ochers, and some greens which will create an "Autumn Tree". **Page 74**

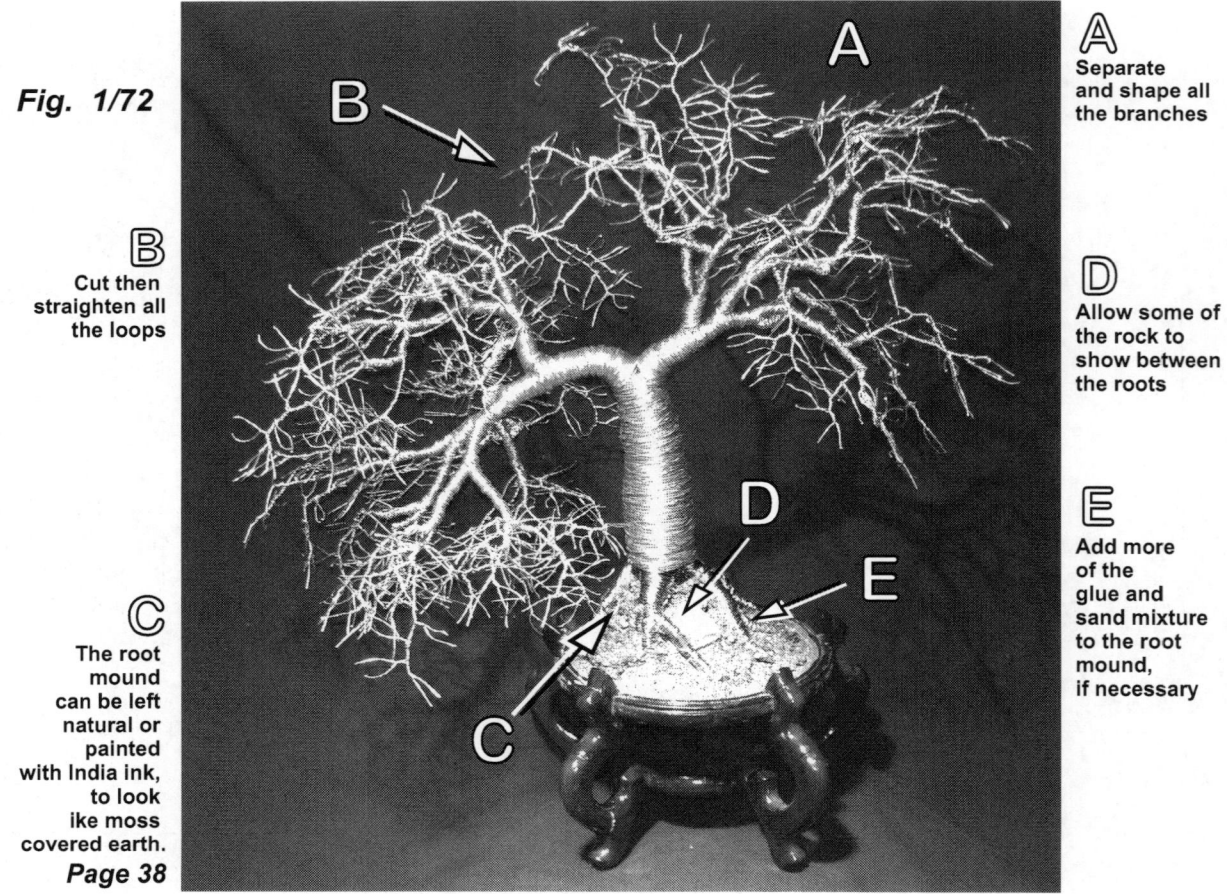

Fig. 1/72

Ⓐ Separate and shape all the branches

Ⓑ Cut then straighten all the loops

Ⓒ The root mound can be left natural or painted with India ink, to look ike moss covered earth. *Page 38*

Ⓓ Allow some of the rock to show between the roots

Ⓔ Add more of the glue and sand mixture to the root mound, if necessary

Creating the Leaves

To create the flat leaves you will need the ball peen hammer, or any small hammer, and a larger hammer head or a flat piece of steel or a jewelers anvil. The large hammer head or flat piece of steel will be used as, and called, an "anvil" on which you will hammer the ends of the twigs **Fig. 1/73** Place and hold the anvil under and up against the twig and strike it 4 or 5 times flattening it out to about 2 or 3 times it original size. Do not strike the twig too many times, this may cause the end of it to break off. **Fig. 2/73** Repeat this process for all the twigs on the tree. As you are creating the leaves use the flat nose pliers to bend and twist some of the flattened leaves. I usually bend and twist about 2/3 of the leaves and leave 1/3 flat. This creates a very nice variety and a realistic look. **Fig. 3/73**

Fig. 1/73
Place twigs on an anvil or the side of a large hammer head

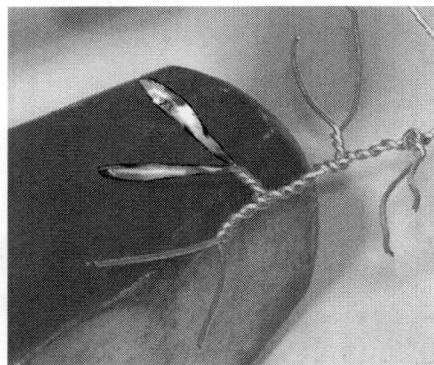

Fig. 2/73
Hammer the twigs flat.

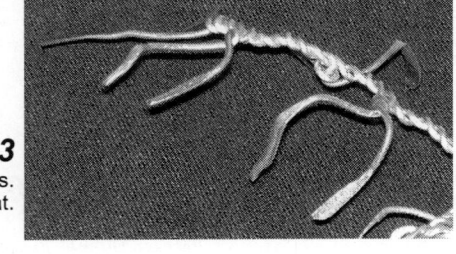

Fig. 3/73
Bend some leaves. Leave some flat.

Adding Color to the Root Mound, Leaves and the Tree

After you have finished shaping all the leaves, and before you give the tree its final shape, you will need to decide about color for the root mound and the tree itself. The first decision is about the root mound. You can leave it in its natural state or paint it using India ink to give the appearance of moss covered earth. For complete instructions for painting the root mound **See page 38** If you are going to paint the root mound you should do so before the final shaping of the tree. The next decision is whether to paint the individual leaves or let them remain as "metallic". Painting the leaves is a 4 step process and is very time consuming. However I think the results are well worth the effort. To paint the leaves or any other part of the tree it is best to use oil based gloss enamel paint. This is the type of paint that is used for model cars and is readily available. Since you are only covering a small area on each leaf, the smallest jars will be plenty to start with. You will also need paint thinner or brush cleaner for your brushes, or if you get any paint where you don't want it. You also will need several small artist brushes, # "0" or # "1". I use one brush for each color.

SUMMER LEAVES. Colors needed: Dark Green, Light Green, Yellow, White.

1. Dark Green (100% Coverage). Paint each leaf top and bottom. I have found it's best to do a small section of leaves at a time, about 10 to 20 leaves. Then you can move the unpainted leaves out of your way as you work on painting the others. Do not "overload" your brush with paint. It is much better to use a "dry brush" than a "wet brush" approach.

Try to cover the entire leaf, on both top and bottom with the dark green, this is the base coat. It is not as important to cover the bottom of the leaves with all 4 colors. And do not be concerned if you miss some areas on the leaf. It is much better to miss some areas on the leaf, than to have the paint dripping off the leaves. Be sure each color is dry before you start the next. I let each color dry overnight.

2. Light Green (50% Coverage). Paint on the light green color trying to repaint about 50% of the area that you painted with the dark green. That means try to let about half of the dark green show with the light green color.

3. Yellow (40% Coverage). Paint on the yellow color at the base of the leaf and onto the leaf stem. That means try to let the yellow cover only about 40% of the base, while letting some of the dark and light green also show.

4. White (10% Coverage). Paint the white on about 10% of the leaf, but only at the tip. This will create a high light on the leaf.

The leaves should now all be painted in Summer colors. If you want an Autumn color tree, use the same technique but replacing the Dark Green with Ocher, the Light green with Orange, the Yellow with a darker Yellow, and use the white as the highlight.

SUMMER COLORS for LEAVES: Dark Green - Light Green - Yellow - White

AUTUMN COLORS for LEAVES: Ocher - Orange - Dark Yellow - White

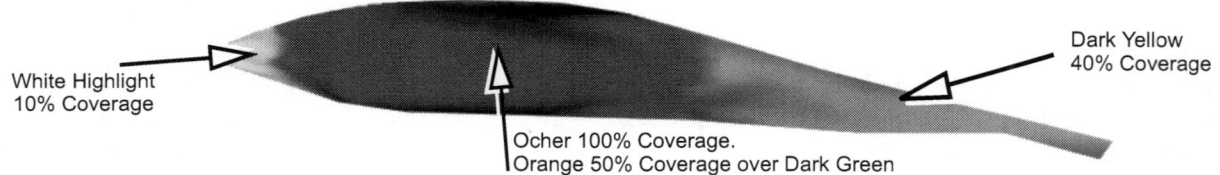

Painting the Entire Tree
As an additional detail you can add to the tree, is to paint the entire tree (not the leaves) in several colors of brown. Again this is a time consuming process, but will add another layer of realism to the piece. I use 3 different shades of brown. Dark, Medium and Light. Start the painting with the darkest color, covering all the bark, then about 40% coverage with the medium color and end with about 20% coverage for the lightest color. Start applying all the colors from the middle of the tree working out toward the end of the branches. Be sure the preceding color is entirely dry, before you start the next. You may want to practice this procedure on a section of scrap wire. Once you have mastered this process I think you will be very pleased with the results.

Adding a Bird Nest to the Tree
As an added element, this type of tree will look very nice with a bird nest in it. **See page 48** for complete instructions on adding a bird nest, or a bird nest with pearl eggs, into the branches of the tree this tree.

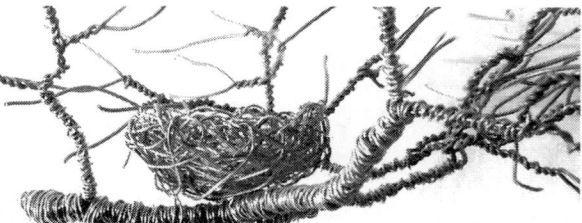

The Final Styling and Shaping the Tree

All the elements of the tree are now in place. The only remaining step left is the shaping of the branches, twigs and leaves. Since the edges of the leaves are sharp, please remember to wear gloves and a long sleeve shirt when working on the tree.

1. The first step is to separate and slightly pull away from each other, any larger branches that may be overlapping each other.

2. Next, since this is a "cascading" tree, divide the branches into an upper and a lower section. The upper section will have less branches than the bottom. There should be a several inch difference between the top of the upper branches and the bottom of the lower branches. Some of the lower branches may extend below the top rim of the base.

3. Place the tree on the floor so you will be able to view it from above. Arrange all the branches so they have a rounded or oval shape.

4. Place the tree back on your work table then turn it completely around slowly so you can view it from all sides. After you are pleased with the shape of the tree, separate any of the twigs or leaves that may be overlapping. You may need the point nose pliers to get to some of the inner twigs or leaves.

5. The final look of the tree sculpture is entirely up to you. You should look at the piece from all views. I sometimes put a piece aside for a few days, then come back to have a look at it with "fresh eyes". Do not hesitate to reshape the tree until you are satisfied with the results.

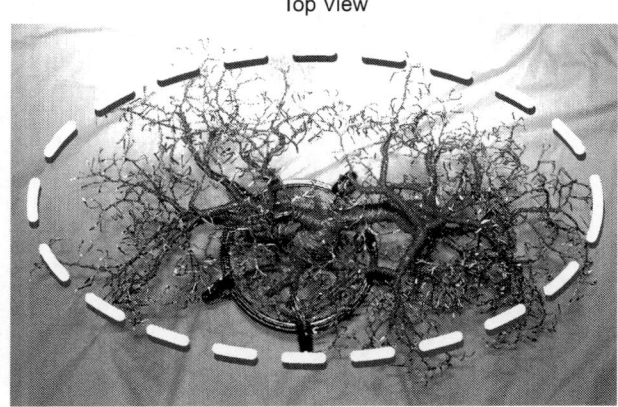
Top View

Back View

Left View

Right View

To see completed pieces in Full Color, visit my website: www.salvillano.com

Mini Jade Leaf Cascade - *9"h X 13"w X 7"d*
Difficulty Scale: *(1 = easy, 10 = difficult)* **this is a 6**

NOTE: Read the entire section for this item before you start, to determine which of the material and tools you need. Some of the items listed here are for optional choices. Have all the material and tools ready before you start to create the piece. For illustrations of tools and material **See page 9 & 10**

MATERIAL CHECK LIST:

__ 18 gauge, 6 strand cable wire, (30 in.)
__ 28 gauge wire, (500 ft.)
__ Electrical or masking tape
__ 2"x6"x18" piece of lumber
__ Electrical staples or 2" nails, (6 each)
__ White cloth or heavy white paper
__ Base to plant tree into **See page 12**
__ White glue
__ Sand and pebble mixture
__ India ink, green, yellow, white
__ Jade leaves, (180)
__ Glass fringe beads (optional)

TOOLS CHECK LIST:

__ Protective eye wear
__ Gloves
__ Long sleeve shirt
__ Large & small wire cutters
__ Large pliers & regular pliers
__ Flat nose pliers
__ Spring clamps, 3
__ Ruler, 24 inch
__ #0, & #1, brushes

To see completed pieces in Full Color, visit my website: www.salvillano.com

Creating the Core Support

1. Cut 3 lengths of 6 strand 18 gauge cable wire into the following sizes: 1 piece 12 inches long, 1 piece 8 inches long and 1 piece 6 inches long. Using the large pliers, bend each of the 3 pieces at a 90 degree angle, 2 inches from any end. Place the 12 inch and the 6 inch piece of cable wire next to each other facing the same direction. Place the 8 inch piece next to the first two facing in the opposite direction. **Fig. 1/77** Tape the 3 pieces of cable wire together at their bases using 1/2 inch black electrical tape. (You can use other types of tape but be sure it is only 1/2 inch wide and strong enough to hold the cable wire together). This tape will be covered with the 28 gauge source wire that you will be using to wrap the entire tree. **Fig. 2/77**

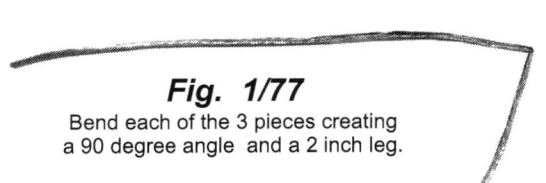

Fig. 1/77
Bend each of the 3 pieces creating a 90 degree angle and a 2 inch leg.

Fig. 2/77
12 inch branch. 6 inch branch. 8 inch branch.
Tape the 3 pieces together.

2. Spread out the 3 root sections equidistant from each other and twist each of the these sections together for one turn. You may need to use one pair of pliers to hold the trunk as you twist the root cables with another pair of pliers. Uncoil the 6 strand cable wire of each root sections, creating 2 groups of 3 strands each. **Fig. 3/77**

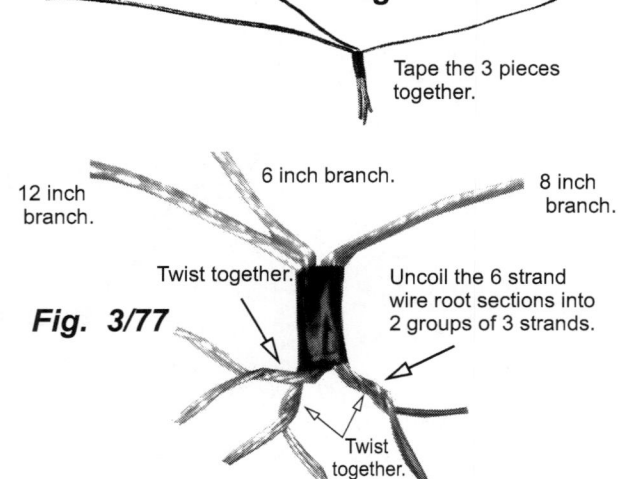

Fig. 3/77
12 inch branch. 6 inch branch. 8 inch branch.
Twist together. Uncoil the 6 strand wire root sections into 2 groups of 3 strands.
Twist together.

Wrapping the Wire (*Also see page 78, Fig. 1/78*)

This entire tree sculpture, plus the structure of the leaves will use only 28 gauge wire. I have selected gold color wire for this piece. Copper wire would also be a good choice. I feel that gold color or copper look best when combined with the jade leaves. You can use any color wire you like just be sure it is 28 gauge.

1. Start by using the wire you have chosen and wrap about 2 inches up any of the branches. Starting near the trunk and working toward the end of the branch. This is done to hold the end of the wire in place as you begin to wrap the rest of the tree. Wrap up and down the trunk and all the roots only, for about 2 or 3 wraps. Use enough wire to partially cover these sections. Don't try to cover all the tape or cable now, we will go back to these sections later for the final wrapping. This wrapping is designed mainly to hold the elements of the tree sculpture together so you will be able to work on it.

2. After the roots and trunk have their primary wrapping completed, wrap up and back the side of the tree that has the 2 branches. Wrap these 2 branches together for about one inch. Wrap the remaining single branch up and back also for about 1 inch.

3. Separate the 6 strand cable wires of the branches into 2 groups. One group with 2 wires and one group of 4 wires. Wrap up and back the group of 4 wires for about 1/2 inch, then separate those 4 wires into 2 groups of 2 wires each and wrap them up and back for about 3/4 inch.

4. Continue wrapping from the single branch and onto the double branch section. Wrap this wire about 1 inch up and back the longer branch, then separate the 6 strand cable wire of this branch and repeat step 3. Wrap down this branch and onto the last branch. Wrap this last branch about 1/2 inch up and back, then repeat step 3.

5. Wrap all the way down from the branches to the root section where you will create 2 root anchors that will help hold the tree onto the base. Do not twist the 2 root anchors together until the tree is ready to be mounted onto the base.

6. Now wrap the entire tree. This time wrap up and back so that the source wire covers and hides the tape and the cable wire. As you wrap up and back, taper the layers of the wrapping so that the trunk of the tree is thicker at the bottom. Taper the roots and branches so they are thinner toward the ends. This tapering is achieved by over wrapping and re-wrapping in the area you want to be thicker. *Fig. 1/78*

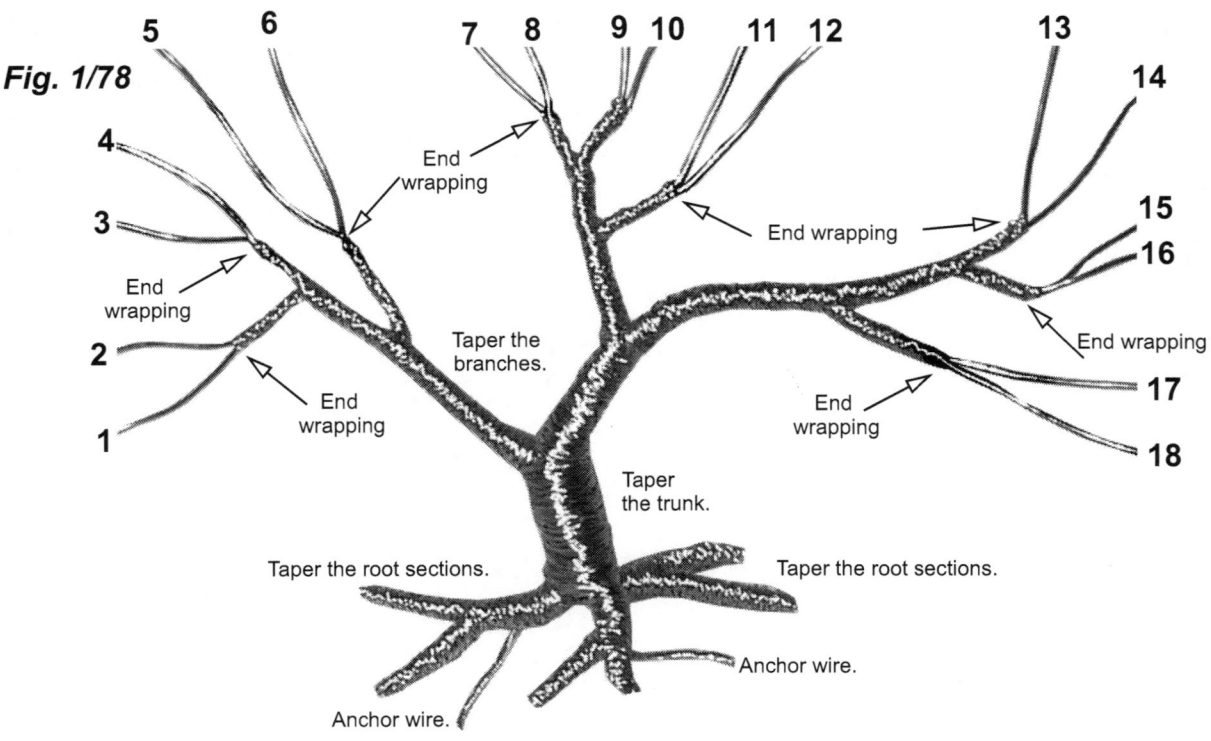

Fig. 1/78

Creating the Jade Leaves

You will need to make at least 180 jade leaves for this tree. You have a choice of using only jade leaves or mixing the jade leaves with glass beads. I will be using all jade leaves for this piece. **See page 53** to learn how to create either type. Follow the instruction, but be sure you use 28 gauge wire to create the jade leaves or the jade and glass leaves.

Attaching the Jade Leaves

1. Use 2 spring clamps, or the wood base mounting option **See page 64, Fig. 3/64** to hold the tree in place and steady it as you attach the individual leaves. I will be using the wood base option. **See page 67** The wood base may take more time to construct, but it will hold the piece securely and will not be in the way as you work on the tree.

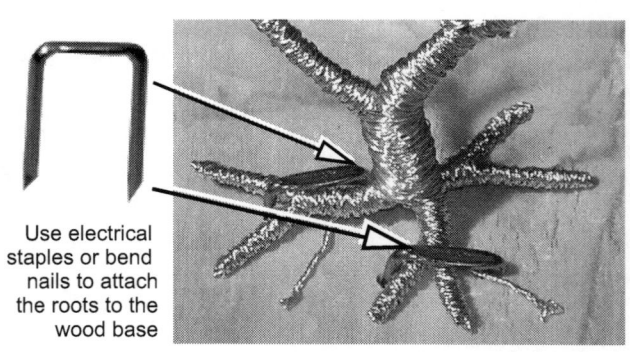

Use electrical staples or bend nails to attach the roots to the wood base

2. Spread out the two legs of a jade leaf and place the base of the leaf stem on top of the branch where you left off wrapping with the source wire. Put this leaf about 1/4 inch onto the branch. Twist one of the leaf legs around the bare cable wire, the loose leg will be left as is and will act as a smaller twig on the branch. **See page 58** If you choose to use the jade leaves with beads on them, the "loose leg" is the leg with the beads on it and should not be wrapped around the cable wire. All the remaining instructions are the same for both types of leaves. Follow the above instructions to wire all the leaves onto each branch. Place the leaves about 1/4 inch apart. The smallest branch will hold about 7 or 8 leaves, the medium about 9 or 10 leaves, and the largest about 11 to 13. Do not be concerned if the leaves, when on the branches, seem loose or flopping, you will secure all the leaves in place when you do the final wrap using the source wire. *Fig. 1/79 & 2/79*. As you finish attaching the leaves to each branch, you can gently bend that branch out of the way so it will be easier to work on the next branches.

3. Using the source wire, wrap up and back on the branch with the leaves on it. It is this wrapping that will hold all the leaves firmly in place. As you are wrapping the source wire, pull gently on it so that it is wrapped tightly onto the leg of the leaf and onto the cable wire. On the return wrap, heading toward the trunk, try to cover the cable wire as much as you can. When you finish one branch proceed to the next, using the source wire as one continuous feed. Wrap all the leaves onto all the branches using the above instructions. After all the leaves are assembled on the tree, remove the tree from its holding base and wrap the source wire from the branch where you ended, onto the trunk and down to the roots. Wrap the source wire about 1/4 inch onto either of the root anchors. End the wrapping, cut the source wire, then twist the two ends of the anchor wires together. *Fig. 3/79* The tree is now ready to be mounted into the base.

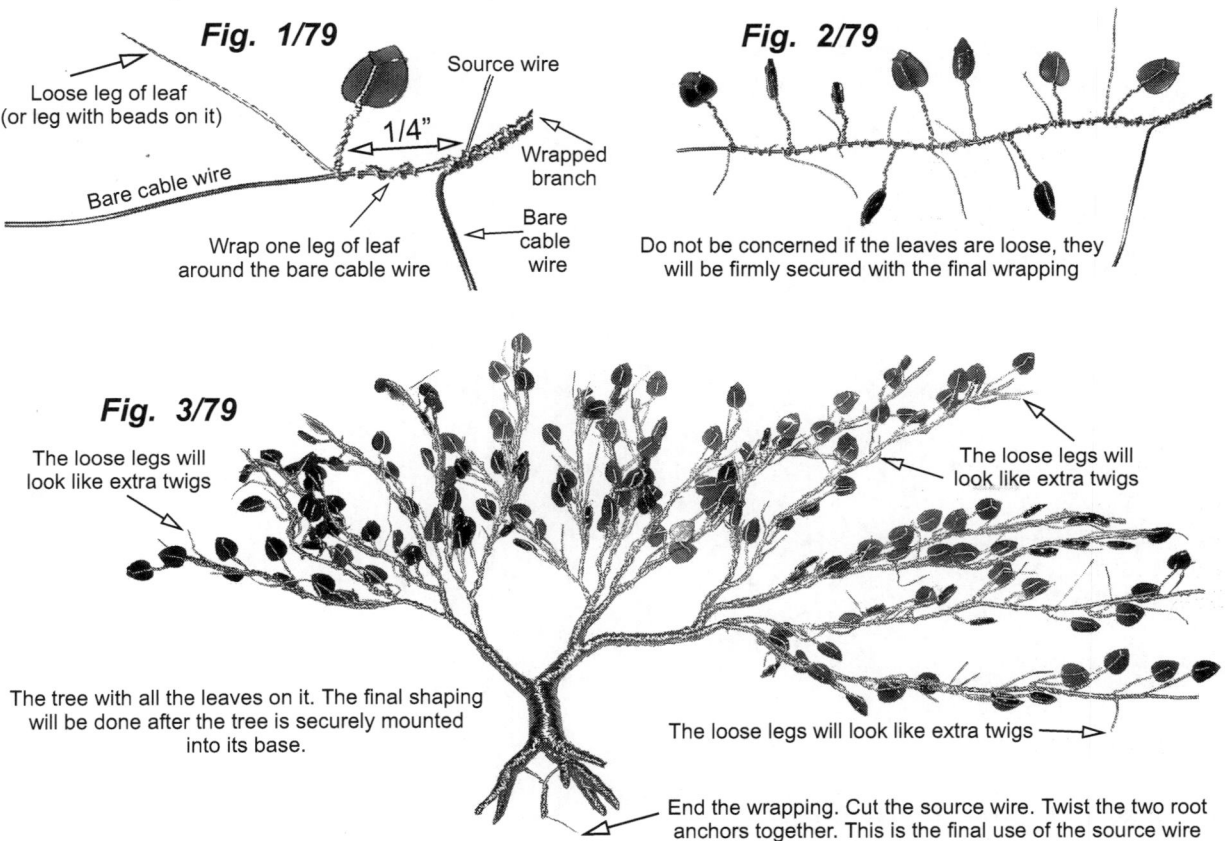

Mounting the Tree into a Base

Select the type of base you want to place your tree sculpture into. **See page 12 for bases.** Be sure the base you select is in proportion to the size of the tree. Before you actually mount the tree, place it into the base to see how it looks. After you have selected your base, follow the instructions on **pages 12 & 35** to mount the tree into the base. Your next decision is whether you want to add color to the root mound, or leave it in its natural sand color. I would suggest that if you have chosen an ornate base, you leave the root mound natural. The plain colors of the sand and pebbles will be an effective contrast to the gold tree color and the green color of the jade leaves. If you choose to add color to the root mound see **See page 38** for instructions. I have chosen a hexagon shaped container 3 1/2 inches wide, by 2 1/4 inches tall. The color is a very dark blue with a gloss finish.

Final Shaping of the Tree Sculpture

Be very sure the root mound is completely dry and solid before you start to shape the tree. As the final step you will now shape the trees branches, twigs and leaves to give it the look of a cascading tree.

1. Fan out all the branches of the left side of the tree. Twist the left group so it is perpendicular to the right group of branches. *Fig. 1/80* Twist all the remaining branches in the left group so that the branch you are twisting is perpendicular to the branch it is emanating from. This action will create the fullness within the tree. Do not spread the leaves out yet, you will do that after both sides of the tree are shaped *Fig. 2/80*

2. Bend down the entire right side of the branches. The longest branch in the group should almost touch the base you are working on. Twist all the branches in the right group perpendicular to each other as you did in step 1 *Fig. 3/80*

3. Starting with the left side of the tree, bend each of the branches so that they are no longer straight but have twists, turns and bends as would a real tree branch. Separate the leaves and point all the leaves in different directions. Be sure there are some leaves on either side of each branch. Follow the same procedure for the right side of the tree. The shape of your tree should be to your liking, do not try to follow the exact shape of the tree I show here. *Fig. 4/80*

Fig. 1/80

Fig. 2/80

Fig. 3/80

Fig. 4/80

To see completed pieces in Full Color, visit my website: www.salvillano.com

Wall Art Sculpture
Difficulty Scale: *(1 = easy, 10 = difficult)* these are 3 to 5

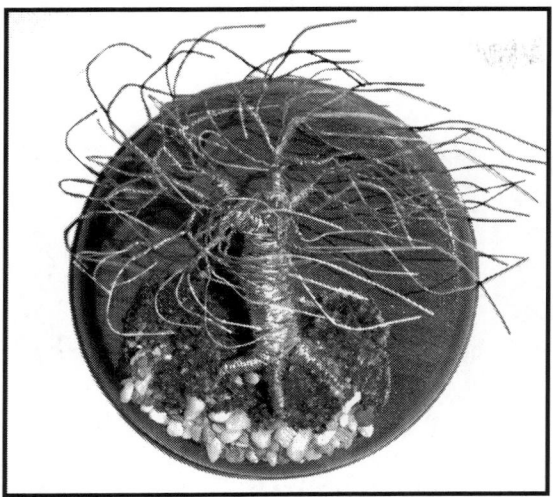

Wind Swept on Round Base
difficulty level = 4

Beaded on Round Base
difficulty level = 5

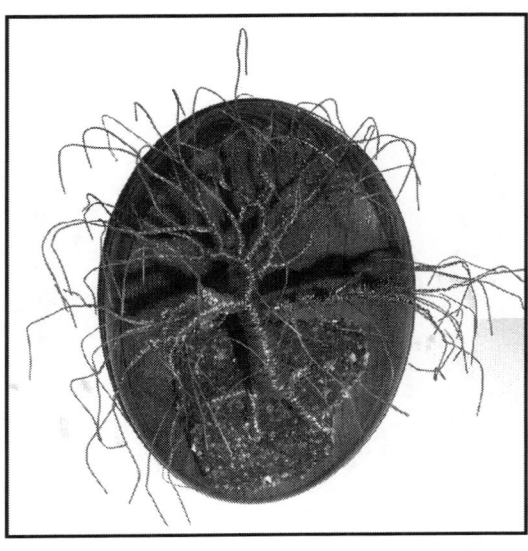

Oak on Oval Base
difficulty level = 3

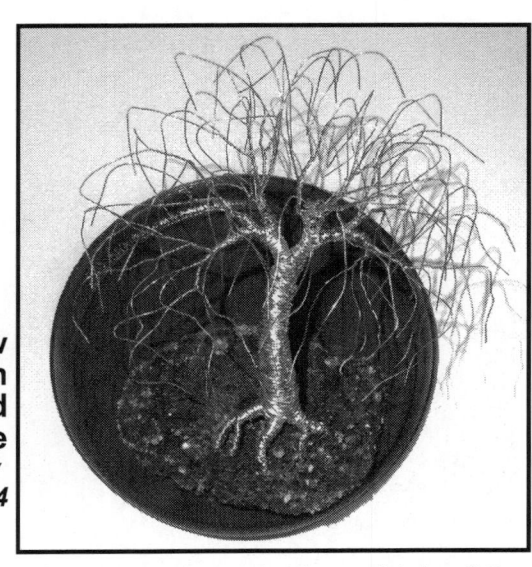

Willow on Round Base
difficulty level = 4

NOTE: Read the entire section for this item before you start, to determine which of the material and tools you need. Some of the items listed here are for optional choices. Have all the material and tools ready before you start to create the piece. For illustrations of tools and material **See pages 9 & 10**

MATERIAL CHECK LIST:
__ 26 gauge wire (400 ft.)
__ 22 gauge wire (400 ft.)
__ Base to plant tree into **See page 12**
__ Electrical or masking tape
__ Saw Tooth Hanger
__ India ink, green, yellow, white
__ Painting leaves **See page 73**
__ White glue
__ Sand and pebble mixture
__ Small rock

TOOLS CHECK LIST:
__ Proective eye wear
__ Gloves
__ Long sleeve shirt
__ Large & small wire cutters
__ Large pliers & regular pliers
__ Point nose pliers
__ Flat nose pliers
__ Ruler, 24 inch
__ #0, #1, & 1" art brushes
__ Ballpeen, or small claw hammer
__ Steel plate or small anvil

To see completed pieces in Full Color, visit my website: www.salvillano.com

The following will show how to create wall art sculpture. I mounted all of the pieces on 6 or 7 inch wood bases. You can mount them on any base material that the glue you are using will adhere to. You can also paint, stain, or leave natural the finish on your base.

Preparing a Base

1. After you have chosen a base, select a hanging device for the back. I use "Saw Tooth Hangers" This type of hanger allows the piece to be shifted to the left or right after you hang it.

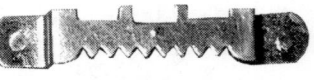
Saw tooth hanger

2. Once you have selected your base and attached the hanger to it you should decide whether you want to stain, paint, or leave natural the surface of the base. This selection should take into account the color of the wire you have selected for the tree. For the best effect try to select colors that contrast each other. For example, gold color wire looks good on a white base, while silver looks best on a dark base.

3. Next you will need to make a sand mound that will hold the tree onto the base. To show the steps for creating this piece I will be using a light color base and dark color wire on an oval wood base. Select a section on the bottom of the base that takes up about 1/3 the area on the base. Paint an irregular shape using the white glue. ***Fig. 1/82*** While the glue is still wet cover this glue area with the sand and pebble mixture. ***Fig. 2/82*** After the glue area is dry (about 2 to 3 hours), create a 1/2 inch high dam around the outside of it, this too should be an irregular shape. Fill the dam with about 1/8 inch of white glue, add a small rock ***Fig. 3/82***, and cover the entire glue area with the sand and pebble mix. Let this dry thoroughly. You can put the base aside as we create the actual tree sculptures.

Fig. 1/82   ***Fig. 2/82***   ***Fig. 3/82***

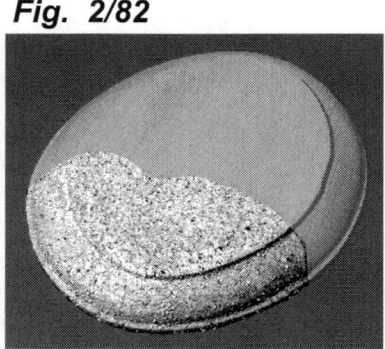
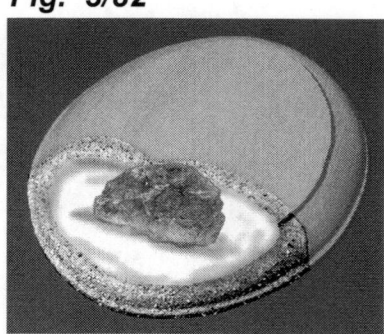

For this project you will be using 22 gauge and 26 gauge wire. The thicker 22 gauge wire is for the structure of the basic tree, and the 26 gauge wire is for the final wrap. I will be using a dark green wire so the color of the wire will contrast the background base, which I have left in its natural wood color. You can use any color wire you like, just be sure the gauges are 22 and 26.

Creating the Tree Structure

1. Using the small wire cutters, cut 40 pieces of the 22 gauge wire to approximate lengths of 10 inches. Do not be concerned about cutting each piece to exactly 10 inches. Slightly different size pieces of the wire will create a interesting final tree. Loosely secure the 40 pieces of the 22 gauge wire together using 3/4 inch masking or electrical tape, about 2 inches from the bottom of the bundle of wire. ***Fig. 4/82***. You will later on be wrapping wire over the tape so it will no longer be visible.

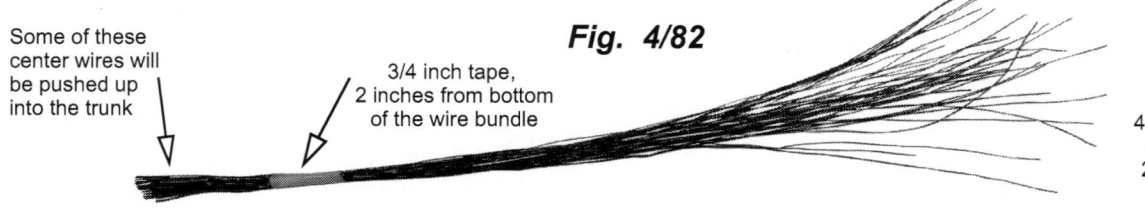

Fig. 4/82

Some of these center wires will be pushed up into the trunk

3/4 inch tape, 2 inches from bottom of the wire bundle

40, 10 inch pieces of 22 gauge wire

2. Hold the wire bundle firmly at the top and bend up the wire to create 4 different groups.(The following steps may seem confusing, so refer to the photos as you follow the instructions.) One group with 6 wires and three groups with 3 wires. Twist the group of 6 wires together about half way toward the end. Then divide this group into 2 groups of 3 wires each and twist them all the way to the end. Twist each of the group of 3 wires together all the way to the end, creating one larger root section of each. When you have finished with this step you will have: one large root with two smaller roots coming off it *Fig. 2/83* (A), two single roots, (B & C) and one root anchor (D) that will be used to help hold the piece onto the base. Use the point nose pliers to push as many of the loose wires at the center of the roots up into the center of the trunk. This will help to create branches of different sizes. Any of the wires that you cannot move up into the trunk should be bent up onto the base of the trunk. This will create a trunk that is thicker at the bottom. *Fig. 1/83*

3. You are now finished using the 22 gauge wire. The rest of the construction of the tree will use only the 26 gauge wire. This wire will now be called the "source wire". Hold the tree firmly by the trunk section and bend down all the roots. This will make it easier to work on the rest of the tree. Twist the end of the source wire around any one of the root sections. Wrap the source wire about 2 inches up the trunk, then back down ending at the top of the root section. Pull the wire snugly as you are wrapping. Divide all the branches into 2 approximately equal sections. Using the flat nose pliers, slightly bend the bottom 1/3 of the trunk away from you. Move the pliers up to the top 1/3 of the trunk and slightly bend this section toward you. This will give the trunk an "S" shape. *Fig. 2/83*

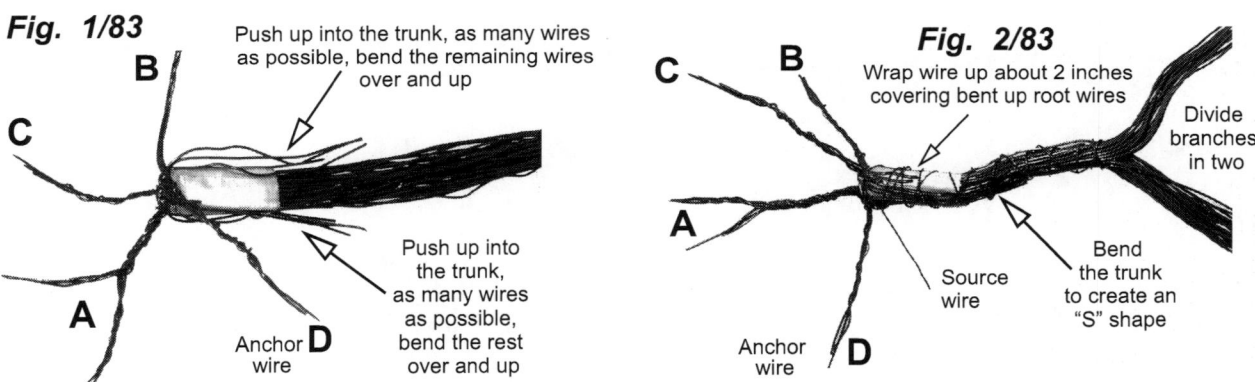

Wrapping the Roots You will be wrapping the root sections first, then the trunk, then the branches. Select any of the single root sections "B" or "C". For this and all other wrapping, do not try to keep all the wraps evenly spaced. It is much better to create an irregular surface pattern as you wrap. Start the wrapping from the trunk base out to the tip of the root. Once out and back all the way to the trunk. Follow the following wrapping sequence for both of the single roots: Out 1/2 on to the root then back to the trunk, out all the way to the root tip then back to the trunk, out 1/2 on to the root then back to the trunk, finally, 1/4 way on to the root then back to the trunk. When you end the wrapping at the base of the trunk, wrap once around the base of the trunk, then proceed to the other single root section and repeat the above steps for this root section. When you finish wrapping the second root, wrap once around the trunk then proceed to the split root section "A". Start at the base of the trunk and wrap out to the tip of one of the smaller root sections, then back to the trunk. Wrap out to the tip of the other smaller root sections then back to the trunk. Wrap out to 1/2 the way of each of the smaller root sections, then back, ending the wrapping at the base of the trunk. This wrapping technique will create roots that are tapered. There is no wire wrapping on the root anchor. *See page 84, Fig. 1/84*

Wrapping the Trunk   Starting at the base of the trunk, where you left off wrapping the roots, wrap up toward the branches and back to the roots 9 times. Pass the wire through the "V" section of the branches each time you get to the branch section. End the 9 &1/2 wrap at the top of the trunk. *Fig. 1/84*

Wrapping the Branches   Start at the top of the trunk and wrap 1/2 up onto either of the 2 branch groups. Divide all the remaining branches in this group into 2 approximately equal groups. Wrap up either of these groups about 1/4 inch, then down and onto the other group and up onto this next group about 1/4 inch. Return wrapping toward, and end at, the trunk. Repeat the above for all the other branch sections, ending at the very top of the trunk. *Fig. 1/84*

Creating the Smaller Branches   Start with any of the branch groups, separate the loose branches into 2 approximately equal groups. Separate each of the groups you just created into 2 more approximately equal groups. Twist the base of the groups up about 1/4 inch. Twist the remaining wires up about 1/4 inch. Repeat the above for all the remaining groups of wires. If you end up with uneven wires in any of the groups, just leave them as loose single branchs. *Fig. 1/84*

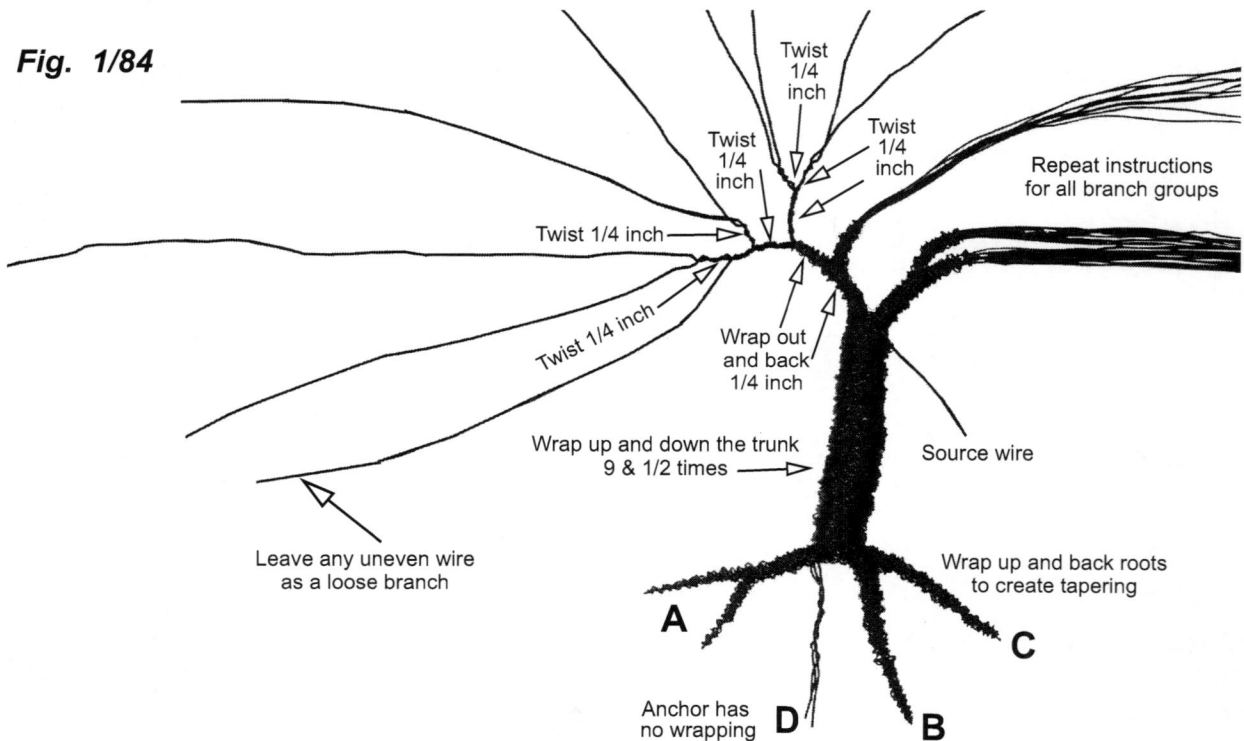

Fig. 1/84

Thickening the Trunk and Roots

THE TRUNK - For the final look of the tree you will need to wrap more wire onto the trunk and roots to thicken these areas. Start at the top of the trunk where you ended wrapping all the branches. Wrap all the way down to the base of the trunk, then wrap up 3/4 of the way toward the top of the trunk, then back down all the way to the base of the trunk. Wrap up 1/2 of the way toward the top of the trunk, then back down to the base of the trunk. The trunk is now finished. You will see that the trunk has a taper from the thinner top to the thicker bottom. *Fig. 1/84*

THE ROOTS - Start wrapping onto any single root, "B" or "C", from where you left off wrapping the trunk. Wrap out to the tip of the root and back, wrap out 1/2 of the way to the tip and back, wrap out 1/4 of the way to the tip and then back, wrap 1/4 out again and back, ending the wrapping at the base of the trunk. Wrap once around the base of the trunk then onto the other single root section. Repeat the above steps for the other single root section. When you end the wrapping of the second single root section at the base of the trunk, wrap once around the trunk then onto the split root section. Wrap out to the tip of either of the smaller roots, then back to the base of the trunk. Wrap out to the tip of the other small root then back to the base of the trunk. Wrap 3/4 of the way out onto the larger main root section, then back to the trunk. Wrap 1/2 of the way out onto the main root section then back to the base of the trunk. Wrap once around the base of the trunk and onto the root anchor. Wrap the source wire several times around the anchor, then cut it. You are now finished with the source wire and the tree is ready to be mounted onto the base.

Mounting the Tree onto the Base

The tree must be securely mounted onto the base before you shape the branches to create the type of tree you want.

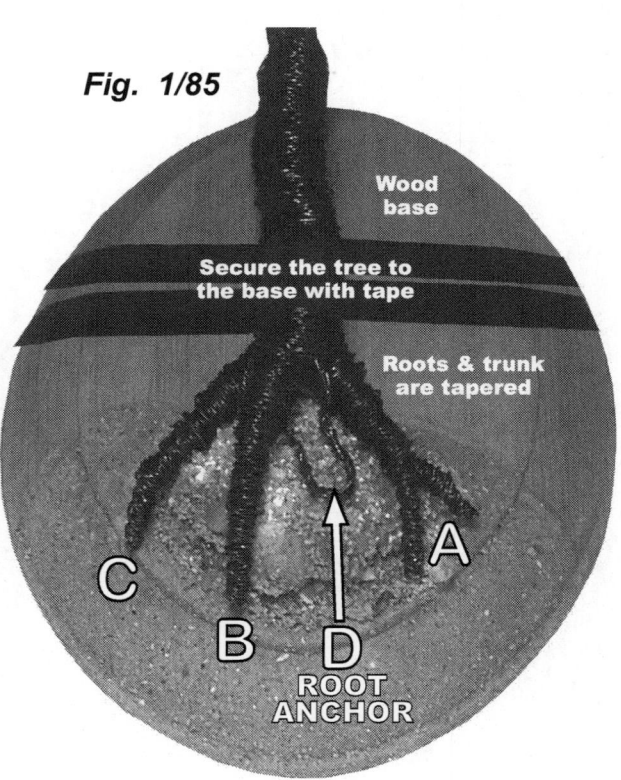

Fig. 1/85

Create the root mound around all the roots

1. Bend all of the branches up so it will be easier to work on the root section. Bend up and coil in the root anchor. Bend down all the root sections. Position the tree on the rock so that the trunk of the tree is parallel to the base. Bend down all the ends of the roots so that they seem to be hugging the rock and the sand mound. When you are pleased with the positioning of the tree onto the root mound, secure the top of the trunk with masking or electrical tape. Use enough tape, and wrap it tightly onto the base, so that the root section will not move as you are working on it. *Fig. 1/85*

2. Create a sand dam around the roots. Be sure the root anchor is included into the center of the dam. Follow steps 1 to 6 on *Page 71* to construct the sand dam and to complete building the root mound.

Completing the Base You must now decide whether you want to leave the root mound natural, with no added color, or have it look like moss covered earth. If you wish to keep the root mound natural, with no color, skip this step and proceed to shaping your tree. If you wish add color to the root mound. *See page 38*

Shaping the Tree Sculpture Using the basic shape you just created, you will be able to shape and add to the tree to create many different types of trees: **Weeping Willow, page 39, Upright Willow, page 40, Beaded, page 41, Wind Swept, page 46, Oak, page 44, Bonsai with Leaves, page 47**

You may also want to consider adding a BIRD NEST among the branches of the finished tree **See page 48**

To see completed pieces in Full Color, visit my website: www.salvillano.com

Tree on Sea Shell - *8"h X 10"w X 8"d*

Difficulty Scale: *(1 = easy, 10 = difficult)* this is a **6**

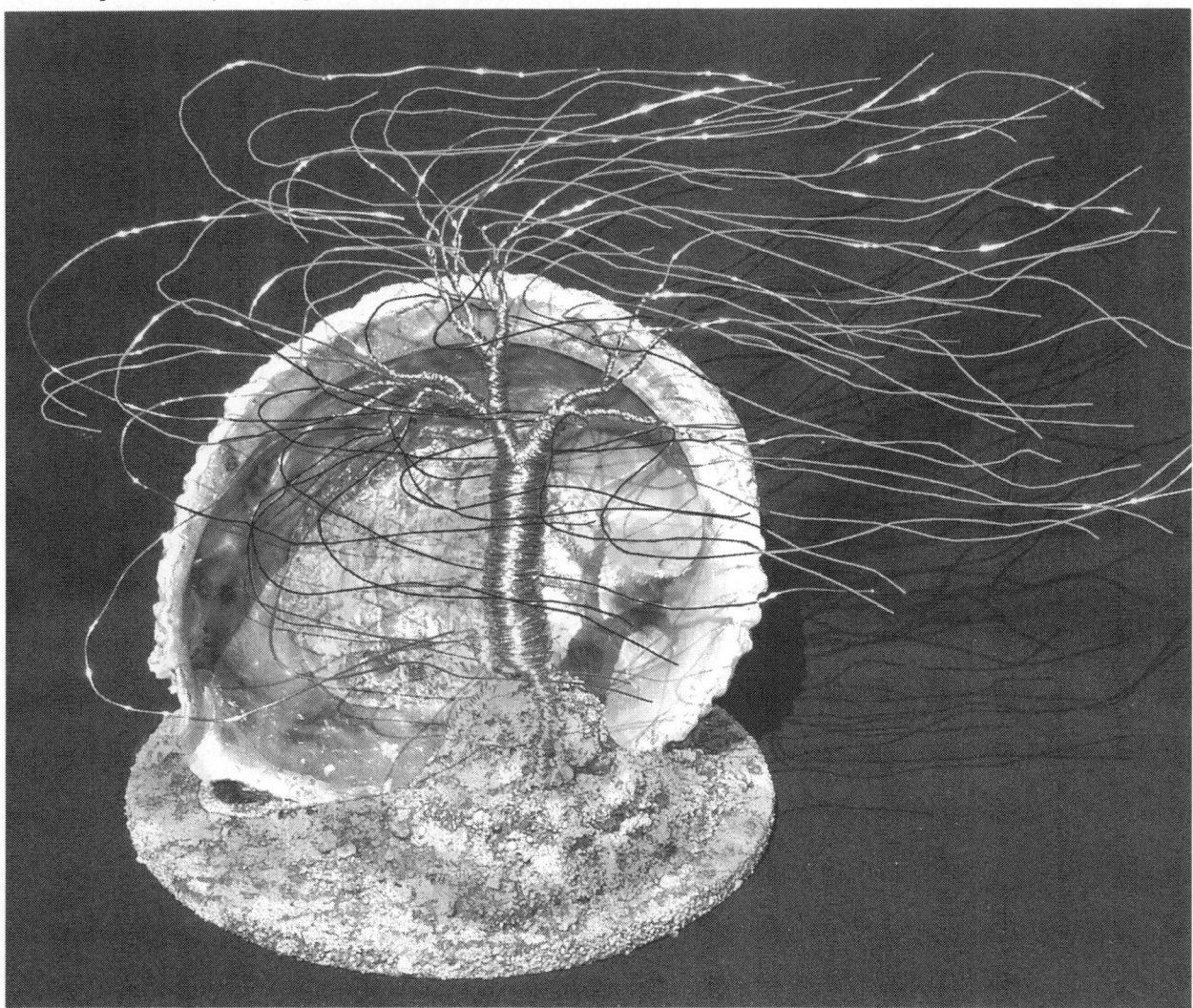

NOTE: Read the entire section for this item before you start, to determine which of the material and tools you need. Some of the items listed here are for optional choices. Have all the material and tools ready before you start to create the piece. For illustrations of tools and material *See pages 9 & 10*

MATERIAL CHECK LIST:

- 24 gauge wire (50 ft.) Gold color or color of your choice
- Abalone shell 6"w X 5"h X 2"d or assorted sea shells
- 6" round cork base or your choice of different base
- Several small rocks 2" to 3" wide
- Sand and pebble mixture
- White glue
- India ink, green, yellow, white
- Electrical or masking tape

TOOLS CHECK LIST:

- Protective eye wear
- Gloves
- Long sleeve shirt
- Large & small wire cutters
- Large pliers & regular pliers
- Point nose pliers
- Flat nose pliers
- Ruler, 24 inch
- #0, #1, & 1" art brushes

To see completed pieces in Full Color, visit my website: www.salvillano.com

I will be describing how to create a tree sculpture on an abalone sea shell. This type of shell contains many different iridescent and reflective colors. I will be creating this piece using gold color 24 gauge wire. The gold color of the wire will add to the overall very interesting mix of colors and reflections. I have chosen to create this piece in the "Wind Swept" style. To me it evokes the image of a lonely windy beach covered with many sea shells. Of course, you may mount the tree sculpture on the base of your choice, and shape the tree into any shape you like. Another choice of a base, (that I do not show in this book), is to use a pile of different size and shape sea shells, with the tree mounted on top. For other types of bases, *See page 12*

Before you start to create this piece, you should first create the base. This is done for two reasons. The first is that since a considerable amount of drying time is needed for the base, rock and sand mound to be bonded together, you can work on the rest of the piece while all the other elements are drying. It is important that all the parts of the base are dry and solid before you mount the tree. The second reason is, by completing the base first, you will be able to fit and make adjustments to the root system and have a very good idea how the final piece will look before you bond the roots to the base.

Preparing the Base

1. Paint on a thin layer of white glue, enough to cover the entire surface and the edges of the cork base. Before the glue is dry, cover the entire surface and the edges with the sand and pebble mixture. Let the glue and sand mixture thoroughly dry overnight.

2. After you are sure the glue and sand mixture is dry, position the shell onto the base toward the edge of the cork. Use a small rock to support the back of the shell so that it is it is as perpendicular to the cork base as you can get it.

3. Create a sand dam around the outer edge of the cork, then fill the entire inner surface of the cork base with about 1/8th inch of white glue. Be sure the base of the shell, and the base of the rock are included in the glue area. Cover the entire area where the glue is with a thick layer of the sand and pebble mixture. Let the entire base assemblage thoroughly dry for at least 3 days. *Fig. 1/87*

4. After all the elements of the base are thoroughly dry and solid, you will prepare the root mound upon which you will place the tree. Place a rock in front of the shell and create a sand dam around it. Fill the inside of the dam with about 1/8th inch of white glue, then cover all the glue in a thick layer of the sand and pebble mix. Be sure all is dry before you proceed *Fig. 1/87*

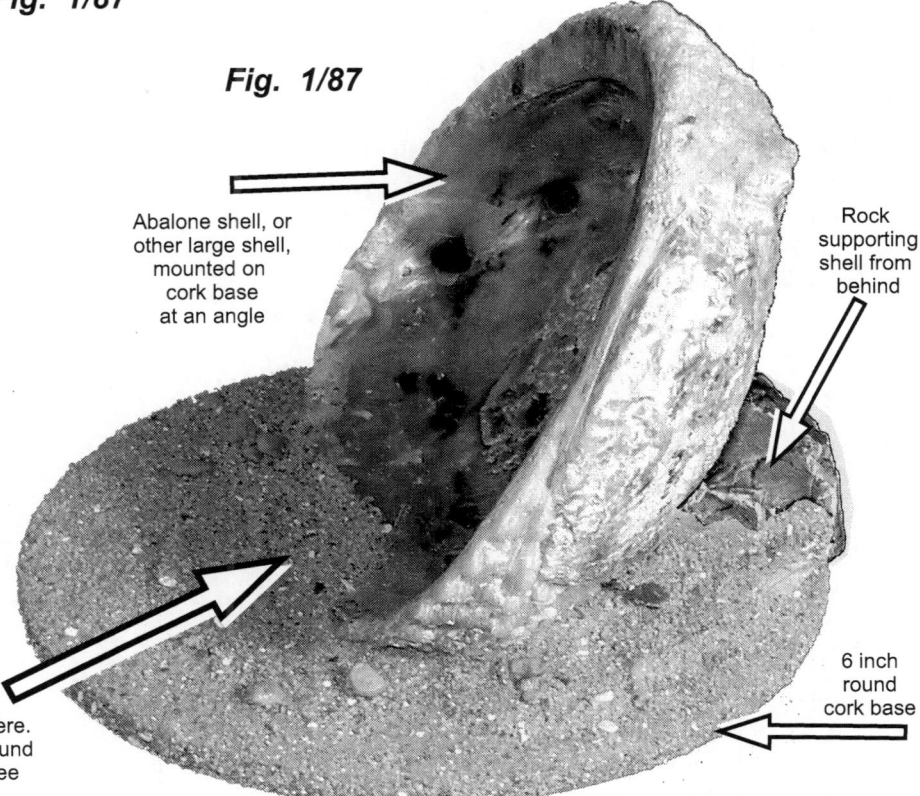

Fig. 1/87

Abalone shell, or other large shell, mounted on cork base at an angle

Rock supporting shell from behind

6 inch round cork base

Position a small rock here. This will be the root mound that will support the tree

Creating the Basic Tree

As I said at the beginning of this section, I will create the Wind Swept tree sculpture to show in the abalone sea shell. After you have created the basic tree described here, you will be able to alter the shape and add to it to create other types of trees.

1. Using the small wire cutters, cut 50 pieces of the 24 gauge gold color wire to approximate lengths of 10 inches. Do not be concerned about cutting each piece to exactly 10 inches. Slightly different size pieces of the wire will create a very interesting final tree. Loosely secure the 50 pieces of the wire together using 3/4 inch masking or electrical tape, about 2 inches from the bottom of the bundle of wire. *Fig. 1/88* You will later on, be wrapping wire over the tape so it will no longer be visible.

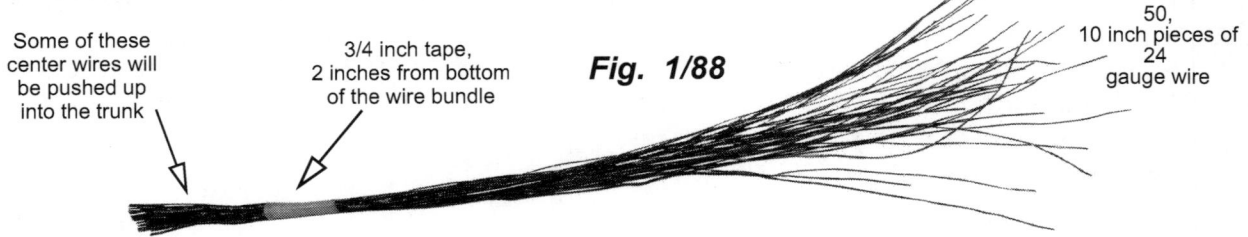

2. Hold the wire bundle firmly at the top and bend up the wire to create 4 different groups.(The following steps may seem confusing, so refer to the photos as you follow the instructions.) One group with 6 wires and three groups with 3 wires. Twist the group of 6 wires together about half way toward the end. Then divide this group into 2 groups of 3 wires each and twist them all the way to the end. Twist each of the group of 3 wires together all the way to the end, creating one larger root section of each. When you have finished with this step you will have: one large root with two smaller roots coming off it *Fig. 2/88* (A), two single roots, (B & C) and one root anchor (D) that will be used to help hold the piece onto the base. Use the point nose pliers to push as many of the loose wires at the center of the roots up into the center of the trunk. This will help to create branches of different sizes. Any of the wires that you cannot move up into the trunk should be bent up onto the base of the trunk. This will create a trunk that is thicker at the bottom. *Fig. 2/88*

3. From now on, the 24 gauge wire be called the "source wire". Hold the tree firmly by the trunk section and bend down all the roots. This will make it easier to work on the rest of the tree. Twist the end of the source wire around any one of the root sections. Wrap the source wire about 2 inches up the trunk, then back down ending at the top of the root section. Pull the wire snugly as you are wrapping. Divide all the branches into 2 approximately equal sections. Using the flat nose pliers, slightly bend the bottom 1/3 of the trunk away from you. Move the pliers up to the top 1/3 of the trunk and slightly bend this section toward you. This will give the trunk an "S" shape. *Fig. 3/88*

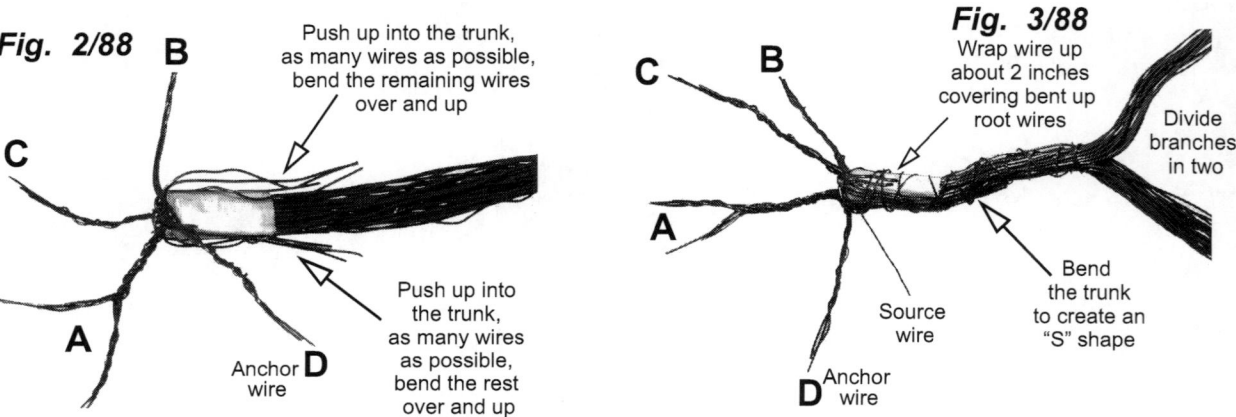

Wrapping the Roots Select any of the single root sections "B" or "C". For this and all other wrapping, do not try to keep all the wraps evenly spaced. It is much better to create an irregularities as you wrap. Start the wrapping from the trunk base out to the tip of the root. Once out and back all the way to the trunk. Follow the following wrapping sequence for both of the single roots: Out 1/2 on to the root then back to the trunk, out all the way to the root tip then back to the trunk, out 1/2 on to the root then back to the trunk, finally, 1/4 way on to the root then back to the trunk. When you end the wrapping at the base of the trunk, wrap once around the base of the trunk, then proceed to the other single root section and repeat the above steps for this root section. When you finish wrapping the second root, wrap once around the trunk then proceed to the split root section "A". Start at the base of the trunk and wrap out to the tip of one of the smaller root sections, then back to the trunk. Wrap out to the tip of the other smaller root sections then back to the trunk. Wrap out to 1/2 the way of each of the smaller root sections, then back, ending the wrapping at the base of the trunk. No wrapping on to the root anchor.

Wrapping the Trunk Starting at the base of the trunk, where you left off wrapping the roots, wrap up toward the branches and back to the roots 9 times. Pass the wire through the "V" section of the branches each time you get to the branch section. End the 9 &1/2 wrap at the top of the trunk. *Fig. 1/89*

Wrapping the Branches Start at the top of the trunk wrap 1/2 up onto either of the 2 branch groups. Divide all the remaining branches in this group in 2 approximately equal groups. Wrap up either of these groups about 1/4 inch, then down and onto the other group and up this group about 1/4 inch. Return wrapping toward, and end at the trunk. Repeat the above for other branch sections, ending at the top of the trunk. *Fig. 1/89*

Creating the Smaller Branches Start with any of the branch groups, separate the loose branches into 2 approximately equal groups. Separate each of the groups you just created into 2 approximately equal groups. Twist the base of the groups up about 1/4 inch. Twist the remaining wires up about 1/4 inch. Repeat the above for all the remaining groups. If you end up with uneven wire, leave it as a loose branch. *Fig. 1/89*

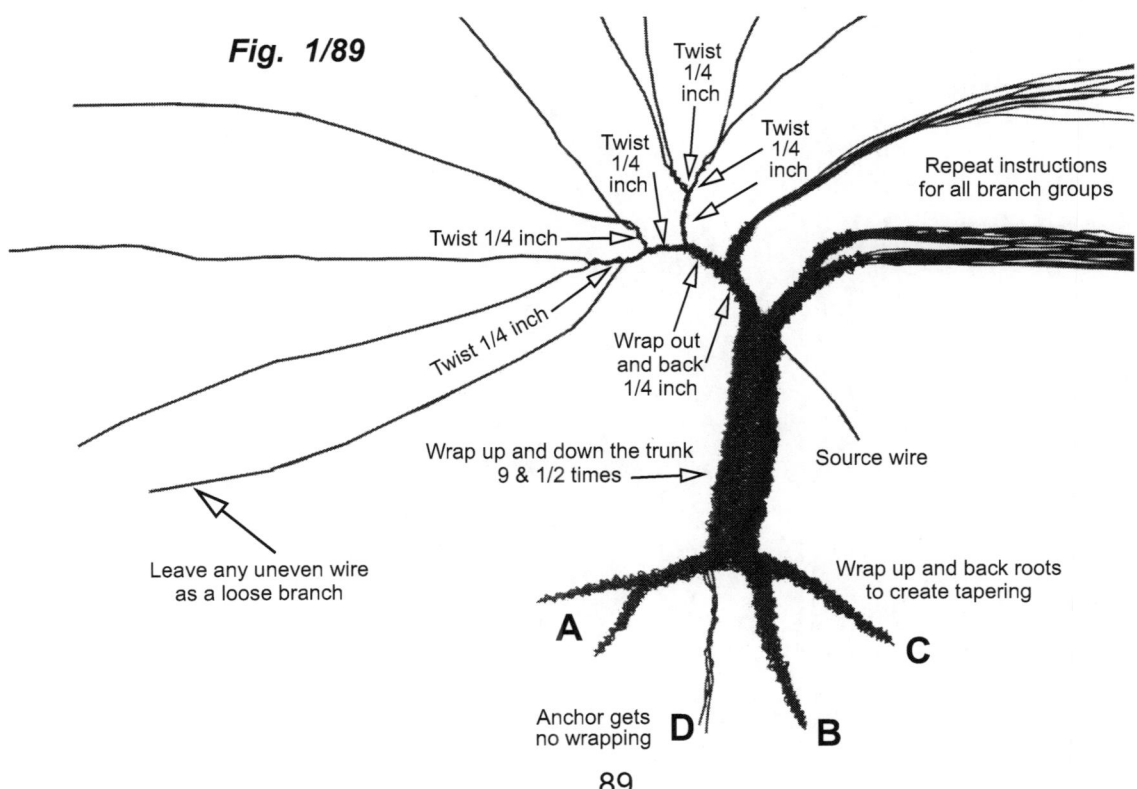

Fig. 1/89

Thickening the Trunk and Roots

THE TRUNK - You will now need to wrap more wire onto the trunk. Start at the top, where you ended wrapping the branches, wrap all the way down to the base of the trunk, then wrap up 3/4 of the way toward the top, then back down all the way to the base. Wrap up 1/2 of the way toward the top, then back down to the base. The trunk is now finished. The trunk has a taper from the thinner top to the thicker bottom. *See page 89, Fig. 1/89*

THE ROOTS - Wrapping onto any single root, "B" or "C", from where you left off wrapping the trunk. Wrap out to the tip of the root and back, wrap out 1/2 of the way to the tip and back, wrap out 1/4 of the way to the tip and then back, wrap 1/4 out again and back, ending the wrapping at the base of the trunk. Wrap once around the base of the trunk then onto the other single root section. Repeat the above steps for the other single root section. When you end the wrapping of the second single root section at the base of the trunk, wrap once around the trunk then onto the split root section. Wrap out to the tip of either of the smaller roots, then back to the base of the trunk. Wrap out to the tip of the other small root then back to the base of the trunk. Wrap 3/4 of the way out onto the larger main root section, then back to the trunk. Wrap 1/2 of the way out onto the main root section then back to the base of the trunk. Wrap once around the base of the trunk and onto the root anchor. Wrap the source wire several times around the anchor, then cut it. You are now finished with the source wire, and the tree is ready to be mounted onto the base.

Mounting the Tree onto the Shell Base

1. Bend all the branches up so it's easier to work on the root section. Bend up and coil in the root anchor. Bend down all the root sections. Position the tree on the root mound where you think it looks centered and balanced. Bend down all the ends of the roots so that they seem to be hugging the root mound. Secure the top of the trunk to the shell using masking or electrical tape. *Fig. 1/90*

2. Create a sand dam around the roots. *Fig. 1/90* Be sure the root anchor is included into the center of the dam. Follow steps 1 to 6 on *Page 71* to construct the sand dam and to complete building the root mound.

Completing the Base
You must now decide whether you want to leave the root mound as a natural, with no added color, or have the it look like moss covered earth. If you wish to keep the root mound natural, with no color, skip this step and proceed to shaping your tree. If you wish add color to the root mound and have it look like moss covered earth, *See page 38*

Shaping the Tree
Using the basic shape you just created, you will be able to create many different types of trees: *See page 21*

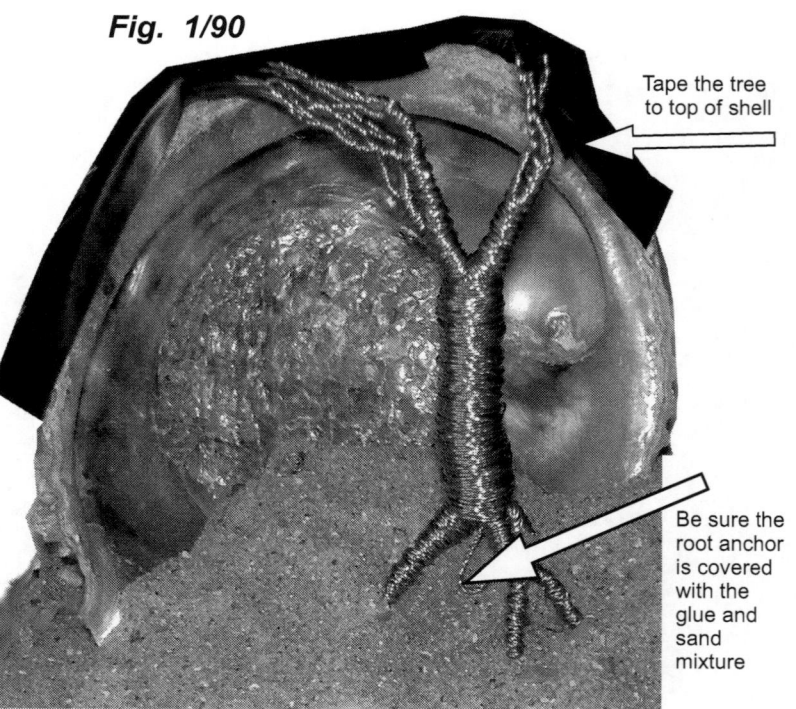

Fig. 1/90

Tape the tree to top of shell

Be sure the root anchor is covered with the glue and sand mixture

Glass Bonsai - *22"h X 21"w X 20"d*

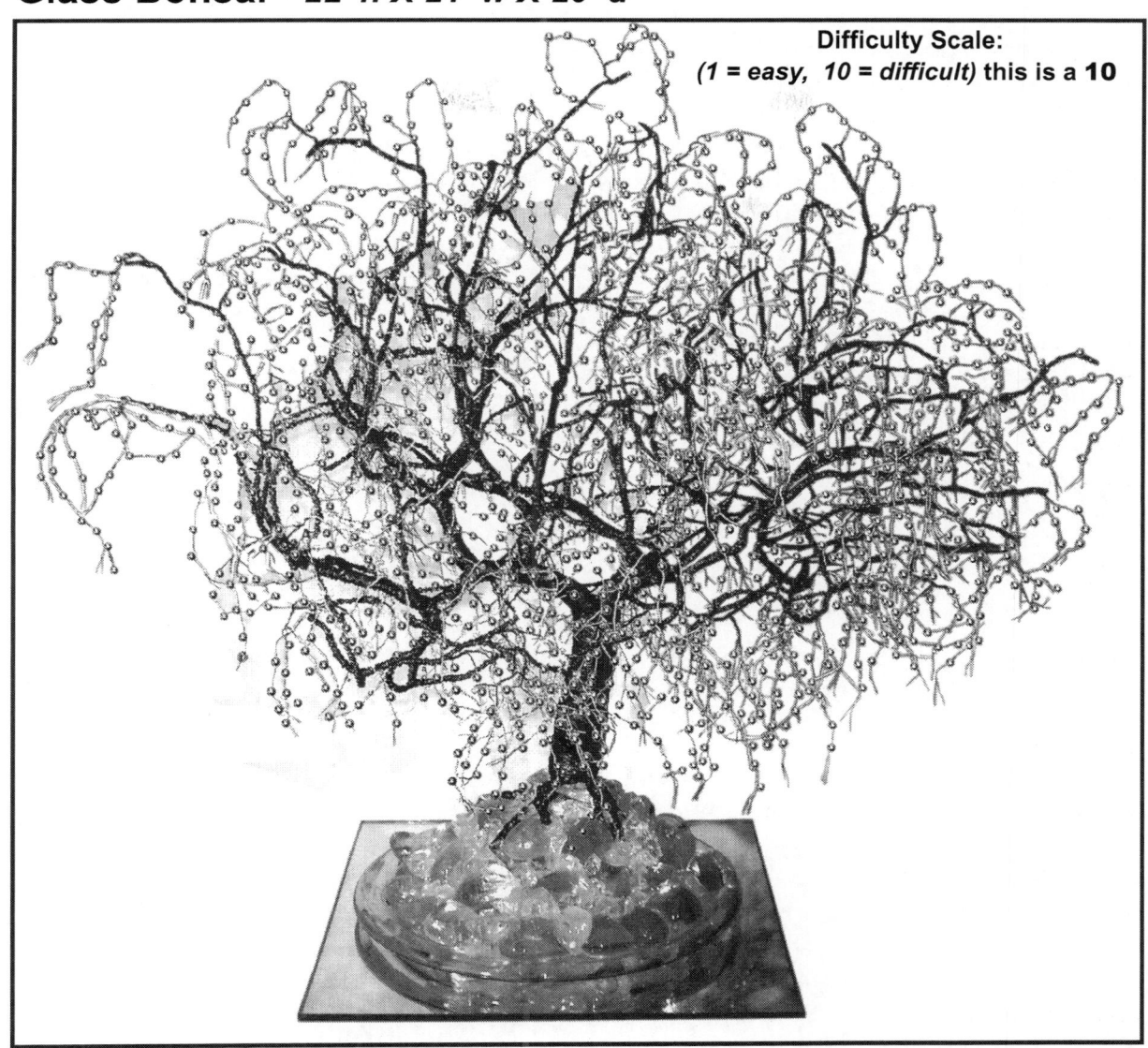

Difficulty Scale:
(1 = easy, 10 = difficult) this is a **10**

MATERIAL CHECK LIST:
- 26 gauge wire (80 Yards)
- 22 gauge wire (7 Yards)
- 6 strand, 18 gauge cable wire (25 ft.)
- 9 inch round glass base
- 20 to 40 pieces of clear glass rocks
- 15 to 30 pieces of irregular shaped glass
- 15 to 30 pieces of small glass pieces

See page 92 for Glass Samples

- E6000 Adhesive, clear, medium viscosity four, 2 ounce tubes.
- Black paint. Liquid 4oz. or spray 6oz.
- Glass clear fringe beads, 7,000
- Electrical or masking tape
- Electrical wire end caps, 20 to 40 (small)
- Optional wood base

NOTE: Read the entire section for this item before you start, to determine what material and tools are needed.

TOOLS CHECK LIST:
- Protective eye wear
- Gloves
- Long sleeve shirt
- Large & small wire cutters
- Large pliers & regular pliers
- Point nose pliers
- Flat nose pliers
- Ruler, 24 inch
- Small metal sculpting tool to spread the E6000 adhesive
- 2 or 3 spring clamps
- Small artist brush (# 0 or #1)

To see completed pieces in Full Color, visit my website: www.salvillano.com

This is one of my most unusual pieces. The entire base is made of glass. It has a mystical look as it reflects and bounces light off the surfaces in the base and the clear glass beads within the branches and twigs of the tree. I have also painted the entire surface of the tree black to contrast the brightness and reflections of all the glass.

Before you start to create the tree for this piece, you should first create the base. This is done for two reasons. The first is that since a considerable amount of drying time is needed for the base and the glass pieces to be bonded together, you can work on the rest of the piece while those elements are drying. It is important that all the parts of the base are dry and solid before you mount the tree. The second reason is, by completing the base first, you will be able to fit and make adjustments to the root system and have a very good idea how the final piece will look before you bond the roots to the base. You will be using "E6000" industrial strength adhesive, which may at first be a little difficult to work with. The E6000 is rather thick and does not easily flow out of the tube, so you may want to use a small metal knife or small metal sculpting tool to work with. I have been using this product for many years, and have found it to be the best for this type of work.

Preparing the Base

1. Apply a thin layer of the E6000 glue to cover the entire inner surface area of the round base. You can apply the glue in large drops then spread it out to cover the entire inner surface. Try not to get any glue on the outer lip of the base.

2. Before the glue is dry, add enough of the glass rocks you have chosen onto the entire area where the glue is. I have selected 1 to 1 1/2 inch glass rocks to use in my base. You can use any type of glass rocks or pieces of glass or clear plastic. The E6000 glue will easily adhere to any of these. Be sure that each of the glass rocks are touching some part of the glue area.

3. Let the base and glass rocks dry overnight, then apply a few drops of the glue in between each of the glass rocks. This will create a solid glass foundation for the tree. You are finished with the base for now, put is aside as you work on the tree. *Fig. 1/92* The other smaller pieces of glass will be used later on to fill in the voids between the roots of the tree and the large glass rocks.

Fig. 1/92
Apply a thin layer of E6000 glue on the entire surface of the round glass base

Try not to get any glue on the lip of the base
(If you do, let the glue dry, then scrape it off)

Add additional glue between glass rocks

1 to 1.5 inch large round glass rocks

Various sizes of irregular shaped glass to fit between the larger glass rocks

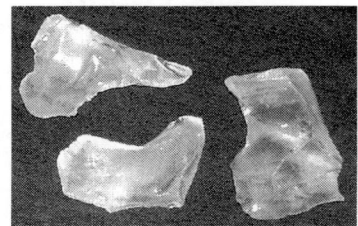

Small glass rocks to fit between the larger glass rocks

Creating the Basic Tree Structure
The basic structure of the tree will be created, then painted, then mounted onto the glass base, then the fringe beads will be added and then the tree will have it's final shaping.

1. Use the large wire cutters to cut 15 pieces of the 6 strand 18 gauge cable to 20 inch lengths. Try to uncoil and straighten each length, as much as possible. This will make the cable easier to work with. If you want, you can put electrical end caps on the end of each cable to prevent the cable from cutting into your hands or wrists. *Fig. 1/93*

2. Divide the cable into: 2 groups of 3 cables (A) & (B), 1 group of 4 cables (C), and 1 group of 5 cables (D). Step up the cables in groups (A), (B), and (C) so that there is about 1/2 inch difference in the length of the cables within that group. Keep all the cables in group (D) the same length. Use tape (electrical or masking) to hold the cables together. The tape will be covered with wire, and will not show. *Fig. 1/93*

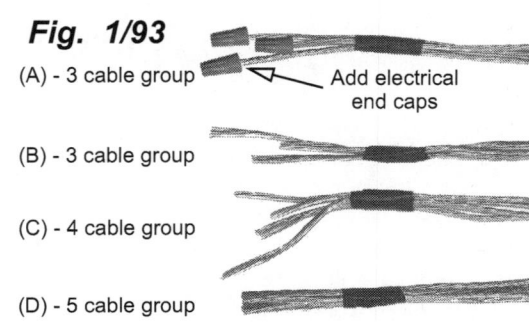

3. Line up all the cable groups as shown in *Fig. 2/93*, then tape all the groups together as shown in *Fig. 3/93* Extend the taping up from the bottom for about 4 inches. This section will become the trunk structure of the tree.

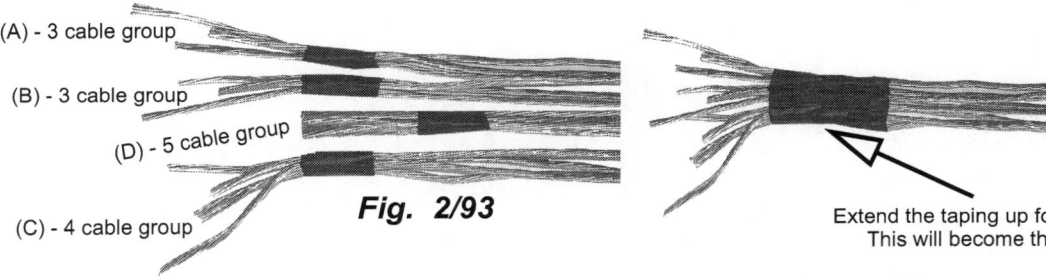

Making the Root System

1. Separate the cable wire into 3 different groups. 2 groups of 3 cable wires (A) & (B), and 1 group of 4 cable wires (C). *Fig. 4/93*

2. Starting with cable group (C), twist two of the 4 cable together for about 1/2 inch. Do the same for the other 2 cables in this group You may need to use the large pliers to twist these cables. Also twist cable groups (A) and (B) out for about 1/2 inch.

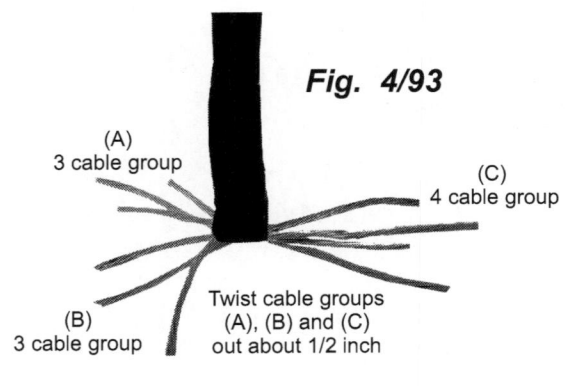

Wrapping the Wire

1. The under-wrapping of the wire will start with 22 gauge steel galvanized wire, and will finish with 26 gauge steel galvanized wire. The 26 gauge wire is where the beads will be affixed to the tree branches. Uncoil about 4 feet of the 22 gauge wire. let the source of the wire rest on the floor, this will make it easier for the source wire to unwind as you use it. *Fig. 5/93*

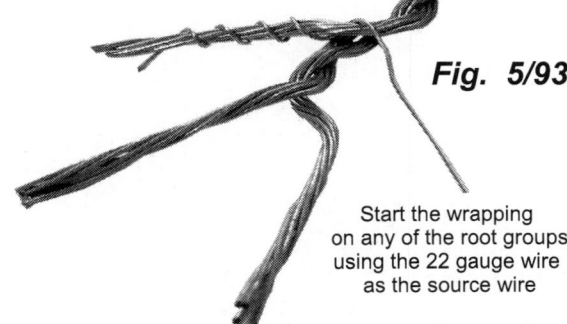

2. Starting at any group, twist the 22 gauge wire source around the single piece of the cable wire. This will secure the wire as you proceed. Hold the trunk of the tree firmly and begin to wrap the source wire around the entire root section. Wrap the wire over any tape you see on the root section, and all the way to the base of the trunk. Continue to wrap the wire until this entire root section is covered and you can no longer see the cable wire or the tape. Wrap the wire all the way to the tip of each root section, then back. This is the first wrapping, you will return to this and all other sections of the tree to add more wire which will create the actual tree shape. Repeat the above instructions to complete the other two root sections. *Fig. 1/94*

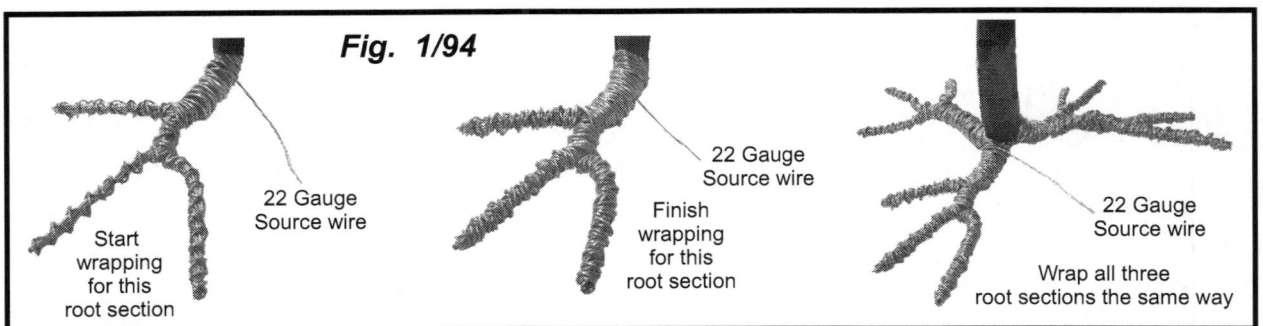

Fig. 1/94

Creating the Trunk Before you start wrapping the trunk, hold the top of the trunk firmly and give the middle part a slight bend. If you are unable to bend the trunk by hand you can use pliers or you can bend the trunk on the edge of a table. Giving the trunk this slight bend will create a more natural and less rigid tree. Start wrapping the trunk at the bottom where you ended wrapping the root sections. Wrap the wire up and down the trunk 4 times ending the top wrap just above the tape. This time do not try to hide all the tape with the wire, the tape will all be covered in the final wrapping. *Fig. 2/94*

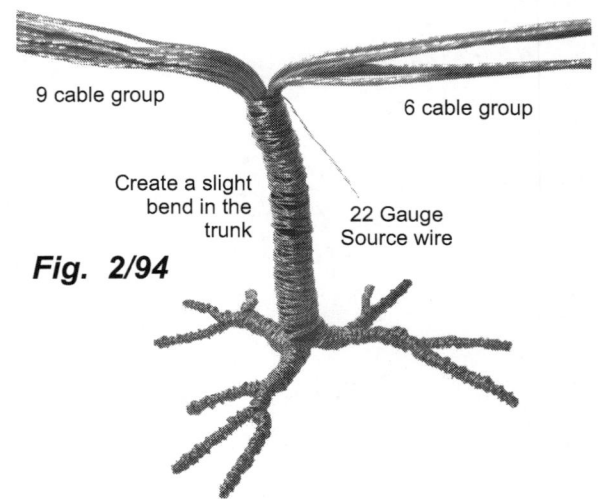

Fig. 2/94

Creating the Branches Separate all the cable wire at the top of the trunk into two groups. One group with nine cables and the other with the remaining six. For the next few steps, you will be wrapping the branches starting at the top of the trunk, wrapping the length of the branches, then returning to where you started. When you get to the section in the branch where you will start to return the wrapping, wrap the source wire through the "V" created by the cable wires. This will help to create a much stronger branch. Next, wrap the group containing the 6 cable wires 2 inches up, then divide this group into 4 cables and 2 cables and wrap these about 1 more inch up. Continue wrapping until you return to the top of the trunk where you started. Now, wrap the group of 9 cables about 2.5 inches up, then divide this group into one group of 6 and one group of 3. Divide the group of 6 into 1 group of 4 and one group of 2. The wrapping distance for these groups is about 1 inch as stated above. The group with the 3 cables is then divided into a group of 2 and 1 single cable wire. After you have created all these groups, wrap the wire back to the starting point at the top of the trunk. The above steps may seem confusing, but I am sure you will see how this is done when you look at *Page 95 Fig. 1/95* I use this method that employs the use of 6 strand cable wire to create many of my larger tree sculptures. When completed, the strength of the tree, branches and twigs is amazing.

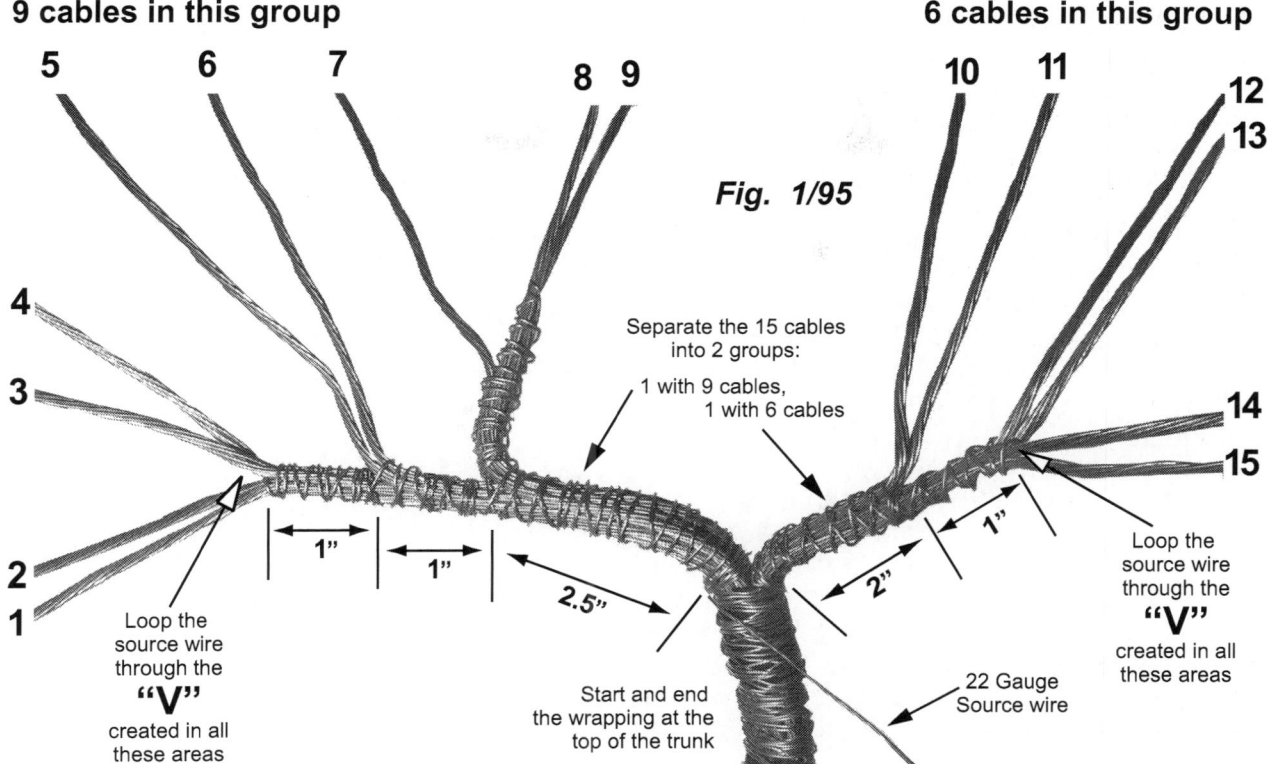

9 cables in this group — 5, 6, 7, 8, 9
6 cables in this group — 10, 11, 12, 13, 14, 15

Fig. 1/95

Separate the 15 cables into 2 groups: 1 with 9 cables, 1 with 6 cables

Loop the source wire through the "V" created in all these areas

Start and end the wrapping at the top of the trunk

22 Gauge Source wire

Loop the source wire through the "V" created in all these areas

Wrapping the Branches

Holding the base of each pair of wire cables, twist the pair of wires for about 1 inch up. Repeat this for all of the pairs of wires. To get a better grip, you may want to hold the cable wire with the standard pliers as you twist. Leave the one single cable wire as is. *Fig. 2/95*

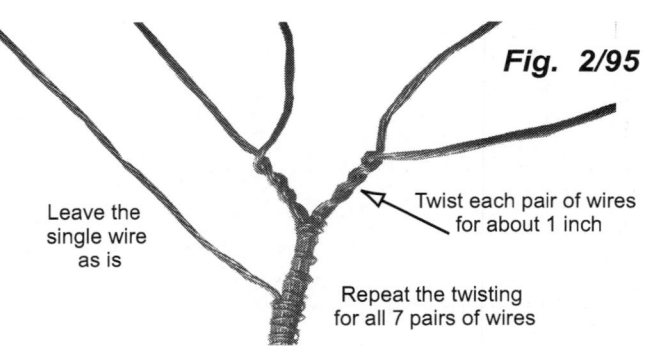

Fig. 2/95

Leave the single wire as is

Twist each pair of wires for about 1 inch

Repeat the twisting for all 7 pairs of wires

Wrapping the Tree

Use a few spring clamps attached to the root section to securely hold the tree in place as you work on it *Fig. 3/95* Once again, starting at the top of the trunk, wrap the source wire out toward the end of the cable branches. When you get to the "V", loop the source wire through the "V" in the new pairs of wires you just made. *Fig. 4/95* Wrap all the branches as described above, ending where you started. You can tape the branches after completed, to keep them out of the way as you work. *Fig. 5/95*

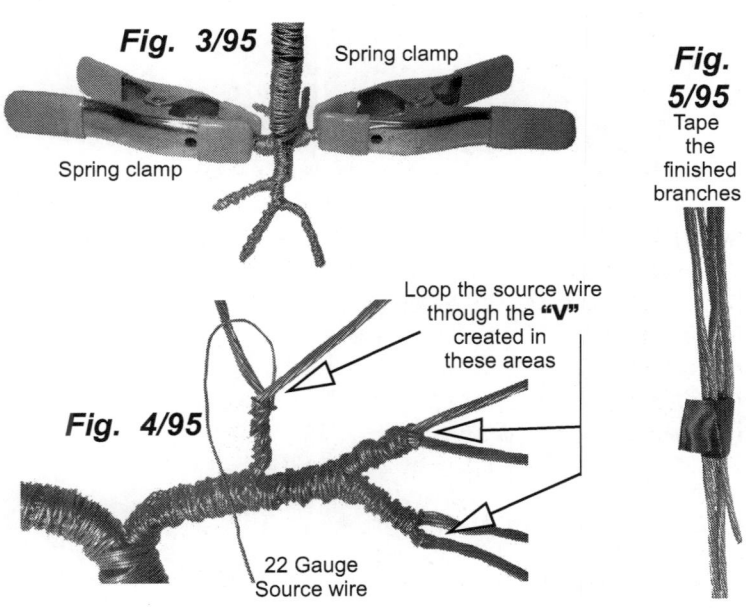

Fig. 3/95 — Spring clamp

Fig. 4/95 — Loop the source wire through the "V" created in these areas — 22 Gauge Source wire

Fig. 5/95 Tape the finished branches

Wrapping the Trunk Start at the top of the trunk where you left off wrapping the last branch. Wire down the entire trunk and back up 6 times. For the 7th wrap, wrap down to the roots then wrap 2 times 3/4 of the way up and back, then 2 times 1/2 of the way up and back. End this wrapping at the base of the trunk. Each time you end the wrapping at the top and bottom of the trunk, loop the wire through the "V" as you did with the branches. Do not wire the roots with this wiring. The roots are finished with the 22 gauge wire, but will still need to be wired with the 26 gauge wire. *Fig. 1/96*

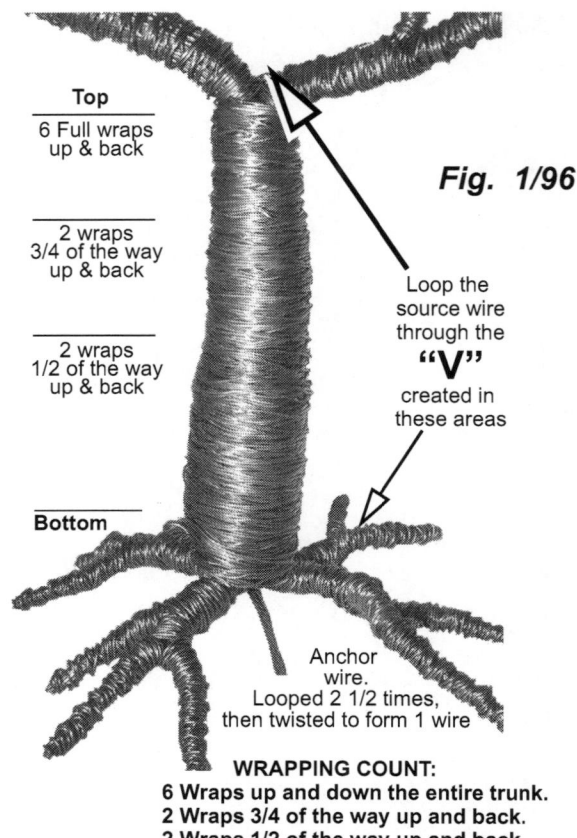

Fig. 1/96

Loop the source wire through the "V" created in these areas

Top — 6 Full wraps up & back
2 wraps 3/4 of the way up & back
2 wraps 1/2 of the way up & back
Bottom

Anchor wire. Looped 2 1/2 times, then twisted to form 1 wire

WRAPPING COUNT:
6 Wraps up and down the entire trunk.
2 Wraps 3/4 of the way up and back.
2 Wraps 1/2 of the way up and back.

Creating an Anchor Make a 2 inch long loop around any of the root sections at its top. Wrap the wire 2 1/2 times then cut it. Twist all the loops together creating one wire. This anchor is used to secure the tree to the base. *Fig. 1/96* This is the final use of the 22 gauge wire. For the rest of the tree, and adding beads to the branches, you will be using only 26 gauge wire. The 26 gauge wire will now be called the source wire.

Final Wrapping

1. The Roots Start at the end of the anchor and securely attach the source wire to it by wrapping it around several times. Wrap out onto any of the root sections all the way out and back to the base of the trunk. Do this one time for each of the root sections. This will cover all the 22 gauge wire with one wrap of the 26 gauge wire. Wrap the wire slowly and try to fit the 26 gauge wire in between the 22 gauge wire.

2. The Trunk Starting at the base of the trunk, where you left off wrapping the roots, wrap the trunk 4 times up and 3 times down, ending at the top of the trunk. Once again, loop the source wire through the "V" in the branches. Once the root and trunk sections are completed you can use a few clamps **See page 95**, or wood base option **See page 67** to hold the tree in place as you work on the branches.

3. The Branches Start wrapping onto either of the 2 main thicker branches covering all of the 22 gauge wire then wrap out onto the 6 strand cable wire for about 1/2 inch. Stop wrapping and separate the 6 strand cable wire into one group with 2 wires and the other with 4 wires. Twist the group with 2 wires together for about 1/2 inch. Twist the group with the 4 wires together for about 1/2 inch. Finally, twist the 2 pairs of wires in the 4 wire group together for about 1/4 inch. *Fig. 2/96* You may want to go back and thicken the branches, just go back and forth with the source wire so that the branches closest to the trunk are the thickest. This will create a more realistic look for the final tree.

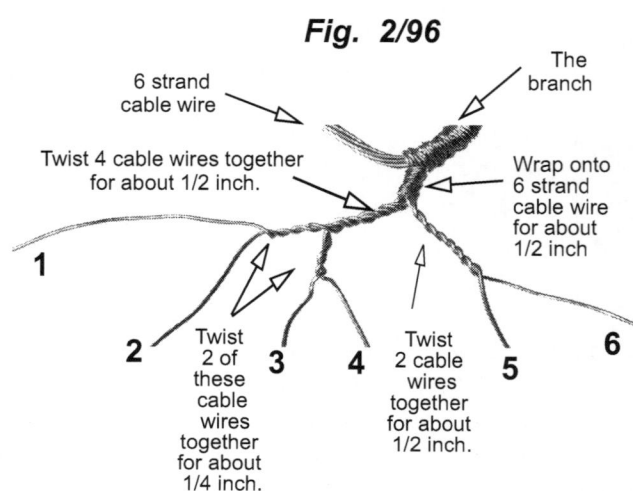

Fig. 2/96

The branch
6 strand cable wire
Twist 4 cable wires together for about 1/2 inch.
Wrap onto 6 strand cable wire for about 1/2 inch
Twist 2 of these cable wires together for about 1/4 inch.
Twist 2 cable wires together for about 1/2 inch.

4. The Twigs Wrap out all the way to the end of any of the individual twigs. When you get to the end of the twig, return wrapping toward the trunk for about 1/2 inch. Create 3 separate, 6 inch loops over the top of the twig. Use the bent nose pliers to twist the 3 loops together for about 1/2 inch. Then, twist one of the loops for about 1/2 inch. Next twist the 2 remaining loops together for about 1/2 inch. Finally, twist the 2 last loops for about 1/2 inch each. When wiring all the following loops onto the twigs, vary the spaces between each of the 3 loop groups from about 1/2 inch to 1 & 1/2 inch. This will create a more natural looking tree structure. Repeat steps **3** and **4** for all the branches and twigs. *Fig. 1/97*

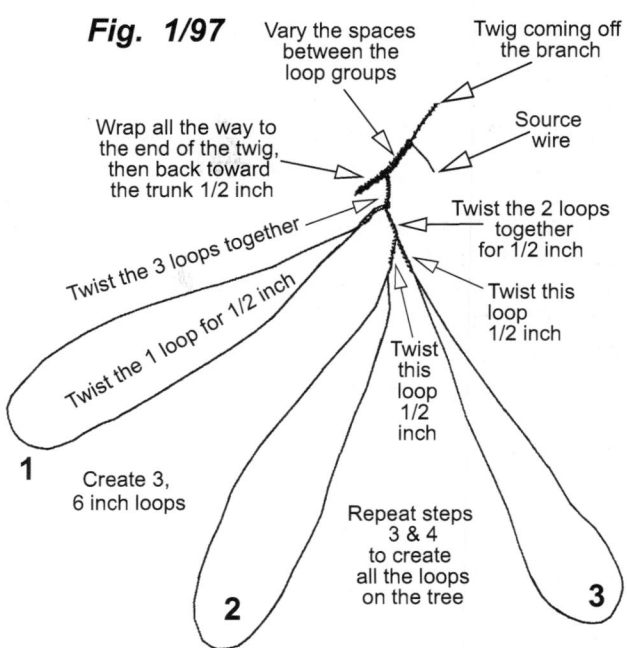

NOTE: If you do not want to create this tree sculpture using glass beads, you can eliminate the beads, cut the loops and twist the loose wires together to create a thicker twig.

5. Final use of the Source Wire When you have created all the loops on all the branches, end the use of the 26 gauge source wire by wrapping one last time down the trunk then onto the root anchor. You are now finished with the wiring of the tree.

Painting the Tree I have chosen to paint this tree using a flat matt black paint. I have created other tree sculptures using clear glass fringe beads and a glass base, and I really like the effect of the contrast between the reflective glass and the flat black matt color of the paint. You can paint the wire on the tree either using spray paint or a brush. I prefer the brush because I do not want to cover every square inch of the tree but want to let some of the color of the wire to show through and act as highlights. Be sure the paint you select will adhere to the metal tree. You can, If you want, choose not to paint the tree and leave the wire as is. If you do not want to paint the tree, skip this section and continue onto "Adding Beads to the Twigs". **NOTE:** Before you paint the tree, try to clean as much of the wire surface as you can using paint thinner or alcohol.

1. Using a Brush Use a small artist brush number 1 or 2, and start painting the tree from the bottom up. If you are using clamps to support the tree, remove them one at a time, paint that area, let it dry, then replace the clamp. If you are using the optional wood base to hold the tree up, paint the entire tree, let it dry, remove the staples or nails that are fixed to the roots. Go back and paint the areas that were unpainted. Use less paint rather than more. You can always go back and add more paint if you need to. Do not be concerned about painting the area of the 26 gauge wire that makes up the loops. This wire will be twisted around the clear fringe beads and you can go back and touch up any of the twisted wire that you feel is showing too much of the bare wire. Remember, leaving some small areas of this wire unpainted, will add to the highlight effects.

2. Using Spray Paint Be sure the paint you have selected will adhere to metal. Read all the instructions on the spray can before you start. When using spray paint, it is very important to follow the instructions for the proper distance from the object while spraying. and, to spray with many light coats rather than one or a few heavy coats. The spray paint will have a tendency to run if applied too quickly or heavily. Be sure the preceding coat of paint is completely dry before you add another coat. Follow the information in step **1**, to apply paint to any unpainted areas that may need covering, you can do this with a brush.

Adding Glass Rocks to the Base You will be adding two more layers of glass rocks to the first layer that you glued to the glass base. It is very important to be sure the base layer of glass is completely dry and set before you proceed. Before you glue the glass rocks, place all of them loosely on top of the first layer so you can see how they will look. Do not place any of the second layer of glass rocks completely to the edge of the first layer, step the second layer in about the distance of one glass rock. Let the second layer dry completely before you start the next layer. Repeat the above instructions to create the third layer. *Fig. 1/98*

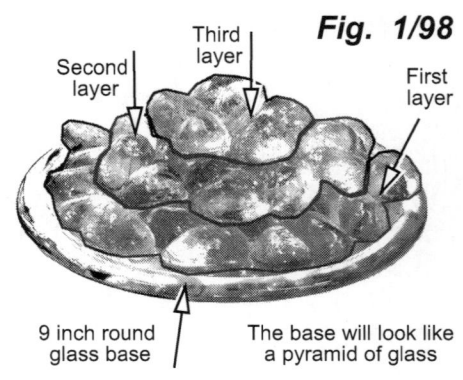

Fig. 1/98

Mounting the Tree onto the Base Whether you are going to add beads to the tree, or not, it will be much easier to work on the tree after it is securely mounted onto the base. Bend all twigs up so that they are not in the way as you work on the base. Bend all the root sections down. Use the point nose pliers to curl the anchor into a circle, this will allow the glue to dry around the root anchor creating a strong bond between the tree and the base. Position the tree on the top of the mound of glass rocks. It does not need to be perfectly centered but can be slightly off to one side of the edge. Use electrical tape that is wrapped several times through the base of the main branches then around the base of the glass base. *Fig. 2/98* You will notice that since you bent all the root sections down, the roots will not lie flat on the top of the glass mound. There will be an empty cavity created under the center of the base of the trunk. This void should be filled with more glass rocks of different sizes, and will help to hold the tree erect and secure it to the base. After you have placed all the various loose rocks in place and they are supporting the tree, glue them using the E6000 glue. After all the various rocks are secured under the trunk, add more assorted glass rocks near and onto the actual roots to add additional bonding between the roots and the base. Let some of the glue seep down between the glass rocks. When you are sure all the glue is dry and the tree is securely bonded to the base, carefully cut away the tape. As a final step and the last time you will be using the glue, add more assorted smaller pieces of glass to fill in between the larger glass rocks, once again let the glue run down between the all the glass pieces. *Fig. 3/98*

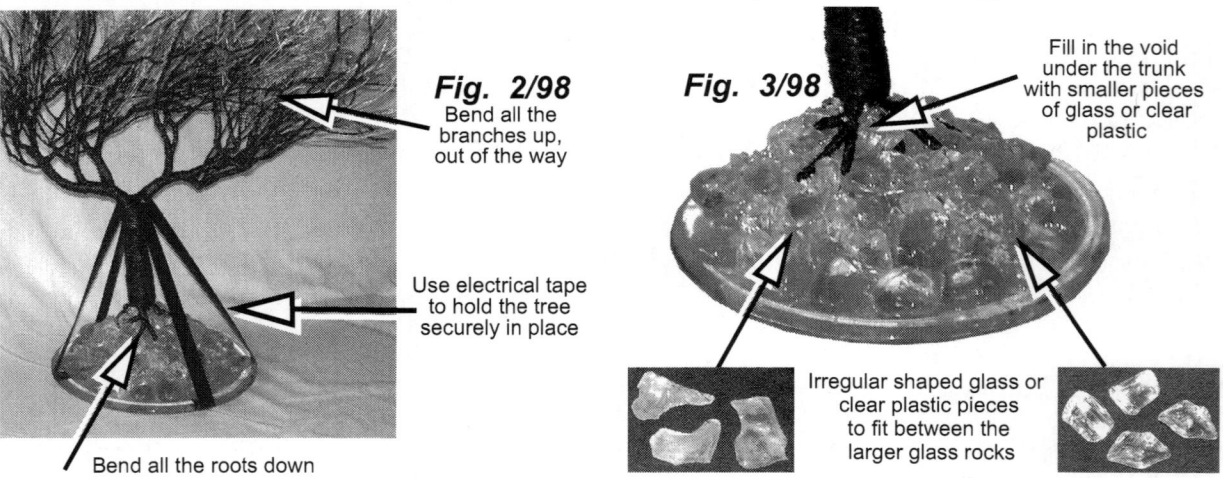

Adding Beads to the Twigs I use "Fringe Beads" I like them because the hole is in the top of the bead allowing the bead to hang from the twig, which gives it a more natural look and lets it move in the breeze so that it can glimmer and reflect the light. You can use any type of bead you like, just be sure the it will fit onto the 26 gauge. **See page 43**

NOTE: If you do not want to create this tree sculpture using glass beads, you can eliminate the beads, cut the loops and twist the loose wires together to create a thicker twig.

Shaping the Tree

1. After all the beads are on all the twigs of the tree it will need to be shaped to create its final look. Separate and spread apart the branches to form a round overall shape of the tree. Look at the tree from above to be sure it is rounded and not flat. The spacing between the main branches should be visually equal. *Fig. 1/99*

Fig. 1/99

Fig. 2/99

2. Starting with any of the branch sections, gently bend all the twigs in that section down at about its mid point and separate them from each other. You can move any of the other branch sections out of the way as you work. *Fig. 2/99*

Fig. 3/99

3. Separate each of the beaded twigs away from each other and bend them up, then down, to create an oval shape. Position some of the beaded twigs on both sides of the branch from which it appears to be "growing" out of. *Fig. 3/99*

4. Continue to shape each of the beaded branch sections as you did in step **3**. As you are creating each of these sections, you may need to push the twigs closer together to make room for the next section. The total amount of branches and twigs will make this a very full tree. *Fig. 1/100*

5. After you have shaped all the branches and twigs, you should once again look at the tree from above to be sure it has the overall rounded look and all of the beaded twigs are separated and are pointing in a downward direction.

6. This tree sculpture, with all its crystal shapes and different angles, will look magnificent when displayed in direct sun or very bright light. As an added effect you can also display the piece with a mirror under the base. *Fig. 2/100*

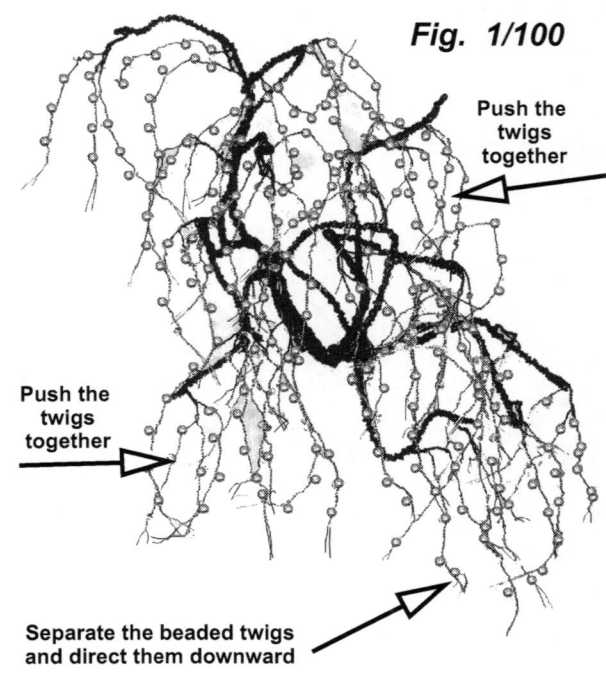

Fig. 1/100

Push the twigs together

Push the twigs together

Separate the beaded twigs and direct them downward

Fig. 2/100

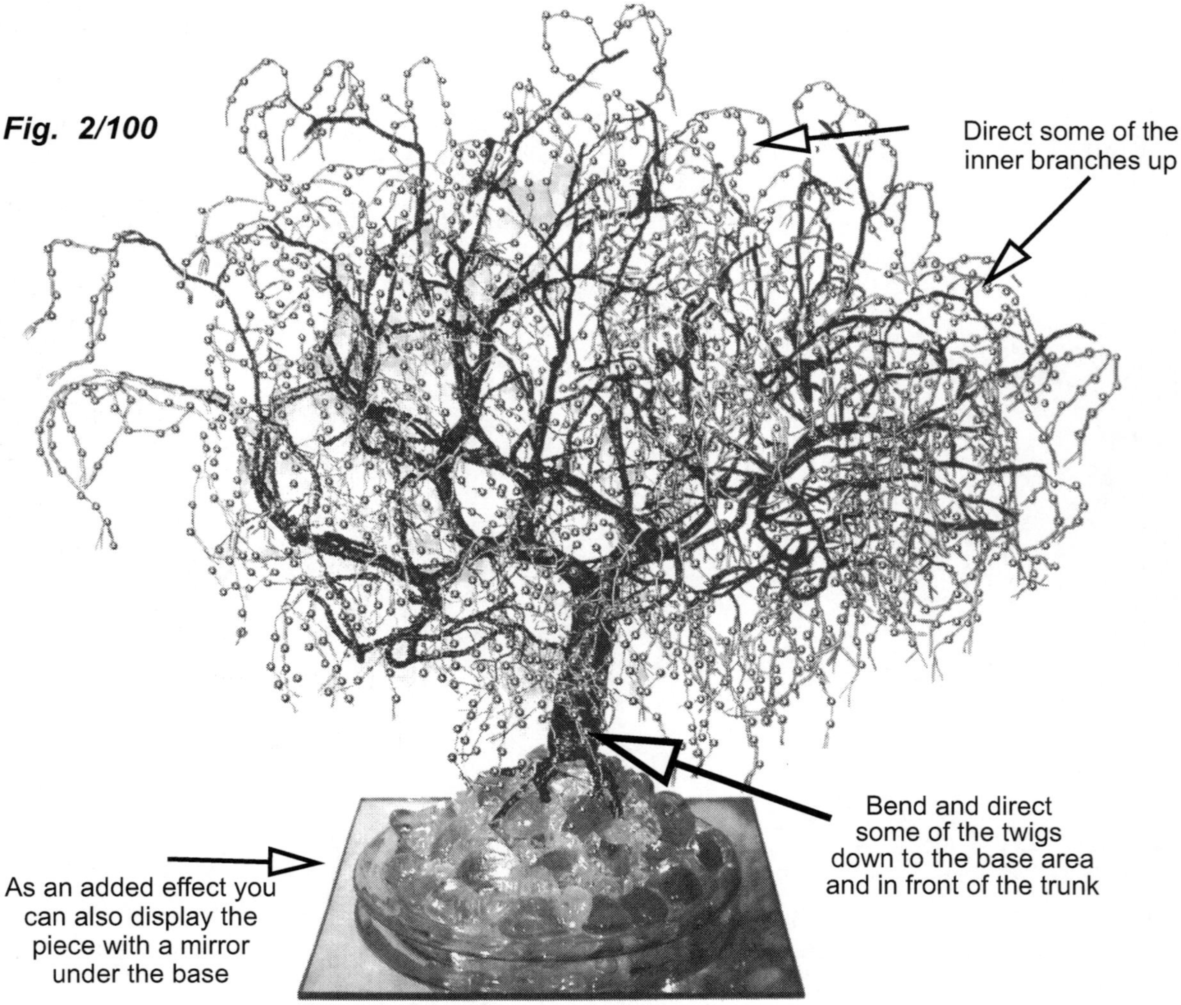

Direct some of the inner branches up

Bend and direct some of the twigs down to the base area and in front of the trunk

As an added effect you can also display the piece with a mirror under the base

To see completed pieces in Full Color, visit my website: www.salvillano.com

Bird Nest in a Branch - *10"h X 10"w X 4"d*

Difficulty Scale: *(1 = easy, 10 = difficult)* **this is a 3**

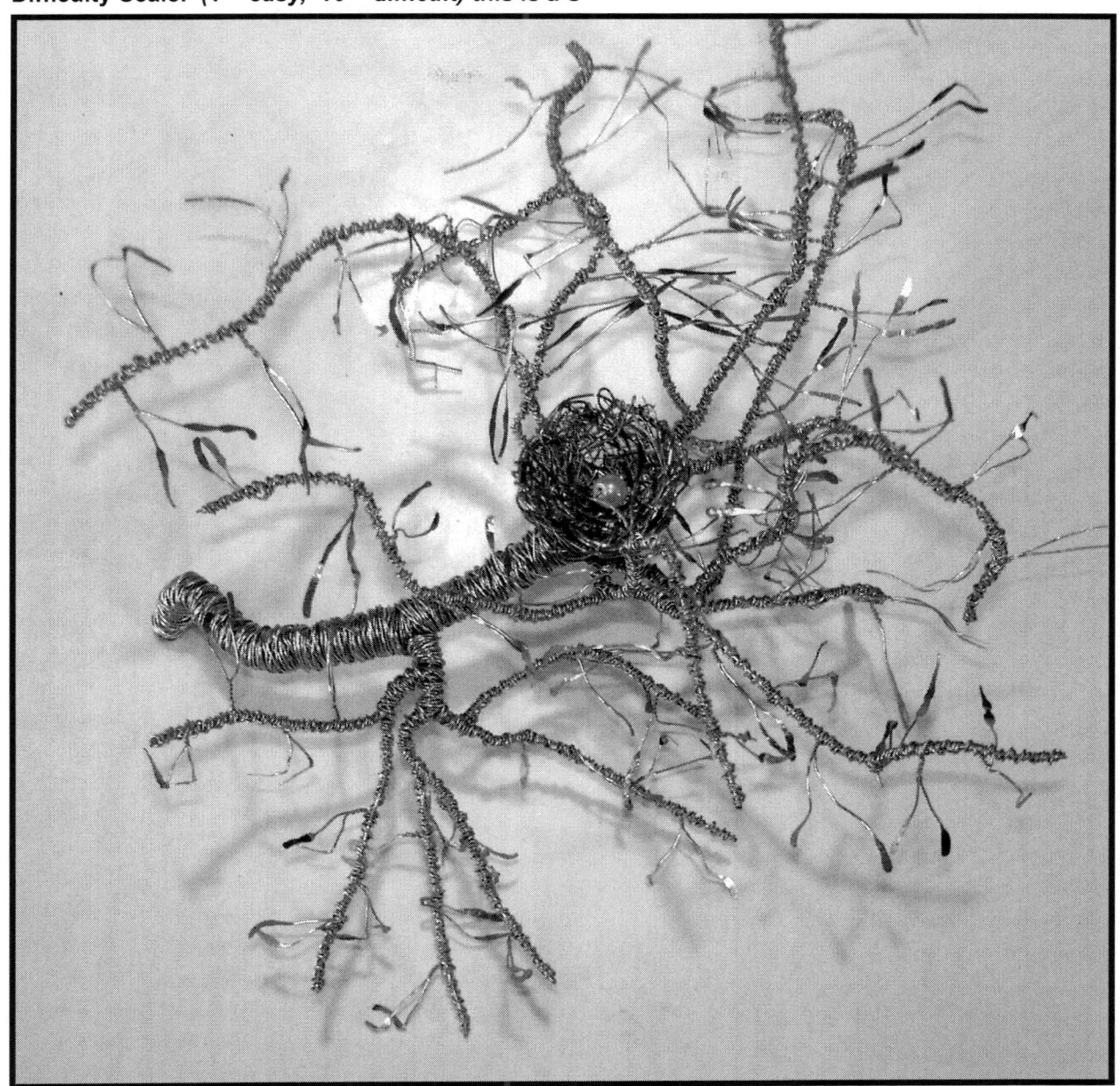

MATERIAL CHECK LIST:

- Three, 6 inch long pieces of 18 gauge 6 strand cable wire
- 26 gauge wire (100 ft.)
- 30 gauge wire (125 ft.)
- Silver or gold leaves (optional)
- Gesso to prime leaves for painting
- Paint for leaves: enamel or spray
- Rock and base for mounting (optional)

TOOLS CHECK LIST:

- Protective eye wear
- Small hammer
- Wide nose pliers
- Bent nose pliers
- Table vise or spring clamps
- Wire cutters, large and small
- Small anvil or flat piece of steel
- 12 inch ruler

To see completed pieces in Full Color, visit my website: www.salvillano.com

This piece is a free standing branch of a tree with a wire nest in among the branches. The nest contains pearl "eggs". I have created many of these pieces that were given as gifts. The significance of the nest containing the eggs is applicable to many important life events such as the birth of a child, a wedding or anniversary and of course Mothers Day. By using gem stones instead of pearls you can apply the piece to many other occasions and events. **See page 125 for gem stone information.** You can also mount the branch on a base **see page 12.** Since spring time represents birth and growing, I have created this piece with green and yellow leaves. You also have the option of adding gems or beads to the twigs to represent buds or fruit s**ee page 43.** Another very interesting effect is to add jade leaves to the branches, instead of painted leaves. **See page 53**

Creating the Branches

1. Cut three, 6 inch pieces of 18 gauge 6 strand cable wire. Using 26 gauge wire, wire the 3 pieces of cable wire together as follows: base piece as is, piece 2, 2 inches up onto the base piece, piece 3, 1 inch up onto piece 2. **Fig. 1/102** Wire each piece for about 1 inch onto the next. (the 26 gauge wire will now be called the source wire)

2. Wrap the source wire up and back over the first wraps 6 times. This will create 3 smaller branches growing out of a larger branch. End this wrapping at the bottom of the branch. **Fig. 2/102**

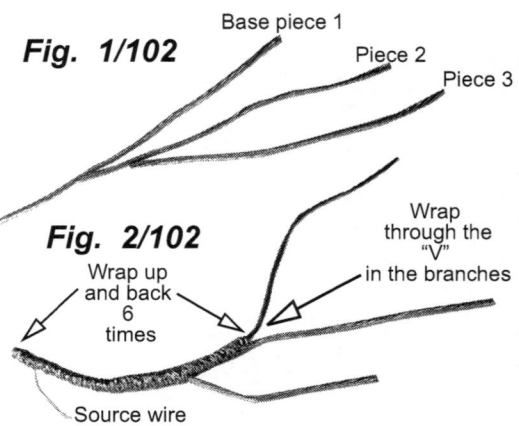

3. Separate the 6 wires of each of the cable wires. Twist all 6 wires of each group together for about 1/4 inch, then 2 for about 1/4 inch, then 4 for about 1/4 inch, then finally the last 4 for about 1/4 inch. This will result in 18 branches. **Fig. 3/102**

4. Wrap the source wire up and onto each twig then back to the bottom one time. End at the bottom of the branch. Wrap this wire through the "V" created where the two twigs separate. **Fig. 4/102**

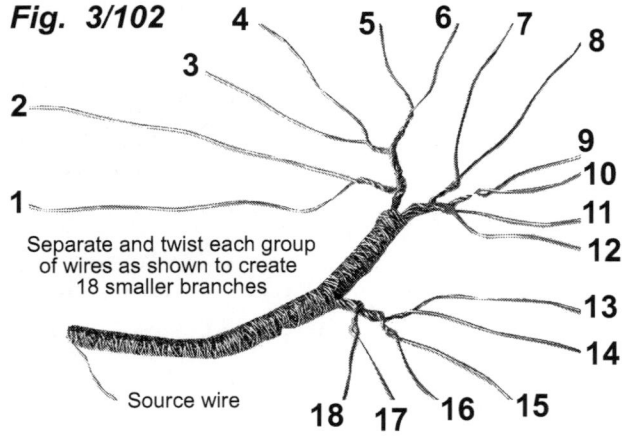

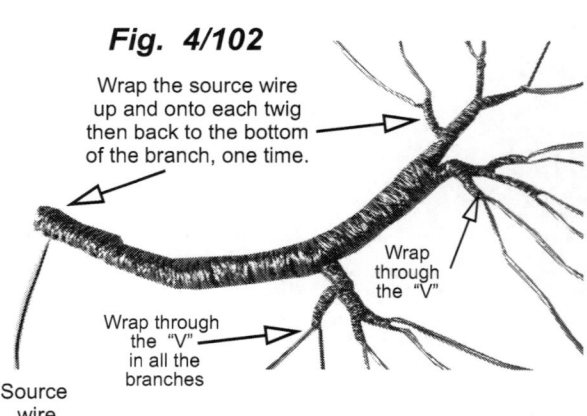

Creating the Leaves

1. Wrap the source wire up the branch then out onto the first twig you come to. Bend any branches or twigs that get in your way as you are working. Continue to wrap the source wire all the way out to the end of the twig. Wrap back toward the branch and stop.

2. Create a 1 inch loop with the source wire. Using the bent nose pliers, twist the base of the loop for 1/4 inch. Continue to wrap for 1/2 inch more and create another loop. Repeat this process for all the twigs. Create as many loops that will fit on the twigs. **See page 103, Fig. 1/103** You may find it easier to work on the leaves by using a table vice or a few spring clamps to hold the branch in place as you work on it.

3. As the final use of the source wire, wrap it all the way down to about 1/4 inch from the end of the main branch. Cut off about 2 inches of the wire and tie it into a knot. Snip off excess wire close to the knot. Bend the end of the wire into the branch and flatten it. *Fig. 1/103*

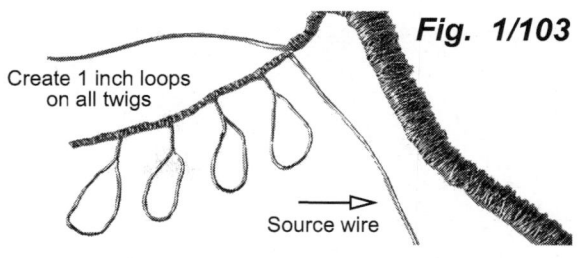

4. Starting with any twig, bend the loops so they are alternately opposite each other. Using the small wire cutters, cut the loops across the tops to create 2 separate pieces of wire that will become leaves *Fig. 2/103*

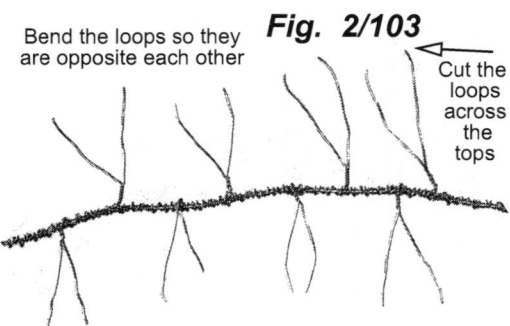

5. Hammer the wire ends on a small anvil, the side of a large hammer, or a flat piece of steel, flattening the ends of the loops. *See page 73* Do not over hammer the wire, each leaf should only require 5 or 6 blows to create a leaf. You may want to practice creating leaves on some scrap wire before starting. Carefully create all the leaves on all the twigs. *Fig. 3/103*

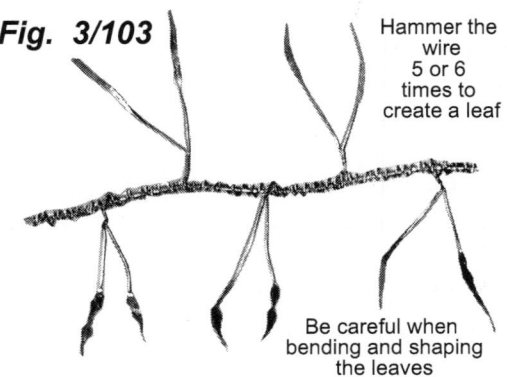

Shaping the Leaves If you are going to paint the leaves proceed to the next step (Painting the Leaves) before you shape the leaves. Be sure all the leaves are totally dry on both sides before you shape them. Using the wide nose pliers, bend or twist most of the leaves in the center to create a more realistic and varied look. Be very careful as you bend or twist the leaves, they are delicate so do not over twist or bend. Once again you may want to practice this on some scrap wire. *See page 73* for more information about creating leaves

Painting the Leaves If you are going to paint the leaves you should do so while they are flat. Be sure the paint you choose will adhere to the flattened metal wire. I like to paint the leaves with a few different colors. What I do is paint all the leaves with a basic dark green base. Then I dab small amounts of lighter green and yellows. As a final touch I paint a very small part of the tip of the leaf white. Of course you can paint the leaves to express any season. Be sure you paint the top and the bottom of the leaves. *See page 74*

Creating a Nest For complete instructions on how to create the nest *See page 48*

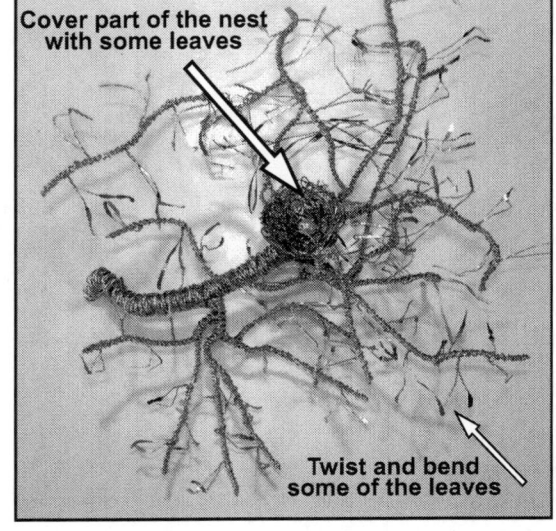

Shaping the Branches After the nest is mounted onto the branch and securely fixed in place, carefully bend some of the twigs over the top of the nest. This will give the piece a very natural look. Most birds want to hide their nests as much as possible. *Fig. 4/103*

To see completed pieces in Full Color, visit my website: www.salvillano.com

Adding Manufactured Leaves to Twigs

Difficulty Scale: *(1 = easy, 10 = difficult)* **this is a 2**

Fig. 1/104

Be sure the leaf has a hole in the bottom

As an alternative to creating the leaves by hammering the ends of the wire flat, you can use small mass produced manufactured leaves. These leaves are very easy to attach to the twigs on your piece. The leaves I show here are Oak Leaves. The size is about 1/2 inch high by 3/8 inch wide. They have a small hole through the bottom of the leaf. There are many different types of leaves that will work fine on your piece. Just be sure the leaf has the small hole in the bottom to attach the wire to. You can purchase these leaves at most large craft stores that sell jewelry supplies or you can go on line to get them. **Fig. 1/104**

Color for the Leaves

I purchase the leaves I need in gold or silver colors. I have used the gold color leaves to create several 50th wedding anniversary pieces, both trees and nests. I use the silver leaves to create pieces for 25th wedding anniversary pieces. You can also use the silver leaves and paint them to create any color leaves you want. To paint the leaves you can use enamel paint (the type that is used to paint models), spray paint or you can use a base of "Gesso". Gesso is a white paint mixture consisting of a binder mixed with chalk, It is used as a base for paint and other materials that are applied over it. Before you paint all the leaves, test one to be sure the paint you are using will adhere to the surface. As you are selecting or creating color for the leaves try to mix different shades of the same color. For example; for summer leaves, do not paint them all the same color green, try to use different shades or hues. This will create a more realistic effect. Do the same for a fall tree. Use yellows, reds, oranges and even leave some of the leaves a pale green.

Wiring the Leaves to the Twigs

1. If you choose to add color to the leaves do so before you add the wire to the leaf that is going to secure the leaf to the twig. Be sure you add the color to both sides of the leaves as described above and the entire leaf is dry. Paint and complete enough leaves for the entire piece you are working on. It is much better to have all the leaves at the ready rather than going back to prepare more. Using the size leaf I describe here, you will need about 1 leaf for each inch of the twig where you are adding the leaves. This is a minimum, you can add more leaves if you want a fuller piece. When I set up to create these leaves, I always make more leaves than I need, and use the extras on other projects.

2. The wire I use for these leaves is 30 gauge. It will be used to create the leaf anchors and also to secure the leaf to the twig. You can use a thicker gauge wire, such as 26 gauge, just be sure it will fit into the hole in the leaves you have selected. Try to use a color wire that will match the color of the twig where you are securing the leaves.

3. Cut a 4 inch length of your source wire (the wire you chose for the leaves) for each of the leaves. Loop the wire in half. Place the looped end of the wire over the bottom section of the leaf. Hold the leaf firmly and turn it over. Pass one end of the wire, then

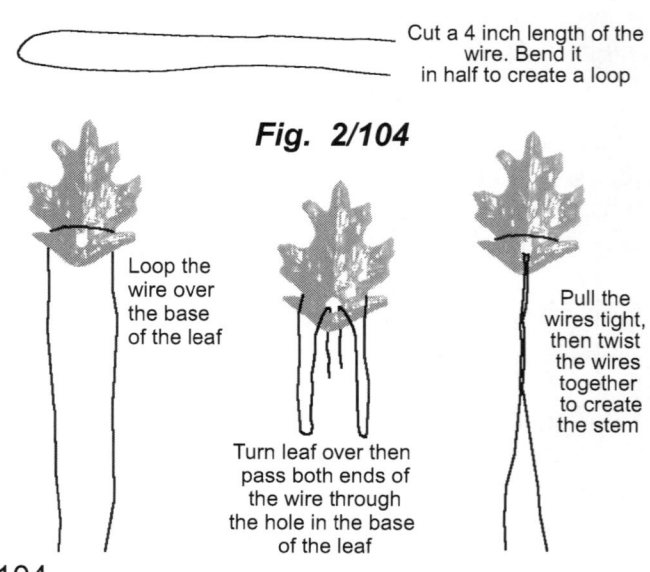

Cut a 4 inch length of the wire. Bend it in half to create a loop

Fig. 2/104

Loop the wire over the base of the leaf

Turn leaf over then pass both ends of the wire through the hole in the base of the leaf

Pull the wires tight, then twist the wires together to create the stem

104

the other end, through the hole in the bottom of the leaf. Hold the leaf in one hand, as you gently pull on the two anchor wires, (if you have difficulty pulling the wires with your fingers, use the flat nose pliers) this action will secure the wire to the leaf. Twist the two anchor wires together for about 1/2 inch. The twisting of the 2 wires will create the stem for the leaf. Repeat the above for all the leaves. **See page 104 Fig. 2/104**

4. Spread the 2 leaf anchors apart so that they are parallel to the twig upon which you are going to attach the leaf. Twist each of the anchor wires onto the twig. Wrap the anchors as tight as you can on the twig. Twist source wire onto the twig and on top of the two anchors. Wrap the source wire to the end of the twig and back once. This action will securely hold the leaf in place and give the twig a texture that will make it look more realistic. *Fig. 1/105* Repeat the above for all the leaves. This method of fastening leaves to twigs can be used on almost any tree you create. You can even go back to a wire tree you have completed and add these type of leaves to it.

Fig. 1/105

Spread the 2 leaf anchors apart so that they are parallel to the twig

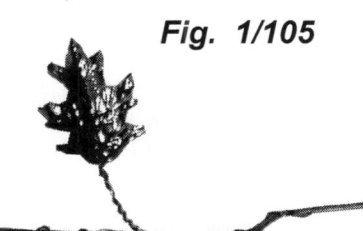

Twist the ends of the leaf anchors wires around the twig

Use the source wire to wrap over the leaf anchors. This will hold the leaves on the twig and cover the leaf anchors

The branch can be left as a free standing piece or mounted onto a base. **See page 12** for base more selections.

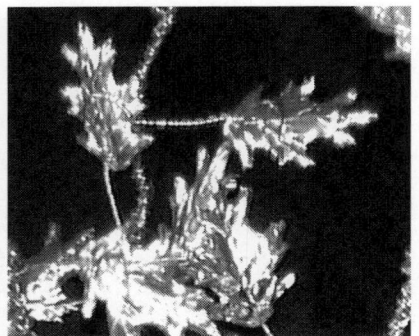

Twist and bend the small twigs that are attached to the leaves.

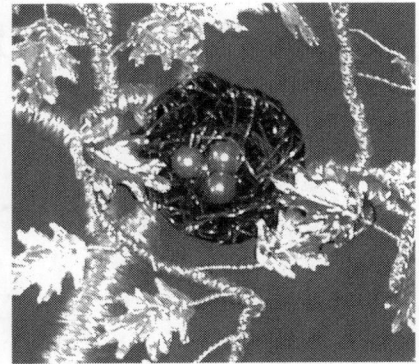

Wire the nest onto a branch, then bend a few of the leave over the top of the nest.

To see completed pieces in Full Color, visit my website: www.salvillano.com

Creating Larger Trees
Many people who have used my other books to create tree sculpture have asked if it is possible to use the same steps that created smaller trees to create larger trees? The answer is a definite yes! I have experimented many times and each of the pieces I created I was very pleased with. The way to do this is to scale up all the sizes and amounts of wire in direct proportion to the piece you want to create. The best way for you to try this is to use a simple smaller tree like the Weeping Willow shown on **Page 39** and double all the size information about the wire lengths while increasing the wire gauge by 2. For example, if the smaller tree is created using 26 gauge wire, you should increase the gauge to 24. (Remember the lower the gauge number, the thicker the wire, so 24 gauge wire is thicker than 26 gauge.) Of course the number of wraps must also be increased. You will have to use your own judgement to determine if you like the amount of wraps on the parts of the tree. You should also keep in mind that the way you wrap the wire may be different than the way I do. As you are wrapping you should periodically stop and look at the piece to see if the proportions are correct. Remember, you can always add more wire, but it is very difficult to remove it.

Working on Several Trees at a Time
At this point in my tree creating career, I find it much easier and more fun to work on several trees at the same time. Since I am working on many trees, I really don't know when each will be finished. This keeps my mind focused on the specific task at hand and not on trying to complete the piece I am working on. I may put a piece aside and not work on it for several weeks, then when I come back to it, I look at it with "fresh eyes" and can really focus on how I want the piece to look. Unfortunately, this system cannot be applied when I am working on a piece that has a deadline.

Completing the Steps
You have now completed all the steps and procedures necessary to create tree sculpture. I hope you are happy with the results. I have tried to make the steps as simple and as clear as possible. Most of what I have learned about creating tree sculpture and working with the wire has come from trial and error, sometimes more "error" than I like to admit. I have always tried to learn something new from the piece I am working on, and the things to do and not to do before I start the next piece.

If you would like to see more of my work, please visit my website listed below. And, once again, I hope you are happy with the your tree sculpture creation. Do not forget to look at the first piece I created on **Page 3** and compare it to your own!

I would be happy to hear from you with any comments, questions or suggestions about my work or this book. You can contact me at:

Sal Villano
PO Box 827 Milford, Ohio 45150

email: salvillano@gmail.com
website: www.salvillano.com

No phone calls please.

Extras

I titled this final section of the book "Extras". Although it is not part of creating tree sculptures, I think you will find it very helpful if you intend to promote and sell your work. You can, if you want, photocopy and use any of the information and forms printed in this section. The topics that I cover are:

Shipping Tree Sculptures	108
Accepting Commissions	109
Offering Your Work on Consignment	110
Art and Craft Shows	111
Keeping Accurate Records	112
Promoting and Selling Your Work	114
Websites Free or Pay	116
Pricing Your Work	118
Master Control Book	119
Photographing Your Work	121
Creating a Website	122
Suppliers List	124
Charts, Tables and Forms	125
Consignment Agreement	126
Certificate of Title	127
Certificate of Authenticity	127
Follow Up Letter	128
Gallery Request	129
Arts Application	129
Art Publication Request	129
Inquiry From a Gallery	130
Price Confirmation and Delivery	130
Thank You Letter	130
Press Release	131
Website Link Exchange	131

Shipping Tree Sculptures

The way I ship my tree sculpture is by using a "box within a box" system. For example, if the sculpture is 8" x 8" x 8", I wire the tree onto the inside bottom and sides of a box that is a least 10" x 10" x 10". The tree sculpture is secured with wire, into the center on the bottom of this inner box so that none of the branches ever touch any of the sides or inside top of this box. The inner box is then sealed and put into another larger outer box and bubble wrap is placed around the sides, top and bottom of the box with the tree sculpture in it. I have been told by some of my customers that boxes have arrived upside down and battered, however, due to the cushioning around all the sides of the inner box, the sculpture arrives safe and sound. I have shipped thousands of tree sculptures of all sizes, as far away as Japan and India, and I have never had any problems or had any of the sculptures returned or damaged.

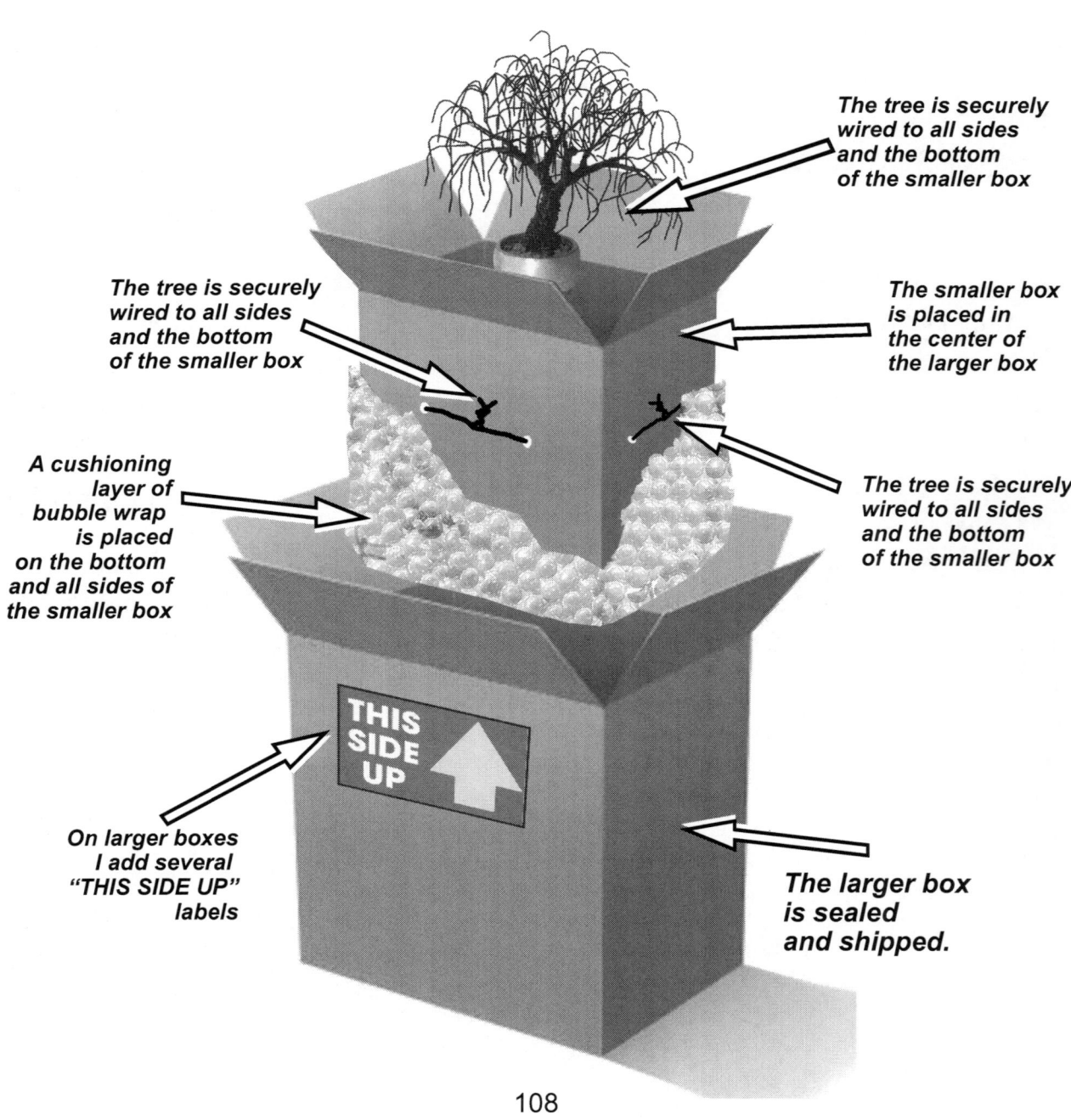

Accepting Commissions

Hopefully, as your art work gets better and better, and you create more and more pieces, someone will ask if you "Do Commissions". Do not be afraid to say yes. But be sure you get all the necessary input before you begin. I have completed many commissions for: anniversaries, weddings, (I created 80 small oak trees that were given as favors to the guests, at my sons wedding) birthdays, child births, and even corporate awards. The first thing I do before I accept a commission is to "lay down" the ground rules, in writing. In fact I have the information about accepting commissions clearly stated on my web site. Since I have a large number of different pieces on my web site, the first step is to ask the person to go to my web site and select the piece on the site that most resembles what they want. I also have a page on my website that says "sold work" with the statement: "This piece is sold, I can create a similar piece in about 6 to 8 weeks." Since I keep records of all the sizes and material used for each piece, it is very easy for me to create a piece similar to one I have also created. If you don't yet have a website, you should have a portfolio of your work. Your portfolio should contain photos, detailed descriptions and prices of every piece you feel is worthy of showing to the public. I would suggest you purchase a professional "artists portfolio" rather then simply placing your work in a 3 ring binder. Remember, the better your work is presented the better your chances of getting a commission.

The following is the Commission Statement that I present on my web site. Feel free to use all or any part of it, if you like. Be sure you insert your name where indicated!

COMMISSIONS

The way I handle Sculpture Commissions ..

1. You describe, in as much detail as possible, the type of sculpture you want me to create, the approximate budget and the time frame.

2. I will give you an exact time frame and final costs. I am currently requiring a 6 to 8 week lead time for all new work.

3. Payment schedule is: 1/3 down to start. 1/3 when I send you photos of the completed piece. Final 1/3 is due before I can ship the piece.

4. Type of payments I accept: PayPal, Bank Check, Money Order.

5. I ship and insure the piece only after payment in full.

6. I offer a full money back guarantee. You can return the piece within seven days for a full refund, exchange or credit, less any shipping.

I have completed hundreds of commissions and shipped them all over the world, and I find this arrangement works best for my clients and me. If you have any questions, please do not hesitate to contact me at:
YOUR INFORMATION HERE.

Offering Your Work "On Consignment"

When you offer your work on consignment you allow someone to sell your work for you but you retain full ownership of the piece until it is sold. Usually the consignment fee to the establishment is 35 to 40 percent of the retail price. I have placed my work on consignment in galleries, gift shops, restaurants, coffee houses, websites, and other retail outlets. I even have my work on two internet sites that sell living Bonsai trees. Before you place your work anywhere, be sure your work fits into the type of work that is offered in the establishment. You should also keep in mind that there are other places that may be willing to show your work, such as office or apartment lobbies, wedding shops, and florists. I even know of an artist who creates very peaceful landscapes and offers them for sale in funeral parlors. If you do decide to place your work on consignment be sure you are very specific with the terms and have everything in writing. Remember if you place a piece on consignment, you are giving them the right to sell the piece before you can offer it for sale again. You should always have a specific length of time that you are willing to leave the work with the consignee. Although I do not mention it in my agreement, you should ask if your work is insured while in their possession. I do not mention it in my agreement because I have all my work insured with a rider policy on my homeowners insurance. Important: never leave any art unless this agreement is signed. *See page 126* for a full size, printable copy of this Consignment Agreement.

NOTE: If you choose to use this form be sure you add "YOUR NAME" where indicated!

CONSIGNMENT AGREEMENT FOR ART

This agreement is in effect from _____ to _____ and may be terminated by either party at any time. This agreement is between **YOUR NAME**_____
and:_____
Located at: _____
The art work described below is owned by **YOUR NAME** while offered for sale at the above named establishment for the full retail price indicated on each piece. The proceeds of each sale are to be divided as follows: _____% for establishment and _____% for **YOUR NAME**. The above establishment is responsible for the sale and the payment of any sales tax due. Notice of sale, copy of sales receipt and payment must be made to **YOUR NAME** within 7 days of the sale. Art work will be shipped to the establishment at the expense of **YOUR NAME** and any unsold art work returned to **YOUR NAME** will be shipped at the expense of the establishment.

LIST OF ART WORK AND RETAIL PRICE:

NAME & ITEM NUMBER	RETAIL PRICE
_____	_____
_____	_____
_____	_____
_____	_____
_____	_____
_____	_____

Total Number of Items_____   Total $_____
Signed for Establishment_____ Print Name _____
Signed by **YOUR NAME** _____ Today's Date _____
Page ___ of ___

Art And Craft Shows

I have been doing art and craft shows for many years. I have found that not only do I sell many tree sculptures and my books, but I also meet like minded artists and some very interesting and helpful people. I still do shows, but after years of wear and tear on my equipment and my body, plus dealing with pouring rain or boiling heat, I now only do indoor events that are close to my home, and only if I have someone to help me. Having said all that, I think attending art shows or quality craft shows is vital to selling your work, meeting new people and promoting yourself. In general, before I enter a show I always try to attend it to see the type of artwork or crafts that are present. Do not hesitate to do a show that is promoted only as a "Craft Show" however it should be a juried show so you know someone is aware of the type of work being submitted. To make preparing for the shows easier and more effective, I have a "Master Show List" of all the things I need to take or do for the show. I change and add to my list before, during and after each show. My master show list is one of the best aids I have ever created!

The following is a list of criteria and other information about attending shows:

1. THE TOTAL COST OF THE SPACE.
When considering the cost of the actual space, you also need to keep in mind travel time and any living or food expenses.

2. IS THE SHOW AN ANNUAL EVENT.
Chances are that the longer the show has been running, the larger the number of people attending and the more time the promoters have had to work out the bugs.

3. HOW LONG HAVE THE PROMOTERS BEEN IN BUSINESS.
Reputable promoters stay in business, bad ones tend to go away!

4. ASK FELLOW ARTISTS HAVE THEY EVER DONE THIS SHOW.
I keep in touch with fellow artists I meet at art shows, and ask them their opinion of the shows they have been in.

5. KEEP ACCURATE RECORDS OF ALL THE SHOWS YOU ATTEND.
I keep records of all the work I sold, the name, address and email of all who purchased any of my work. I also have a "Sign Up" sheet available for anyone who wants to be on my mailing list. I use this list to let people know of my up coming shows.

6. WORK ON YOUR ART WHILE AT THE SHOW.
Every time I set up my booth for a show I always leave some room where I can actually work on my sculpture. People are always interested in seeing an artist at work.

7. BE WILLING AND HAPPY TO ANSWERING ALL QUESTIONS.
I am always happy to answer all the questions people ask. Sometimes I may answer the same few questions 50 or 60 times at one show. I enjoy answering the questions because it shows people are interested in my work. People who visit your booth are unaware of how many times you have answered the same question. You should try to answer it as if this was the first time you heard it!

Keeping Accurate Records

One of the most efficient and important things you can do for yourself is to keep accurate records of all your work. For an artist, this means also taking photographs of all the pieces you create, even if you do not like them! Once you get in the routene of recording all the items you create, it will become second nature and you will do it automatically. I have my system set up so that as soon as I finish a piece, I photograph it, and assign it an item number. Then I write the copy for it, price it, add the website location numbers at the bottom of the page, and add it to my "Master Control Book" see page **See page 119** Finally I put it on the "Home Page" of my website with the heading "New".

The following are some of the other items I keep records of. I keep the different lists in various programs on my computer. Before computers all this information was indexed on 3 x 5 cards, which was much more time consuming and not as accurate. You can create all these lists programs using Microsoft Excel, Microsoft Word, or other similar programs. It also important to keep your lists updated.

GENERAL MAILING LIST

It is very important for you to create and maintain mailing lists (Data Base). There are several very good mailing list programs available, and they are not expensive. I use one called "My Mail List". I find it easy to use, and I can customize it for my own needs. Your lists should include an email address. I have many different list headings yet the program I use enables me to merge all the lists together should I want to create a large master list. I keep all my mailing lists separated by catagories such as:

CUSTOMERS: This is a list of anyone who ever purchased anything from me and any commissions. It contains name, address, phone number, email, website, details of items purchased, where purchased, dates, and an area for any notes I may want to add such as; if they have purchased from me previously.

SUPPLIERS: All the detailed information about all the supplies I use, listed by product, price and date. I also note any person I have contacted within the company.

OTHER ARTISTS: Here I list any, sculptors, painters, photographers and crafters that I have communicated with, and some general information about them. I also note if I have a web link with their site and mine.

INTERESTING WEBSITES: These are websits I find interesting, or sites where I may be able to show my work or I may wish to exchange links with.

WEBSITES SELLING MY WORK: All the websites that offer my work for sale, with all the important information about the site.

GALLERIES SELLING MY WORK: All the galleries selling my work, plus all the information about the gallery and the contact people.

OTHER OUTLETS SELLING MY WORK: This list is any outlet selling my work other than websites or galleries with all the information about the establishment.

DIRECTORIES: There are websites called "Directories". They are simply listings of websites by category. I try to get listed on as many as possible under the headings of artist or sculpture. Most of these sites allow you to describe your website and add your link. Some of them want you to add a link from your site back to theirs, which I always do.

ART & CRAFT SHOWS: Here is where I keep all the information about all the shows I have been in, and the shows I would like to be in. I list all the requirements, direction, costs and add notes about the show after I have been in it.

PUBLICATIONS: All the publications I receive that relate to artists or sculpture, including newsletters and blogs. I keep this information in a list form because when I create a new piece, that I feel it may be of interest to the readers of certain publications, I send them an email with information about piece and I attach a photo. I send it to them in the form of a "Press Release". Most publications are very receptive to this type of information and are always looking for new or different ideas in the art field. I have had my work in publications about Bonsai, Beading, Wire, Sculpture and even a publication from China that specializes in Fantasy Pieces".

AWARDS I HAVE RECEIVED: A list of all my awards. I list the show names, dates, the award I received and any other relevant information. Some art shows ask for this information as part of their application process, so it's a good idea to have it where you can easily get to it.

TESTIMONIALS: Every time someone sends me an unsolicited testimonial about my work I save it. After I list all their information, I add the actual wording of the testimonial to the notes section of the list. I have used testimonials of my work and my books on my site in a section called appropriately, "Testimonials about My Work".

CHECK LIST FOR SHOWS: I keep a check list of all the things I need to do my shows. Everything I need for the show is listed. I have had the same list for years, and have added to it and changed it many times. Having this list makes it much easier and more organized when I have to prepare for a show on a Friday evening that's opening on Saturday morning. I print out my list, then check off the items as I load them.

PURCHASING MAILING LISTS: I have, from time to time, purchased outside mailing lists to try to get more business, but I no longer do. I find them to be too expensive (sometimes ranging from 50 cents to a dollar per name), and not very accurate. Plus, most of the companies who sell these lists will only allow you to use the list once. And I never offer my mailing lists for sale or rent. What I have done if I want a list of, for example, art galleries, is created my own list from the phone book. It takes some time, but once you do it, the list you created is yours to use as often as you like.

A FINAL NOTE ABOUT MAILING LISTS: Your lists are only as good as they are accurate. It is very important to "clean" you list at least once a year. It makes no sense to do a mailing to art galleries, if half of them are out of business! Never loan or sell your mailing list to anyone or any company, your client list is your lifeline to sales!

Promoting and Selling Your Work

Before you attempt selling your work you will need to have a large enough body of work to show variety and consistency of the art you are creating. It is a proven fact that the more pieces you show, the more you will sell. There are many different ways to promote and sell your work. Some are more effective than others. But it's the combination of all the different ways of promoting that will add up to your overall selling success. It may not be possible for you to participate in all of the venues listed, but you should try to do as many as you can, as often as you can. Always try to keep expanding your outlets. It is always a good idea to share with other artists any ideas, successes and failures they may have encountered. Before you start to promote your work you should have printed material at the ready, such as Business Cards, Letterheads, Invoices, Brochures, and Hang Tags. These items are basic tools necessary for anyone who wants to sell their work. The following is a list of some of the ways you can use to promote and sell your work.

GALLERIES: *Full Service Galleries:* These galleries will accept your work and sell it to their clients or the general public. Do not walk into any gallery with your work or your portfolio in hand. Always call them, or email, to ask about how you can present your work for consideration in their gallery. You could also request the gallery to visit your website to determine if your work is for them. Do not get discouraged if a gallery does not want to show your work. Galleries sometimes specialize in certain types of art, and yours may not be a good fit. Usually galleries will take a 40 to 50 percent commission. Some galleries are now not only asking for a commission, but also want to charge you rent to show your work. I never offer my work to galleries that have this as their policy.

Co-op Galleries: This type of gallery is created when a group of artists get together to rent or buy space and share the overhead. This arrangement can work out very well for the artists involved. Usually these galleries have the largest variety of work on display covering every square inch of the walls and floor. As a participant in the gallery, you may be required to spent time in the gallery and act as a salesperson for everyones work. This is called "Gallery Sitting". Sometimes, in very successful galleries, the artists will also hire staff to run the gallery, freeing the artists to create their work. It is important that all the rules, responsibilities, and obligations of all the artists involved, are clearly stated in writing. This is my favorite type of arrangement because of the variety of art and artists.

Rent Space in a Gallery: With this arrangement you rent an area within an existing gallery. Usually the space is about 8 X 10 feet. You pay a monthly rental fee, it can be anywhere from $150.00 per month and up. Plus you also pay a small commission (5 to 10 percent) on the sale of any of your work that is sold by anyone other than you. There may also be a fee to process any transaction that passes through the credit card terminal of the gallery. I have had very good results with this type of gallery. I not only sold my work from my space, but on weekends, when the gallery was much busier than during the week, I would set up a small area in my space and work on some of my smaller pieces. Visitors to the gallery seemed to enjoy seeing "The Artist at Work" and having the opportunity to ask questions. I enjoyed this interaction, and have even gotten some very good ideas from the questions that the visitors asked.

ART REPS: This is a general category of people or organizations that will sell your work for you, for a commission. They could be: Other artists, (a few years ago, I sold my work through a photographer who specializes in photographing only trees. When his photographs were displayed with my tree sculpture, the effect was very impressive, and we both sold many pieces), Art Consultants, Art Brokers, Designers, Decorators. Reps can be anyone who is willing, and able to sell your work for a commission. Their commission can range from 30%, at the low end, to 65% for someone with good connections who is able to sell a great deal of your work. Reps. may also be in the position to obtain commissions for you. You should be sure you have a very clearly written agreement with any rep. you deal with. Before you begin to work with a rep. some of the questions you should ask are: who else do they represent, who are some of the clients they sell to, and how long have they been in business. The rep. should be willing to answer any question you have. Most reps will not represent a new artist unless they have an impressive body of work and a selling record. Or if the artists have been recommended by a client or another artist. Once again, good sources to find a rep. are other artists, the yellow pages of local phone books, or the internet.

RETAIL OUTLETS: Placing your work in other retail outlets can also be a very good way to get more sales. I have offered my work for sale in: Gift Shops, Jewelry Stores, Bead Shops and Craft Stores. As a selling tool I ask the owner of the store if I can use my own display. I have curio cabinets with lights in them, that present my work in a very professional way. I have found that it is much better to keep all my work together, rather than a piece here and a piece there. The owners are usually receptive to this idea since I take care of all the work involved in displaying my work. All the rules that apply to offering your work to galleries, apply here.

STATIONARY: In order to create a professional image for you and your work, you should have you own stationary. It is very easy to do this with the many "Create your own printed matter" websites available. *Vistaprint.com* and *PSprint.com* are two of the larger web sites offering complete printing services and a multitude of products, but there are many more. They offer products from basic business cards to complete website creation. I have used both for various projects, and both are easy to use, offering templates to help you create what ever you need. You can also use a local print shop, if you do not want to go on line to create the products. Your local print shop will most likely charge you more than the on line printers, but you will get personal service from them. I would suggest you keep all your designs simple and easy to read. Be sure to include all the important information about you on all your printed matter. Such as: Name, Address, All Phone Numbers, email address, and your website. If you are in a local gallery, you may also want to include a map on the back of the business card. The items I use to promote myself and my work are: Business Cards, Letterheads, Envelopes, Invoices, Price Tags, Shipping Labels and a simple Brochure showing a cross section of my work and my "About the Artist" information. I also created a flyer that offers 10% off and free shipping in the USA and Canada. I include this flyer whenever I ship any sculpture or books that I have sold.

DIRECT MAIL: This term is used when referring to promotional material that is mailed to your prospective clients. It can take the form of: Post Cards, Brochures, Newsletters, to name a few. With the advent of the internet, and email, this type of promotion has become less effective and more costly. The only type of Direct Mail I now use is Post Cards. I use them to announce new work I created and any gallery or show I am in.

EMAIL PROMOTION: In my opinion this is the most effective way of promoting you, your work, and any upcoming events you are in. I keep separate email lists in various categories to mail to the appropriate recipient when needed.

YOUR WEBSITE: After you have created your website and have it live on line, **See page 122** you will need to promote it. It's not very effective to have a beautiful website but no visitors. You can, of course hire a company to promote your site but this can be very expensive, and much of the services they offer, you can do for yourself. If you want to promote your site on your own, one of the best books on the subject is: *"101 Ways to Promote Your Website"* written by Susan Sweeney, C.A. It is available through Maximum Press at: www.maxpress.com. I have followed the suggestions in this book to promote my website and find it very well written and useful.

ART WEBSITES:

One of the most effective and inexpensive ways to promote and therefor sell your work is through your website. Your website is your 24 hours a day, 7 days a week, 365 days a year gallery, showing all your work and allowing your visitors to easily communicate with you. A very good way to promote your site is on art sites that promote artists and allow you to add a link to your site from their site. Most of these sites are free but some do have a small monthly or yearly charge and charge a small fee to handle the transaction if someone purchases a piece form their site. I have found the sites that charge are worth the money since I have sold work far surpassing the cost of being on the site. I am listed on the following sites. You should visit the site to see if it is a good place to show your work.

ADD www. TO THE BEGINNING OF EACH LISTING.

FREE ART WEBSITES:

ads4world.com
absolutearts.com
alibaba.com
art-3000.com
artabus.com
artavita.com
artbistro.monster.com/
artbracket.com
artbreak.com
artchain.com
artists.de
artfeedback.com
artid.com
artistrising.com
artistsites.org
buy-and-sell-art.com
artprice.com
artmetal.com
artpatron.com
artq.net
artquest.com
artslant.com
arttract.com
artwanted.com
beetlebird.com
behance.net
bluecanvas.com
buysellcommunity.com
celesteprize.com
craftjuice.com
craftori.com
craigslist.com
deviantart.com
ebayclassifieds.com
foundmyself.com
freewebs.com
goodsmiths.com
HGTV.com
imgur.com
importingart.com
ispyart.com
madeitmyself.com
manta.com
market4free.com
merchantcircle.com
midwestartcenter.com
mosaicglobe.com
myartprofile.com
olx.com
123soho.com
picasaweb.google.com
pinterest.com
publicdomainpictures.net
redbubble.com
rtist.com
sanesociety.org
sculptureartists.org
selfpublisherstore.com
sharemyartwork.com
stumbleupon.com
theartsource.com
thebartertown.net
threesistersmarketplace
tripleclicks.com
weebly.com
weiku.com
wetcanvas.com
wotartist.com
yellowbot.com
zamaana.com

PAY ART WEBSITES:

allproartists.org
amazonsellercentral.com
artscad.com
artfire.com
artistsmarketonline.com
artpal.com
artquid.com
authorsden.com
cityslick.net
custommade.com
ebay.com
etsy.com
FineArtStudioOnline.com
handmadespark.com
thebartertown.net
worldartdirectory.com
yessy.com

OTHER ARTISTS WEBSITES: If you are given the opportunity to show any of your work on other artists websites you should consider doing so. This is a very good way to get more exposure for your art. Just be sure the site you are looking at is compatible with your work. You may also need to reciprocate, and show the other artists work on your site. This arrangement can be for a specific time or indefinitely. As I said before, I had a very successful showing when I presented my work along with a photographer who specialized in photographing different types of trees in a very artistically beautiful way.

SHOWS WITH ORGANIZATIONS: I have had some very successful shows at local venues, such as: Church Organizations, PTO Groups, School Craft Shows, Pottery Shows, Historical Societies, and Chambers of Commerce. These shows are usually very inexpensive and mostly run for only one day. Sometimes you may be asked to donate part of your sales to the organization. People who attend these types of shows are there mainly to support the organizations and realize that the cost of the space and part of the sales generated by the show go to support the organization. I found it surprising when I met some of the same people I saw a high end art shows, attending these local shows. That's why I recommend attending and supporting your local organizations.

JOIN ART ORGANIZATIONS: It's very important for you to join organizations and groups related to your art. Not only will you be kept updated about upcoming shows and events, you will also meet, interact and learn from other artists.

NEWSLETTERS: Newsletters should do exactly what the name states: inform people of the "News" about you and your work. To produce a printed newsletter, and mail it, is very time consuming and expensive. A much better way is to produce your newsletter on your computer and distribute it via email. There are many programs that have standard newsletter templates and are very easy to use. If you don't have the time, but still feel this type of exposure would work for you, you can hire a company that will do most of the work for you, and distribute your newsletter to your email list. *Constantcontact.com* is one such company that does this job very effectively.

ART PUBLICATIONS: There are a multitude of publications directed at artists and art lovers. The cost of inserting an ad in one of them can be very expensive. From time to time I have placed ads in them to show a new piece or for a specific events I was in, however, in general I do not think the are a very efficient way to spend you limited advertising dollars. Plus if published monthly, you will need to send them all your information at least two months before the publication date.

BLOGS: Blogs are a relatively new form of on line communications. They are basically a website published and updated by an individual or group of users offering opinions, information, and images on a regular basis. Visitors to the blog can also communicate with the bloggers. If you do choose to use this form of promotion, be aware that blogging is very time consuming and can lead to confrontation. There are many websites that can help you create and maintain a blog.

Pricing Your Work

Perhaps one of the most difficult decisions you can make as an artist is how much to sell your work for. Price it too high and it may not sell, price it too low it will be perceived as "not worth much" and you will never make a profit. . You should also be flexible. If all the comments that are made about a piece are about the high price, the price is most likely too high. On the other hand, if people seem to be purchasing you work at a very brisk pace, you can most likely raise the prices. Another major consideration is the amount of work you are showing. It is a proven fact that the more work you show, the more you will sell. So, before you even consider selling any of you work be sure you have at least 20 to 30 different pieces to display. The following are some formulas used to give you an idea about how to price your work. The numbers stated are just suggestions. I base my pricing on Material, Time, My Hourly Rate, and a Percent Add-On.

MATERIAL:
This is the total cost of all the material used to create the piece, such as; wire, beads, bases, adhesives, rocks, drift wood, in other words all the parts of the piece.

TIME SPENT CREATING THE PIECE:
I keep records of all the time I spend working on a piece, including any research I need to do and any drawings or photographs needed.

HOURLY RATE:
This is the most subjective element of the formula. My rate at the present time is $45 to $60 per hour. I base this on my 35 years experience and the efficiency and speed by which I can now complete a piece.

PERCENT ADD-ON:
I add 100% to the above total I arrive at. This is to allow for any discount I may want to offer to a gallery or a rep commission. This may seem like a lot, but I have learned through the years that if you allow people to make a good profit on you work, they will be much happier selling for you, and you will sell more work. If you find you are selling a lot of work, but you feel you are not making a lot of money, you may need to increase your rates.

MATERIAL:	$ 76.00
TIME (16.5 Hrs X $45.00):	742.50
PERCENT ADD ON (Time total X 2):	1,485.00

The total retail price for this piece is $1,485.00 which leaves me plenty of room to offer a commission on the piece to a gallery or a rep. If someone visits my studio and wishes to purchase a piece, I can also offer them a "Special Price".

Master Control Book Pages

The following is the layout and information I put on my master control book sheets. These sheets can be created in "Word" or any program that will allow you to insert a photo on the page. Every piece I create has its own sheet which I keep in alphabetical order in a standard 3 ring binder. The numbers at the bottom coinside with the numbers in the Rolodex **See page 120** that pertain to the web sites that this piece is on. I circle the numbers in red pencil, so if anything changes, I can erase the circle. When the piece sells, I note on the sheet, the date and information about the buyer and where it sold from. I then remove this page and put into another 3 ring binder titled simply "Sold Work". I have been using this system for years, and find it works very well.

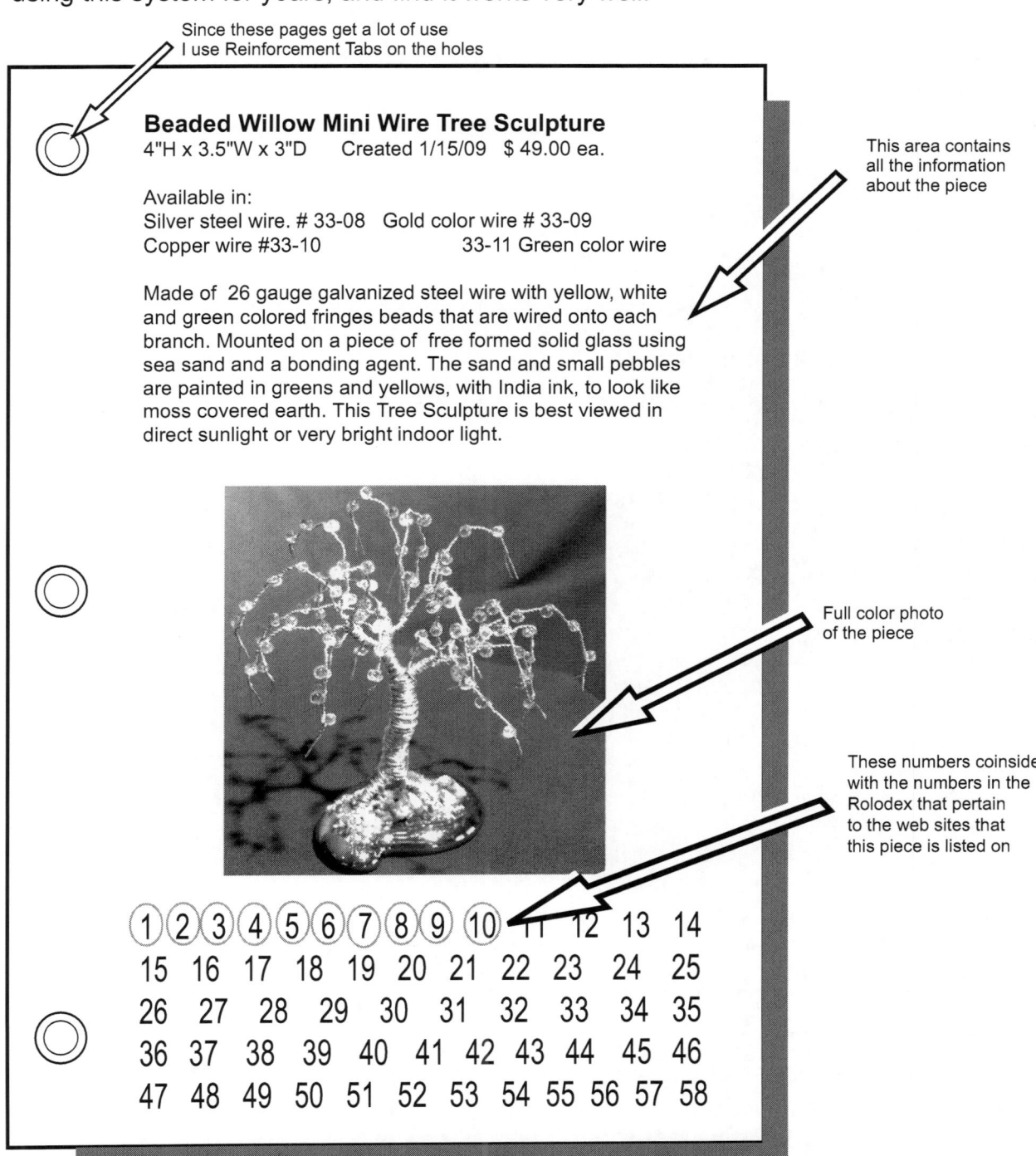

Since these pages get a lot of use I use Reinforcement Tabs on the holes

This area contains all the information about the piece

Full color photo of the piece

These numbers coinside with the numbers in the Rolodex that pertain to the web sites that this piece is listed on

119

Rolodex Set Up

I use a Rolodex card file, shown below, to keep track of all the websites my work is on and other information. I separate the pages of the file into several areas. I find it amazing the amount of information and the ease by which I can get to it using this simple device.

1. Websites listed by name, alphabetically. See illustration below for set up

2. Websites listed by number, these numbers coincide with the website numbers listed in my "Favorites" list on my computer. See illustration below for set up.

3. A section named "Directories" that I only have a listing on.

4. I also created a section listing all my passwords and user names. It is not a good idea to list passwords and user names on your computer. If lost or stolen it becomes very easy for anyone to get at your vital information.

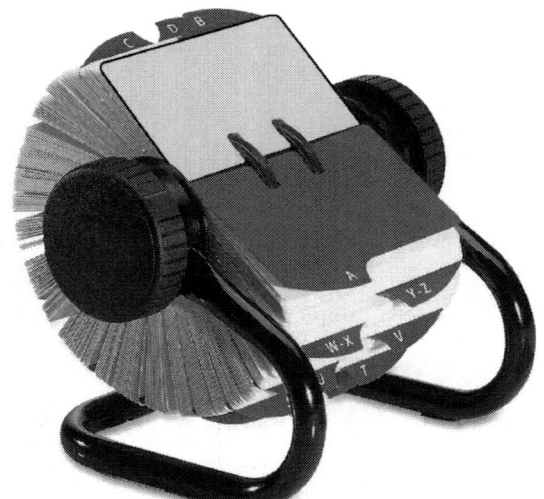

I find it amazing the amount of information and the ease by which I can get to it, using this simple device

Format 1 lists the websites in alphabetical order on the left of the card, and the number of the site in my "Favorites", on my computer, on the right side. It also lists if the site is free or the cost of the listing. Plus my user name, passwords and any other relevant information is also listed on the bottom of the card. If I need more room for other information, it is listed on the back of the card.

FORMAT 1
Websites in alphabetical order on left of card

Format 2 lists the same information as on Format 1, except it lists the number on the left and the alphabetical order on the right. Having each site cross listed saves a great deal of time when I am looking for a particular website. With this system, I can find a site by its name or by its number.

FORMAT 2
Websites in numerical order on left of card

120

Photographing Your Work

With the technology available today it is very easy and It is very important to take a photograph of every piece you create. Not so long ago in order to get into a show or have your work presented in a gallery, you needed to submit slides of each piece. To create the slides you needed all the equipment, then you had to get the slides developed in triplicate. You then needed to present the slides with little arrows showing the recipient the correct way to put each slide into the projector. And you also had to write the name of the piece and your name and date created on the cardboard edge of the slide. As you can surmise, this was sometime an all day procedure. Today with digital everything, is has become very simple to produce, save and transmit images of everything you create. Now if I want to enter a show I simply attach jpeg photos of my work to the email application with instructions stating: "if you are interested in seeing more of my work, please visit my website at www.salvillano.com". I also keep a digital file containing all the information about each piece, such as date of creation, size, material used, time to create and any other bit of information I feel is important. I have used the information in these files many times when I receive a new commission that is similar to an existing piece. This helps keep me from "reinventing the wheel" when creating the new piece and makes the work proceed much faster.

Before you begin to photograph your pieces, it's a good idea to read a few books on the subject, or if you have the time, take a course on digital photography. There is so much information on the web that you can learn all you need to know and purchase all the equipment you need to buy, on line.

Here is the set up I use to photograph all my work. In addition to the lighting set up shown, I also, whenever possible, shoot my work outdoors in direct sunlight or minimal shade. All the photographs presented on my website and in my books, I shot myself.

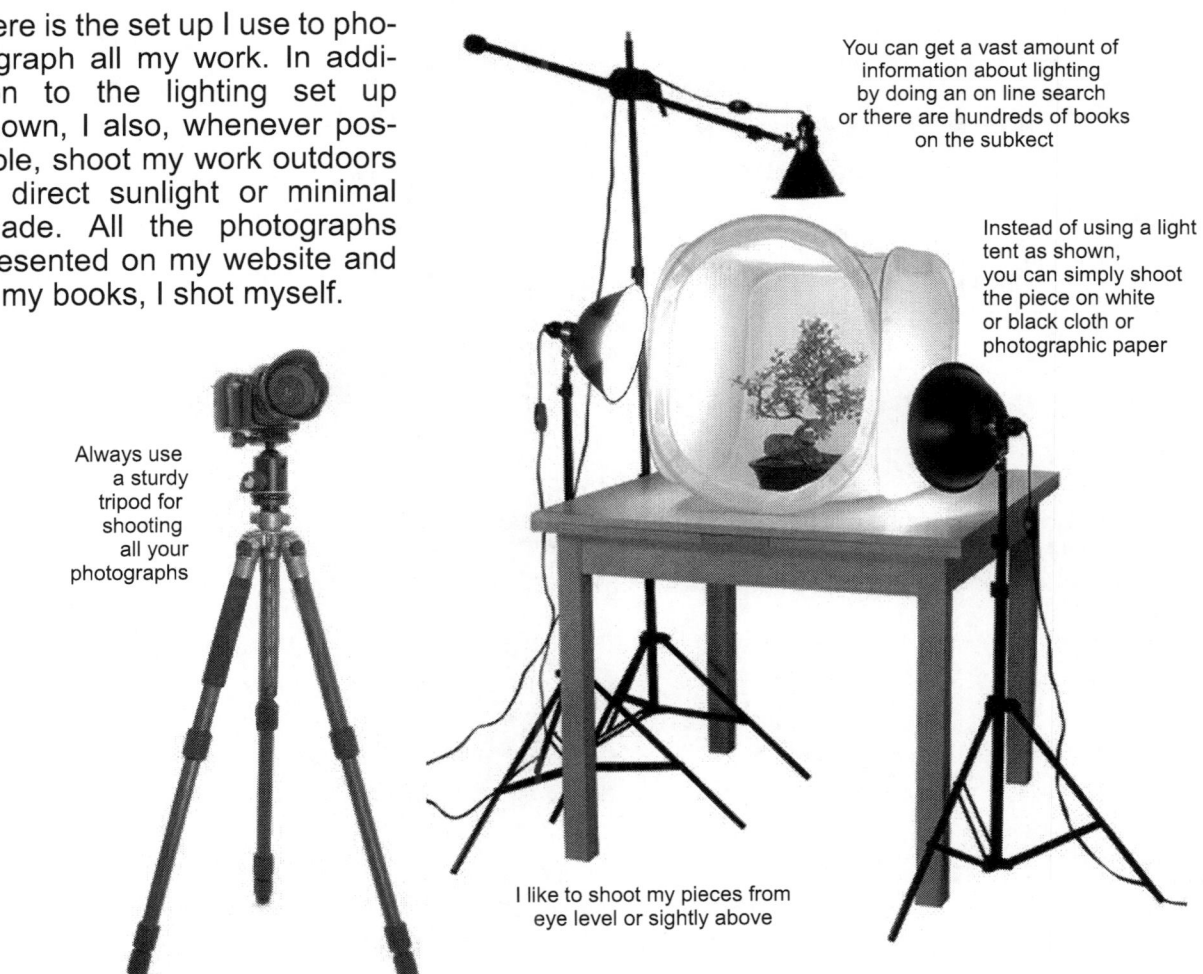

You can get a vast amount of information about lighting by doing an on line search or there are hundreds of books on the subkect

Instead of using a light tent as shown, you can simply shoot the piece on white or black cloth or photographic paper

Always use a sturdy tripod for shooting all your photographs

I like to shoot my pieces from eye level or sightly above

Creating a Website

Creating and maintaining a website is the single most important thing you can do to promote and sell your work. I sell 80% of all my work from my website or other art websites I am showing on. Having your own website is like having a personal store, selling only the creations you make, available 24 hours an day, 365 days a year, in every country on earth that has internet access. With the new web browsers it is now possible to have your site appear in a foreign country presented in their language. I am always amazed to see all the information on my site written in Russian!

If you can afford it, it is much better to hire a web master to create, update and maintain your site. However if you are like most full or part time artists you cannot afford it. Thankfully, there are many inexpensive website creation programs available that enable you to very easily create and maintain your own site. There is, of course a learning curve, but before long you will find yourself in complete control of your site. I created my first website many years ago and I am still using the same program today. The cost of the program was $35.00. There are companies on the web that will help you every step of the way. They will guide you step by step; from obtaining a domain name for you site, creating your pages then launching your site onto the web. Once you master the program, you will find it very easy and rewarding to change and add art to your inventory. After I created and launched my website, I found the best way to keep up with the details associated with my site, was to devote one full day a week to just working on my site. I devote Fridays to adding to and updating the work on my site. I choose Friday so that I could have the site up and running for the weekend when more people are surfing the web. The following are elements that I feel are vital to create a successful website presence.

__ Visit other artists websites to see how they present their work.

__ Keep the pages simple. Do not try to create the best website ever created.

__ Stay away from moving objects or animation, it slows down older computers.

__ Whenever I visit a site that has music, I turn off the sound on my computer.

__ Create a "Navigation Bar" put it on the top and bottom of every page **See page 123**

__ Clearly explain all the details of the piece under its photo.

__ Make it easy to purchase your work by using a "Shopping Cart". I use PayPal.

__ State your "Return Policy".

__ Explain how you ship your work **See page 108**

__ Add a counter to your site. I use "Stat Counter.com". It's free.

__ Show you work on as many "Free" artists web sites as possible. Be sure you add a link to your site. To date I am on 85 free sites, and I am always looking for more.

__ If you are on any social media sites, promote your art there too. A good idea is to let everyone know whenever you add new work to your site.

NOTE: *Be very careful when dealing with anyone on the web. There are many scams aimed at artists. For example, they want to buy your art using a Western Union Money Order, asking to send you much more money than the piece costs, and want you to return the difference. Don't do it, it's a scam. Don't even respond to the email!*

The Navigation Bar on my Website

Click Here for an OVERVIEW of ALL my TREE SCULPTURE						
Gallery 1 *Wire Trees*	Gallery 2 *Bonsai Trees*	Gallery 3 *Beaded Trees*	Gallery 4 *Wind Swept*	Gallery 5 *Bird Nests*	Gallery 6 *Wall Art*	Commissions
Home	About Villano	Order Forms	How to Book	Contact	Links	Sold Work

ELEMENTS OF MY NAVIGATION BAR ON MY WEBSITE

OVERVIEW PAGE:
An "overview" page shows each piece as a thumbnail (small photos) with a link to the larger photo that contains all the information about the piece, including name, description, price and how to order.

GALLERY PAGES 1 through 6:
Separates all your work into specific categories making it easier for the visitor to find different types of pieces they are looking for.

HOME PAGE:
This link is created so the visitors can easily start over at the first page. You should make it as easy as possible for the visitor to navigate back to the first page of the site.

ABOUT THE ARTIST:
Tell everyone about yourself on your "About The Artist" and your "Artist Statement" page. People are interested in you and your work. If you have a photo of yourself, put it on this page.

ORDER FORM:
This is the page to use for a "print out order form". Some people are not comfortable ordering on line, and would rather send the money by mail. If clients wish to send you personal or business checks, you should inform them that you cannot ship the piece until their check clears the bank.

"HOW TO" BOOK:
This is where I sell my books. All the information about the books I sell is here. If you sell anything different than your regular art, create a separate page for it.

CONTACT:
Information telling how people can contact you with any questions or comments.

LINKS:
Links to other sites are very important. Whenever possible offer to exchange links with any website that is compatible with yours, such as artists, suppliers and galleries. The more links you have the better ranking your site will have.

SOLD WORK:
This page shows people that you are selling you art, and it will be very helpful in assisting people who may want you to create a piece for them.

Suppliers List

Following is a list of some of the suppliers I use. I do not endorse any supplier listed, but if I have ever had any issues with a supplier, they would not be listed here. If you don't find an item you are looking for on this list, the best thing to do is a Google Search for the item. When doing a search add as many details to the search entry as you can. Be sure to also search on ebay.com and amazon.com

ADD www. TO THE BEGINNING OF EACH LISTING.

ART SUPPLIES:
- dickblick.com
- cheapjoes.com
- createforless.com
- hobbylobby.com
- jerrysartarama.com
- michaels.com

BASES:
- bases4all.com
- crateandbarrel.com
- orientalfurniture.com
- save-on-crafts.com

BEADS:
- artbeads.com
- auntiesbeads.com
- beadaholique.com
- firemountaingems.com
- pandahall.com

BONSAI CONTAINERS:
- bonsaiboy.com
- bonsaioutlet.com
- booksamillion.com
- dallasbonsai.com
- forever-bloom.com
- hiwtc.com

BOOKS:
- amazon.com
- bn.com
- ebooks.com
- gohastings.com
- half.com

COLOR INKS:
- dickblick.com
- cheapjoes.com
- createforless.com
- hobbylobby.com
- jerrysartarama.com
- michaels.com
- rexart.com

DISPLAY CASES:
- displays2go.com
- fixturedepot.com
- storesupply.com

DRIFT WOOD:
- buydriftwoodforsale.com
- coastaldriftwood.com
- petsolutions.com

FLORAL SUPPLIES:
- fss.com
- michaels.com
- michaelsfloralsupply.com
- wholesalefloral.com

GEMS:
- artbeads.com
- firemountaingems.com
- gemselect.com
- jewelrycentral.com
- wholesalersusainc.com
- youpearl.com

GLASS:
- factorydirectcraft.com
- mosaicartsupply.com
- save-on-crafts.com

JADE LEAVES:
- jojojade.com
- rashiinc.com

PACKING & SHIPPING:
- esupplystore.com
- packagingsupplies.com
- shippingsupply.com
- uline.com

PEDESTALS:
- pedestalsource.com
- pedestalexpress.com
- homedecorators.com

PHOTOGRAPHY:
- adorama.com
- bhphotovideo.com
- calumetphoto.com
- cowboystudio.com
- samys.com

PRINTING:
- psprint.com
- uprinting.com
- vistaprint.com

ROCKS:
- astrogallery.com
- azgardens.com
- marcorocks.com
- storeforknowledge.com

SAND:
- completely-coastal.com
- marinedepot.com
- petsmart.com
- petco.com

SHOW TENTS:
- buyshade.com
- ecanopy.com
- elitedeals.com
- impact-displays.com

TOOLS:
- duluthtrading.com
- homedepot.com
- lowes.som
- micromark.com
- pjtool.com
- sears.com
- smalltools.com
- 2spi.com

WIRE:
- artisticwire.com
- darice.com
- factorydirectcraft.com
- parawire.com
- whimsie.com
- widgetsupply.com

Charts, Tables and Forms

The following pages consist of information and forms that I feel you may find useful. If you wish to photocopy and use any of the forms or information for your personal use, you may do so with my permission.

WIRE GAUGE CHART

Remember: The lower the gauge number is, the thicker the wire is

Gauge		
0	0.3065	7.7851
1	0.283	7.1882
2	0.2625	6.6675
3	0.2437	6.19
4	0.2253	5.7226
5	0.207	5.2578
6	0.192	4.8768
7	0.177	4.4958
8	0.162	4.1148
9	0.1483	3.7668
10	0.135	3.429
11	0.1205	3.0607
12	0.1055	2.6797
13	0.0915	2.3241
14	0.08	2.032
15	0.072	1.8288
16	0.0625	1.5875
17	0.054	1.3716
18	0.0475	1.2065
19	0.041	1.0414
20	0.0348	0.8839
21	0.0317	0.8052
22	0.0286	0.7264
23	0.0258	0.6553
24	0.023	0.5842
25	0.0204	0.5182
26	0.0181	0.4597
27	0.0173	0.4394
28	0.0162	0.4115
29	0.015	0.381
30	0.014	0.3556
31	0.0132	0.3353
32	0.0128	0.3251

METRIC CONVERSION

millimeter	X .039	=	inches
meters	X 3.28	=	feet
meters	X 1.09	=	yards
kilometers	X .621	=	miles
inches	X 25.4	=	millimeter
feet	X .305	=	meters
yards	X .914	=	meters
miles	X 1.61	=	kilometers

ZODIAC SIGNS

Aries	March 21-April 19
Taurus	April 20-May 20
Gemini	May 21-June 20
Cancer	June 21-July 22
Leo	July 23- Aug. 22
Virgo	Aug. 23-Sept. 22
Libra	Sept. 23- Oct. 22
Scorpio	Oct. 23- Nov. 21
Sagittarius	Nov. 22-Dec. 21
Capricorn	Dec. 22-Jan. 19
Aquarius	Jan. 20-Feb 18

BIRTHSTONE CHART

Month	Birthstone
January	Garnet
February	Amethyst
March	Aquamarine
April	Diamond
May	Emerald
June	Pearl
July	Ruby
August	Peridot
September	Sapphire
October	Opal
November	Topaz
December	Turquoise

ANNIVERSARY CHART GEMSTONE

1st	Peridot	16th	Red Spinel
2nd	Red Garnet	17th	Carnelian
3rd	Jade	18th	Aquamarine
4th	Blue Zircon	19th	Garnet
5th	Pink Tourmaline	20th	Yellow Diamond
6th	Turquoise	25th	Tsavorite
7th	Yellow Sapphire	30th	Pearl
8th	Tanzanite	35th	Emerald
9th	Amethyst	40th	Ruby
10th	Blue Sapphire	45th	Cat's Eye
11th	Citrine	50th	Imperial Topaz
12th	Opal	60th	Star Ruby
13th	Moonstone	65th	Blue Spinel
14th	Agate	70th	Smokey Topaz
15th	Rhodolite	75th	Diamond

Consignment Agreement

YOUR NAME
YOUR ADDRESS
YOUR PHONE   EMAIL ADDRESS   WEBSITE

CONSIGNMENT AGREEMENT FOR ART

This agreement is in effect from _____ to _____ and may be terminated by either party at any time.
This agreement is between:_____**YOUR NAME & ADDRESS** _____
and:_____
Located at:_____
The art work described below is owned by **YOUR NAME**. while offered for sale at the above named establishment for the full retail price indicated on each piece. The proceeds of each sale are to be divided as follows: _____% for establishment and _____% for **YOUR NAME**. The above establishment is responsible for the sale and the payment of any sales tax due. Notice of sale, copy of sales receipt and payment must be made to **YOUR NAME** within 7 days of the sale. Art work will be shipped to the establishment at the expense of **YOUR NAME** and any unsold art work returned to **YOUR NAME** will be shipped at the expense of the establishment.

LIST OF ART WORK AND RETAIL PRICE:

NAME OF PIECE	RETAIL PRICE
1._____	$_____
2._____	$_____
3._____	$_____
4._____	$_____
5._____	$_____
6._____	$_____
7._____	$_____
8._____	$_____
9._____	$_____
10._____	$_____
11._____	$_____
12._____	$_____
13._____	$_____
14._____	$_____
15._____	$_____

Total Number of Items_____   Total Retail Value $_____
Signed for Establishment_____   Print Name_____
Signed by **YOUR NAME**_____   Today's Date_____

Page _____ of __ ___

Certificate of Title

Sometimes you may receive a request, from a buyer for a "Certificate of Title". This is a written document signed by you and the buyer stating that you created the piece and are now transferring ownership to the buyer. This is proof that the buyer purchased the piece.

YOUR NAME
YOUR ADDRESS
YOUR PHONE   EMAIL ADDRESS   WEBSITE

CERTIFICATE OF TITLE

I_____PRINT YOUR NAME HERE_____certify that I am the sole creator of the artwork entitled_____NAME OF PIECE_____ using my item number_____ size_____medium_____ This art work was created on____DATE___ and has been in my possession since its creation. I_____PRINT YOUR NAME HERE_____ on this date am transferring full ownership to:
_____PRINT NAME OF NEW OWNER_____
_____PRINT ADDRESS OF NEW OWNER_____
_____SIGNATURE OF NEW OWNER_____
_____SIGN YOUR NAME HERE_____
_____DATE HERE_____

Certificate of Authenticity

A Certificate of Authenticity provides the buyer with a written, signed guarantee that art work you are presenting is real and was created by you.

YOUR NAME
YOUR ADDRESS
YOUR PHONE   EMAIL ADDRESS   WEBSITE

CERTIFICATE OF AUTHENTICITY

I_____PRINT YOUR NAME HERE_____certify that I am the sole creator of the artwork entitled_____NAME OF PIECE_____ using my item number_____ size_____medium_____ This art work was created on____DATE___ and has been in my possession since its creation.
_____PRINT YOUR NAME HERE _____
_____PRINT YOUR ADDRESS HERE_____
_____DATE CREATED____   TODAYS DATE_____
_____SIGN YOUR NAME HERE _____

Sample Letters

The following is the text of specific letters you may need to communicate with various organizations or individuals. These letters should always be sent out on your letterhead or by email. Always keep a copy for your records. The first sample letter (Follow up Letter) shows all the elements of the letter and the layout. The following letters show only the text needed. You can, of course, add any other information you think is relevant. However, it is a good idea to keep the letter as short as possible.

Follow Up Letter:

YOUR LOGO HERE IF YOU USE ONE
YOUR NAME
YOUR ADDRESS
YOUR PHONE   EMAIL ADDRESS   WEBSITE

Date Here 00/00/00

Mr.. John Doe
144-86 Any Street
Town, State Zip

Dear Mr.. Doe

It was very pleasant speaking with you yesterday. As per our conversation, I am enclosing the following items you requested:

My Resume, My Artist Statement, and Several Press Releases.

If you need any additional information or images of my work, please do not hesitate to ask. You can also view all my work and further information on my website at: www.yoursite.com.

Sincerely,

Sign Your Name

Type your name here

Gallery Request:

Gallery Name
Mr. John Doe
144-86 Any Street
Town, State Zip
Date Here 00/00/00

Dear Mr. Doe

I recently visited your gallery and I would like the opportunity to show my work to you so that I may be considered for representation in your gallery.

Enclosed please find: My Resume and Artist Statement, Shows I have exhibited in, and some Press Coverage I have received.

I will be calling you in a few days to see if you are interested in arranging an appointment,

If you need any additional information or images, please do not hesitate to ask.
You can also view all my work and further information on my website at: www.yoursite.com.

Sign Your Name

Arts Application Request:

Art Council Name
Mr. John Doe
144-86 Any Street
Town, State Zip
Date Here 00/00/00

Dear Mr. Doe

Please send me, by return mail or email, information and any applications necessary to apply for admission to your Art Council. I would also appreciate any brochures about your organization.

For your convenience I have enclosed a postage paid envelope. Thank you for your help.

Sign Your Name

Art Publication Ad Information:

Art Publication Name
Mr. John Doe
144-86 Any Street
Town, State Zip
Date Here 00/00/00

Dear Mr. Doe

Please send me, by return mail or email attachment, your complete media package.
I am interested in advertising my art work in your publication. If possible, please also include any recent issues available.

Sign Your Name

Inquiry From a Gallery:

Gallery Name
Mr.. John Doe
144-86 Any Street
Town, State Zip
Date Here 00/00/00

Dear Mr.. Doe

Thank you very much for your interest in my work. The piece in question is (Give full detailed information about the piece). The retail price is $ 00000. I offer a Gallery discount of 00% plus shipping. I can also accept commissions and can offer you a 00% discount .

If you need any additional information or images, please do not hesitate to ask.
You can also view all my work and further information on my website at: www.yoursite.com.

Sign Your Name

Price Confirmation & Delivery of Art:

Acmy Corporation
Mr. John Doe
144-86 Any Street
Town, State Zip
Date Here 00/00/00

Dear Mr. Doe

This letter is to confirm the details of our verbal agreement of 00/00/00. In reference to (Give full detailed information about the piece).

As we agreed, I will deliver the piece to your company on 00/00/00. Payment in full of $0000 is due upon delivery. Thanks again for your purchase and I look forward to our next meeting.

Sign Your Name

Thank You:

Mr.. John Doe
144-86 Any Street
Town, State Zip
Date Here 00/00/00

Dear Mr.. Doe

Thank you very much for your purchase of (Name of Piece). As agreed, I will be shipping the piece by UPS on 00/00/00 and I will forward you the tracking number when it is issued. I will also include in the package, information about my upcoming shows in your area, and I look forward to hopefully seeing you again at one of my shows.

Thanks again for your interest in my work.

Sign Your Name

Press, (*News*) Release:

A Press Release, more accurately now called a "News Release", is written information sent directly to media outlets. The release contains detailed information and images about any topic you think may be of interest to the publications readers. It can cover such areas as: your upcoming shows, awards you recently received, new work completed, important commissions, or any other information you think may be of interest. The format of the release should be presented so that the recipient can simply copy, then publish it with no additions necessary. Your release can be delivered by US Mail, email or posted on your social media site. Posting your release on a social media site is a very good way for your family and friends to "spread the word" about you and your career. Once again, you should keep your copy short and direct. These days most people don't have the time to read long wordy announcements. The following is a release about an upcoming show.

YOUR LOGO HERE IF YOU USE ONE
YOUR NAME
YOUR ADDRESS
YOUR PHONE   EMAIL ADDRESS   WEBSITE   TODAYS DATE

P R E S S   R E L E A S E

FOR IMMEDIATE RELEASE   CONTACT: (YOUR NAME, PHONE, EMAIL HERE)

"Local Artist, (YOUR NAME), to be featured in a ONE-PERSON SHOW"

Local artist (Your Name Here) will present 12 new pieces at a One-Person Show entitled (Name of show), open to the public (Dates Here) at the (Gallery name address, hours and wedsite Here) Opening reception will be (Date & Time Here).

(IN THIS AREA, place no more than three or four lines of copy containing details about you, your work and other shows or events. Not your entire bio.)

Additional information about the artist, and other upcoming shows, is available on the artists website at: www.yourwebsite.com

Thank You!

Link Exchange Request:

Whenever I visit a website that I find interesting, and would like to exchange links with, I have this email pre-written that I send to see if they want to exchange links with me.

Hi. (Name of Person if you know it)
Please visit my website at: (www.yourwebsite.com) to determine if you would be interested in exchanging links with my site.
Thank you. (Your name here)

The inspiration for creating my sculpture grew from a lifetime love of trees. As I study each tree, I am in awe of the stately presence and silent majesty they posses. I find the structure of trees to be one of the many perfections of nature. With their roots intertwined, imbedded in, and embracing the earth;

*in winter they show their structure,
in spring a burst of gentle buds,
in summer an incredible canopy of green,
and in fall, a magical kaleidoscope of ever
changing color.*

Beauty, pure beauty.

About SAL VILLANO

Sal Villano was born in New York City in 1944 into a large extended family of many artists. So, he was always very aware of art in his life and was naturally attracted to expressing himself visually. He attended public grade school, high school and college. He also studied at The Art Students League in Manhattan. While still in college he assisted his uncle Charles Santaniello, a sculptor, in creating commercial displays for many New York businesses. And, he also helped his uncle create human figures and animal characters for parts of an exhibit for the World's Fair in Europe.

It was this time he spent working with his uncle that he realized he too wanted to be a sculptor. After graduating college he went to work as a commercial artist for a large toy company in New York City. In 1969, after several years at this position he started his own art studio with another artist, this very successful partnership provided him the opportunity to produce a wide verity of commercial work both two and three dimensional.

It was at the time he spent at the Art Students league that Sal created his first wire tree sculpture. While constructing an armature to support a clay figure, he noticed that the wire he was using could also be bent, twisted and wrapped to create a tree sculpture. Since that day, many years ago, he has created thousands of tree sculptures of various wire types and gauges and each carefully placed onto a base that is a vital part of the total presentation of the piece.

Whether viewed in direct sunlight casting harsh shadows or in soft candle light creating a gentle form, the tree sculptures created by Sal Villano each take on a personality of their own. And, as in nature, no two trees can ever be created alike.

All the sculpture of Sal Villano can be viewed at: www.salvillano.com

Printed in Great Britain
by Amazon